MICHAEL C. J. PUTNAM

Virgil's Epic Designs

EKPHRASIS IN THE *AENEID*

Yale University Press   New Haven and London

Copyright © 1998 by Yale University.
All rights reserved.
This book may not be reproduced, in whole or in part, including illustrations, in any form (beyond that copying permitted by Sections 107 and 108 of the U.S. Copyright Law and except by reviewers for the public press), without written permission from the publishers.

Printed in the United States of America.

Library of Congress Cataloging-in-Publication Data

Putnam, Michael C. J.
Virgil's epic designs : ekphrasis in the Aeneid / Michael C. J. Putnam.
p.   cm.
Includes bibliographical references and index.
ISBN 0-300-07353-4 (alk. paper)
1. Virgil. Aeneis. 2. Epic poetry, Latin—History and criticism. 3. Aeneas (Legendary character) in literature. 4. Description (Rhetoric) 5. Rhetoric, Ancient. 6. Virgil—Technique. 7. Ekphrasis. I. Title.
PA6825.P844   1998
873'.01—dc21   97-43717
                                                                                    CIP

A catalogue record for this book is available from the British Library.

The paper in this book meets the guidelines for permanence and durability of the Committee on Production Guidelines for Book Longevity of the Council on Library Resources.

10 9 8 7 6 5 4 3 2

For my nieces and nephews

Contents

Preface / ix
Acknowledgments / xi

Introduction / 1
1 Dido's Murals / 23
2 The Cloak of Cloanthus / 55
3 Daedalus' Sculptures / 75
4 Silvia's Stag / 97
5 The Shield of Aeneas / 119
6 The Baldric of Pallas / 189
Conclusion / 208

Notes / 215
Bibliography / 245
Index / 253

Preface

An extraordinary feature of the poetics of the *Aeneid* is the degree to which several aspects of the poem's presentation press against its nominal contents. We read an epic poem that takes us on a narrative tour of Aeneas' adventures, from the demise of Troy to the death of Turnus. Virgil makes masterful use of standard epic devices, like catalogues of heroes, to enhance his plotline, and seizes three important opportunities to extend his story line into a future beyond the purview of the epic itself, as he looks to the history of Rome and, in particular, of the emperor Augustus' rise to and consolidation of power, a time during which the poem itself was written.

But these very intimations of allegory and the layerings of history they suggest, by causing the reader to pause and ponder parallels between then and now, work to some degree against the forward momentum of plot. The same can be said of Virgil's rich allusivity to his poetic past, beginning with Homer, or of his use, say, of lyric and elegiac devices as commentary on narrative events. This book deals with another such device: ekphrasis. Ekphrasis, the topos of "speaking out" in order to describe a person or animal or landscape or, most usually, a work of art, inevitably generates a pause in the narrative when art looks at and continues art, and when the artisan of words, who works on our imaginations by his own verbal constructions, manufactures artifacts within his text for us to see with our mind's eye. As art describes art, we linger, not to escape the story's flow but to deepen our understanding of its meaning, to watch metaphor operating on a grand scale where epic text and one of its grandest synecdoches work as didactic complements to each other.

Virgil's longer ekphrases, especially those devoted to the murals in Dido's temple to Juno and to the shield of Aeneas, have long histories of scholarly discussion. But this is the first study that analyzes all of the poet's ekphrases of works of art (with the addition of one further essay on an animal ekphrasis). Though in the book's conclusion I make some general inferences about Virgilian descriptions that might prove useful to students of ekphrasis in general, my primary focus is on Virgil's text and on how ekphrasis helps us plumb its particular meanings.

In pursuing this endeavor I have been aided by numerous scholars, past and present, whether their chief area of interest was ekphrasis, or the poetry of Virgil, or both. I have striven to recognize them in the pages which follow. It remains to note here personal debts of gratitude. My colleagues, especially Joseph Pucci, and my students at Brown, both present and former, have been an unfailing source of help and advice. From the latter I am particularly indebted here to Robert Gurval, Stephen Scully, and Sarah Spence. Christine Perkell gave the manuscript a perspicacious reading which prompted, among many ameliorations, a much improved conclusion. Other friends, in particular, Alessandro Barchiesi, Leonard Barkan, Glen Bowersock, Rachel Jacoff, Helen North, Georgia Nugent, Barbara Pavlock, Matthew Santirocco, Charles Segal, Eugene Vance, John Van Sickle, Rosanna Warren, and James Zetzel, have been generous with aid and encouragement. It is a pleasure also to thank Noreen O'Connor of Yale University Press for her astute editing. As always, Ruthann Whitten brought both humor and efficiency to her assistance. Kenneth Gaulin provided the setting in which much of the manuscript was written and offered unfailing support. My continuing obligation to my family I happily acknowledge elsewhere.

Acknowledgments

I would like to thank these journals and publishers for permission to reprint in revised form the following articles: "Dido's Murals and Virgilian Ekphrasis," *Harvard Studies in Classical Philology* 98 (1998). Reprinted by permission of the Department of the Classics, Harvard University, and the President and Fellows of Harvard College. "Ganymede and Virgilian Ekphrasis," *American Journal of Philology* 116 (1995): 419–40, and "Daedalus, Virgil and the End of Art," *American Journal of Philology* 108 (1987): 173–98. Reprinted by permission of *American Journal of Philology* and the Johns Hopkins University Press. "Silvia's Stag and Virgilian Ekphrasis," *Materiali e discussioni per l'analisi dei testi classici* 34 (1995): 107–33. Reprinted by permission of Professor Gian Biagio Conte and *Materiali e discussioni*. "Virgil's Danaid Ekphrasis," *Illinois Classical Studies* 19 (1994): 171–89. Reprinted by permission of *Illinois Classical Studies*.

Introduction

This book examines Virgil's use of the rhetorical figure of ekphrasis throughout the *Aeneid.* The trope of "speaking forth" is of particular service for the poet at a moment when narration must apparently pause to recount, and in the process bring understanding of and clarity to, an entity of interest to the story line as it progresses.[1] Such a *descriptio,* for instance, can be concerned with a piece of landscape. Virgil's first example of the figure in the epic epitomizes the magic and menace which the Trojans both confront and engender as they moor in Dido's harbor at Carthage, while at the same time the poet brilliantly makes use of Homer to toy with his reader. (Has Aeneas arrived at Ithaca, or Phaeacia, or the land of Circe or Calypso? we first must ask.) Or ekphrasis can elaborate the biographical background of a person necessary to explain his or her future action, as, for example, in the expansive portrait of Camilla in book 11, with its powerful reversal of male and female roles. The poet also utilizes ekphrasis in book 7 to look at a feral creature such as Silvia's stag, and to suggest, *in parvo,* a complex meditation on the relationship of human and animal, or of nature and culture, and their mutual corruptibility, at a moment in the poem when war comes to Latium and human deterioration is the order of the day.

The stag and its meaning will be the subject of a subsequent chapter, but my primary concern in the book will be with what John Hollander has entitled "notional ekphrasis," which is to say with works of art which, however palpable in the text, are figments of Virgil's imagination.[2] Six of these scattered throughout the *Aeneid* make varied appearances from the first book to the last. Three are elaborate—the description in book 1 of the murals that decorate Dido's temple to Juno, the view that opens book 6 of the sculptures which Daedalus crafts for his temple to Apollo, and, most expansive of all, the vision in book 8 of the shield of Aeneas, fashioned by Vulcan for the hero. There are three shorter descriptions, of the cloak given Cloanthus for his victory in the boat race of book 5, of the shield of Turnus in book 7, and, as final example in the poem, of the sword belt of Pallas in the tenth book. All except the shield of Turnus will receive separate treatment in the subsequent pages, but I will also use this last as illustration here of some of the special attributes of Virgilian description.

It will be my presumption that all of Virgil's notional ekphrases are in consequential ways metaphors for the larger text which they embellish and that, individually and as a group, they have much to teach the reader about the poem as a whole.

Ekphrasis, especially when utilized for the depiction of works of art, is often treated as mere decorative figuration. We tend, on first reading at least, to look on such descriptions as engendering a moment of respite, in the case of the *Aeneid,* in epic action, a digression, and at times even a relief from the story line, bringing more aesthetic entertainment than spiritual enrichment to the searcher after meaning. Such an approach is abetted by the very atemporality of art itself. Though time passes, of course, as we read an ekphrasis and as our eye moves from line to line down the page, we are still bearing witness to an artifact, an apparently tangible, stable object, made visible to the inner eye through the charm of words. Murray Krieger is on the mark in asserting that the ideal, but unrealizable, goal of ekphrasis is to stop time, to place narrative momentum in a subservient position to the object under scrutiny, which we are meant to grasp in a flash of comprehension, just as we would react when first seeing a painting or a piece of sculpture in a museum.[3]

This reading is supported by a concomitant emphasis on what we might call the "objectness" of the artifact involved, through which we attend not only to the work of art but to its maker and manufacturing, as well as to its role as something whose essence is absorbed visually. The reader is made to watch viewer or viewers both within the text and without, as the object or objects are seen by the poem's protagonists and by readers at any point in its later history. We behold the murals in Dido's temple through the eyes of Aeneas and react with empathy as he responds to the scenes which he surveys of Troy's last days and with understanding when he imputes a parallel compassion to Dido whose workmen (the Latin word is *manus,* "hands") created the total ensemble. And with the still larger shield of Aeneas we are made to observe not only Vulcan as artisan and Aeneas as viewer but also the materiality of the object, its overall shape, its contents, the placement of those contents, and the metals that give them being. This concreteness is reinforced by an arsenal of rhetorical and narrative gestures, ranging from apostrophe and a series of addresses to "you," the viewer-reader, to ring composition which at once reflects shield, the poem in which it is embedded, and Virgil's total oeuvre. With these lyric, antinarrative (which here is to say antiepic) signals, the poet, too, uses the particularities of language to retard time in favor of art's momentary, physical luminosity.

In his important book on ekphrasis, James Heffernan has added gender to the discussion, viewing the stationary object as passive and therefore feminine, at the mercy of the masculine, controlling word upon which it becomes dependent as an author enters the ekphrastic mode.[4]

I would like to take my start from these considerations, using Heffernan's cogent reminder that "a verbalized depiction . . . serves as an interpretive signpost for the reader."[5] For by its very act of disruption, ekphrasis forces itself on the reader as a generative moment, as two types of narrativity confront each other. For Virgil this instant of intersection, of destabilization and at times transgression, is the overture not for a digression from the heady onslaught of epic narrative but for a meditation on one art as mirror of another, on Virgil's descriptions of examples of the fine arts as synecdoches for that larger manifestation of artistic accomplishment which is the poem itself. It is my thesis in the following chapters that all the ekphrases of the *Aeneid,* even the shorter descriptions in however circumscribed a capacity, represent the poem itself and afford us deeper ways of reading which we may plumb only through the actuation of sight into insight.

I will argue this point by returning to some of the themes I have discussed earlier, to the placement and content of the descriptions, to the role of the viewer, and to the multivalent frictions which ekphrasis creates. Let us look briefly again at each ekphrasis, taking them, as this book will, in order of appearance. As Aeneas views the scenes from the Trojan past on Dido's temple to Juno, he reacts in sorrow as well as in appreciation of the Carthaginian queen's empathy, but the all-knowing reader contemplates the reiteration of violence and deadly action, especially taken against the young and unsuspecting, that claims a series of victims, the majority at the hands of the best of the Achaians, Achilles. The list ends with Penthesilea, still alive in the ekphrasis and blending easily into the continued narrative of the poem proper through the figure of Dido. Ekphrasis, like the art it describes, is both static and in motion, while Dido—woman as heroic leader, *dux femina facti*, masculine founder of a burgeoning city—because of the arrival of Aeneas-Achilles, soon becomes feminized, as she loses command of herself and her world, and the suffering, passive offering to Rome in progress. She who orders the creation of art is symbolically and literally destroyed in it and by it. The deaths which the ekphrasis details are taken up in Aeneas' seductive, destructive narrative and lead inexorably to her suicide. Juno's temple and its murals harbor and monumentalize the goddess' violence in ways only the reader-viewer, and not the poem's protagonists, can comprehend. Art, we thus learn, may elicit an emotional reaction based on memory of the past, but it also shrouds some deeper universal truths that are applicable to the poem as a whole.

The Ganymede ekphrasis, brief though it is, furthers several parallel motifs. We linger, for a moment, in contemplation of the tale of a young Trojan hunter beloved by the king of heaven, but instead of a finale where mortal becomes immortal by transformation into the cup-bearer of the gods, we find only the lamentation of his guardians at their loss and the rage of the dogs for their absent master. There is neither erotic satisfaction for Ganymede within the ekphrasis nor pleasure for the reader in a climactic rounding off of the tale. Instead, appropriately enough for ekphrasis, stasis predominates over motion and disjunction replaces continuity in a personal history where roles are inverted as hunter becomes hunted, and, again, active is exchanged for passive. We end by asking what it means for a champion to carry away as a prize this story of loss and incompletion, and therefore what the ekphrasis, however limited in scope, can tell us of the larger poem-artifact we call the

Aeneid and what it in turn says of the relation between victory and victims.

Aeneas is witness to Dido's murals and the bestower of the cloak on Cloanthus. He is also the viewer of Daedalus' autobiographical sculptures, which he comes upon, at the start of book 6, soon after his arrival in Italy. He would have read through all the panels, says the narrator, had not Achates and the Sibyl whisked him away from what she styles *spectacula,* mere display to delight the eye, lacking any reason for the hero to delay his journey to the Underworld and to dwell on them in detail and in depth. But this is exactly what ekphrasis asks of readers and what, again as in the case of Dido's murals, differentiates what readers glean, and what the narrator's knowledge and prejudice help them to ascertain, from what Aeneas may not.

The Daedalus ekphrasis documents the only instance in ancient literature where an artist tells his own tale solipsistically in art, appropriating his own creativity for a final burst of inspiration. In essence it is the story of an artist who uses his craft to deceive (Pasiphaë's bull, the Labyrinth), then through pity unravels that deception (the story of Ariadne, and his own implicit, equally crafty, airborne escape from Crete). But the climax of the description, where the narrator's apostrophe to Icarus suggests that we conflate him with Daedalus as dual creators, leaves ekphrastic art still incomplete, with only the narrator's exclamation hinting at what its conclusion might have been.

The growing emotionality of the artist leads only to the disclosure of art's ability to dissimulate, to the sometimes disastrous nature of artistry, and, finally, to the inability of the artist to create. Icarus' daring and death are rewarded only by the absence of art because *dolor,* the suffering and resentment that come to the father through the fall of his son, render this artist a failure. And what does this say of Daedalus-Virgil? His epic is marked with the deaths of young heroes which bring grief to their parents. It comes to an end with an example of what *dolor,* here arising from the death of Pallas, can provoke in the actions of Aeneas, actions which contravene the most ethically importunate command his father, Anchises, had laid upon him—to spare the defeated and war down the proud. Moral father can no more create moral son, Virgil may be suggesting, than poet can complete the life of that son after his final display of anger and violence.

Aeneas is shunted past the *spectacula* of Daedalian art, perhaps lest prolonged scrutiny reveal to him the passions and deficiencies of his life to come, or of any life for that matter. It is readers, with their privileged leisure for meditation, who again can make the connection between a poem's ekphrases of art and the artful poem itself and can ponder what each can tell us of the other. Aeneas is also the voyeur of the shield which Vulcan crafts for him and whose ekphrasis is by far the longest in the poem. Aeneas admires (*miratur*), before the ekphrasis begins, the "untellable weaving of the shield" (*clipei non enarrabile textum*), and, after its finish, he once more admires it, while this time "he rejoices in the image, ignorant of the matter [which he sees]." The phrasing is ambiguous. Aeneas may find pleasure in the image even though he is uncomprehending of what he sees. He is, after all, looking at what he could not know, at the whole history of Rome miraculously compressed onto an iconic shield.

This history extends from the doings of Ascanius' sons to the aftermath of the battle of Actium, excerpts from which comprise the ekphrasis proper. But Aeneas could also rejoice because he does not know what the future of Rome entails. Here again we face the disparity between, on the one hand, omniscient crafter (Vulcan), narrator, and reader, and, on the other, the hero who in this instance could not understand what was before his eyes, even were he allowed time for contemplation. For what the all-knowing reader absorbs from an ekphrasis that begins with human twins suckled by a feral wolf and ends with a river in Armenia protesting its apparent bridging by the emperor is a tale of inexorable evolution toward the glory of Augustan Rome, but one which in the process tells of freedom and subjugation, of violence and mourning, of pride and loss.

Once more ekphrasis and epic complement and analogize each other, as do Virgil and Vulcan. Each begins with a scene in a cave that either suggests or directly projects negative power into a future near or distant, and ends with a hero and river indignant that their individuality has been suppressed. The *Aeneid* embraces this encapsulation of Roman history in its larger narrative and yet at the same time serves as a minuscule synecdoche of it. However forward the thrust of epic poem and iconic shield, each also finally deals in the circularities and repetitions that offer honest evidence of human nature at work, whether in epic narrative or ekphrastic description or in the larger Virgilian career that takes us from the smoking rooftops that speak of the ruin (as well as the beauty) of the pastoral idyll in the first eclogue, to the smoking rooftops which Aeneas threatens to visit on the city of Latinus as his epic nears its finale.

Here also, familial and erotic relationships play vital roles in the deployment of the ekphrasis. As in the case of the Daedalus description, we are dealing with a parent-child bond which, if not a putative part of the artifact, forms a crucial aspect of its reception. Even here, as mother Venus delivers the shield to her son, the erotic element is not totally absent. "She offered herself [to him] of her own accord" (*se . . . obtulit ultro*), says the narrator about the goddess of love, echoing a line from the third eclogue where one lover submits himself to another.[6] Venus must apparently exert her sexual potential as she presents the history of Rome to her son. She is merely extending the tactic she had earlier used on Vulcan at the engendering of the shield, where the metaphoric flame of love soon becomes the literal fire of the artisan at work. There, too, she must bring her sexual wiles to bear against a husband who hesitates before agreeing to her request. Just as an ambiguous tone touched the aftermath of the ekphrasis, so in its introduction the reader is also left with a sense of unease. Why must Venus seduce both husband into creating, and son into accepting, the shield, if nothing is amiss in its production? To forge the shield is to forge the chronicle of Rome, with all that this implies.

There is also role reversal of another sort, which reminds us of the ekphrasis of Dido's murals. As Vulcan sets out to make the shield he is likened to a Roman *matrona,* keeping her life and her family chaste as she works her wool. On the one hand Virgil's irony, which was not lost on his ancient critics, reminds us of what an adulterous "husband" Venus had been in her dealings with a (presumably) faithful Vulcan. More à propos still, in the begetting of the shield the woman is both in charge and the source of equivocal inspiration, while it is the masculine creator, Vulcan, the lord of fire himself, who is feminized—a submissive devotee of Minerva, according to the simile. The artifact itself may be passive and feminine, subject to the domination of the male word, but in the setting of Virgil's two most expansive ekphrases it is the woman who is in power and who, especially in the case of the shield, lords it over the creator at the incipience of its manufacture. It is no accident that the feminine potential to stir up violence is a major theme of the poem, ranging full circle from the storm Juno launches in book 1, as destructive incorporation of her inner irrationality, to Aeneas' use of Junonian language when he prepares to kill in anger as the epic ends.

Finally, we have the line-and-a-half ekphrasis in book 10 devoted to the sword belt of Pallas on which is depicted "the band of youths, foully slaughtered on their single night of marriage and the bloodied wedding chambers," which is to say the brutal massacre of the forty-nine sons of Aegyptus by an equal number of daughters of Danaus. The briefest of Virgilian ekphrases is in some ways his most hyperbolic. The shield of Aeneas may magically enclose all of Roman history from which the narrator excerpts notable scenes, but there is something particularly horrifying about a *balteus* worn into battle by a young warrior that contains more than four dozen killings catalogued, we must imagine, without discrimination, on the limited compass of a belt. War, here, appears as a series of concentrated, immoral murders of unremitting violence and victimization which, at least in Virgil's case, have no resolution. It is also, more particularly still, an ugly complement to martial battling. Again we are concerned with a relationship between parents and children, here of a father in the background who urges his daughters on to acts of revenge. But the protagonists themselves, when we turn to the erotic tale itself, can be seen in two ways, as Greeks killing barbarian pursuers (and as analogues to those engaged in a foreign war) or as cousins murdering cousins (and therefore as prototypes for fighters in a civil conflict). I will return to this point in a moment. Suffice it to attend to what Virgil's alter ego here, the artisan Clonus, "Battle-Din," has accomplished in crafting a definition of war itself as a source of hideous inversion: the incessant, treacherous killing of virgin males by virgin males, where one party is finally at the mercy of the other and where the action itself is driven by brutality and the lust for revenge.

A reference back to Greek tragedy is also critical here. We are fortu-

INTRODUCTION

nate to have preserved the *Supplices*, the first drama in Aeschylus' Danaid trilogy, where Danaus' daughters plead for asylum from their trackers, and we can hypothesize that, either during the second play or between it and the last, the murders took place. More significant, however, is the fact that we possess a fragment from the concluding drama where Aphrodite sings the praises of marriage and its concomitant fertility. We can likewise assume, therefore, that Hypermestra, the one of Danaus' offspring who spared her husband, is forgiven her disobedience to her father and blessed in her marriage to the husband she had saved. There is no sparing in the *Aeneid*, no act of pardon, no marriage consummated, no equivalents as emblems of a return to societal order. The Danaid tragedy is parallel to Virgil's other direct allusions to Greek tragedy. To take one example from earlier in the epic, Dido, as her madness grows and as she prepares for suicide, is likened to Orestes driven by his mother across the stage as the avenging Furies sit by.[7] No *Eumenides* is forthcoming, for Dido or for similar individuals elsewhere in the poem, bringing redemption through peace and reconciliation.

In this connection we must note another link between sword belt and shield besides the powerful conciseness of their contents. They are the poem's only objects described ekphrastically which are in motion, as it were, across the poem. We read of the shield at the end of book 8, but we soon see it again in all its brilliance in book 10 when Aeneas arrives downriver with his new Etruscan allies to do battle with the Latins. Virgil compares the golden fires its boss spews forth to the funereal red of comets at night or to the thirst and disease which the Dog Star brings to ill mortals as it saddens the sky.[8] At the start of Roman history, as we watch its prototypical hero at work in the epic's final books, we find ourselves immersed in a series of killings that lead directly into the animality and ferocity of the shield's opening vignettes. The parallel progress of the *balteus*, subject of a static ekphrasis propelled into activity by war's mayhem, begins in book 10 where it is worn by Pallas and donned by Turnus in a moment of pride after killing the young hero. It is this baldric that, in the epic's final lines, Aeneas sees around the shoulder of his opponent. This vision, a reminder, in Virgil's words, of the passionate grief he had experienced at Pallas' death, impels Aeneas, "set aflame by furies and terrifying in his wrath," to kill his suppliant antagonist as the epic ends.[9]

This is the last, most succinct occasion where Virgil brings Aeneas into conjunction with an object that has been the focus of ekphrasis, in this case two books before. Here, too, we are given a response on his part as he reacts to this *monumentum*, the tangible artifact that serves also as a monument and a reminder. The narrator tells us only of Aeneas' ferocious reaction to the sight, not whether he pondered the possible meanings of what he saw (his occasion to pause had come a moment earlier in reaction to Turnus' plea for clemency). The reader must not only adjudicate the difference between Aeneas' furious but superficial response to the belt's content and its deeper meanings. He or she must also watch the object as it moves from Pallas, to Turnus—like Pallas earlier, now active attacker become passive victim—to Aeneas' observant eyes. As the force of the ekphrasis is brilliantly transferred from book 10 to book 12, the reader absorbs the constancy of vendetta and, in particular, the brutality of fraternal strife. It is not the clemency of Hypermestra but the need for unremitting, Danaidic vengeance and slaughter that grips Aeneas as his saga closes.

Virgil's ekphrases, therefore, in no sense prove to be rhetorical interruptions of the plot line for nonessential digression but rather function as foci where smaller synecdoches suggest ways in which the larger text can be interpreted and reinterpreted, where the imaginative power, ambiguity, and deceptiveness of visual art play off against, and illuminate, the multivalent richness of the grand verbal artifact for which they also operate as metaphor. As two types of narrativity collide, it is the poet, imaginer of these double visions, who in his role as Daedalus offers us ways to solve the labyrinthine complexities of his own literary accomplishment through depictions of art. Virgilian ekphrases always occur at crucial moments of intersection in the text, even on the most literal level, as Aeneas meets Dido, for instance, or prepares to enter the Underworld, or accepts the destiny of Rome as summarized on Vulcan's shield. But the resulting friction, as we pursue the act of criticism through differentiated ways of reading, is vital for our comprehension of the poem as a whole.

I will come back shortly to further examination of the creative challenges which ekphrasis offers to the central text and to the reader's enjoyment as he or she observes Virgil engaging with past examples of ekphrases and setting up generic tensions that arise from this conjunction. First I would like to dwell briefly on the relation between ekphrasis and simile. The two devices have in common the fact that each stands as a metaphorical way to review the context in which it is placed and to shed new light on it. When Dido is compared to a wounded, incautious deer and Aeneas to a hunter who has shot his prey unwittingly, the reader conflates the text's eroticism (and moral ambiguity) with a pursuit that will soon turn from figurative to a redoubled literalness, first as the hunting lovers take shelter from the storm and then as Dido commits suicide with Aeneas' sword. But Dido is also compared, earlier in her misadventure, to Diana and, as the denouement approaches, to Pentheus and, as we saw, to Orestes acting their parts on the stage. Both analogies give her tale important mythical precedents, associating her personal history, in its early moments, with divinity's immortal freedom and, as it develops, with human madness reprojected in the permanence of tragedy and its performance.

But Dido is also Penthesilea, as the ekphrasis of Troy's demise and of Achilles' unceasing ferocity comes alive in the ensuing narrative. It is the resulting expansive community of exemplariness with the imagined palpability of art that sets ekphrasis apart from simile. Simile is a momentary, however sharp-edged, way of reimagining its context. The ekphrases in the *Aeneid,* of Ganymede, say, or of the Danaids, are equally brief, but their association with a tangible artifact gives them a symbolic dimension missing ordinarily from simile. We presume that Cloanthus not only admires but wears the cloak, with all that its decoration implies, and that the Danaid *balteus* works its fatal way through the text, touching the lives of Pallas, Turnus, and Aeneas. Moreover, simile, for all its enriching potential as a trope, lacks the multiple perspectives offered especially by the more expansive examples of ekphrasis, where the points of view of the narrator (and even of the poet behind his sometimes third-person extension), of commissioner and creator, of viewer or viewers within the text, of readers from the early years of the Augustan principate on to the present, have each much to tell us.

One factor which Virgilian ekphrasis and simile often share is a common heritage in earlier poetry. No reader can fully comprehend the force of the final simile in the epic, for instance—where Turnus, as his energy flags before his final confrontation with Aeneas, is compared to someone who dreams of his incapability of action—without looking back to the inspiration behind the verses. The reader is expected to compare this simile to a parallel one in *Iliad* 22, where Homer likens Hector, chased by Achilles, to a man who dreams he (barely) escapes his pursuer while the latter nearly catches him. Among Virgil's brilliant alterations to his model is the introduction of the first-person plural into the analogy: Turnus is like us, and we are like Turnus, as we seem to wish to move when, in fact, we are incapable of action. We readers share in the famous Virgilian empathy at work.

We must for a moment also watch Virgil's ekphrases from the point of view of the *Aeneid*'s literary background, and particularly of other ekphrastic texts in earlier Greek and Latin literature. I will be looking in some detail at such parallels in the chapters which follow. I need only point out here the most salient examples. The longest, which also has the hoariest tradition of scholarly reaction, is Virgil's emulation of Homer's shield of Achilles in the kindred artifact that Vulcan crafts for Aeneas. Virgil is at pains to have us observe both similarities with and differences from his Homeric model. In content, for example, Homer illustrates what might be styled universal elements in ordinary life—cities at peace and at war, seasonal activities, a dancing floor. The forward thrust of the epic forms a contrast with the circularity of the shield and with the notion of recurrence its contents imply: the balanced cities, the passage of the seasons, the dancers, and the potter's wheel to which they are likened.

We tend to compare and contrast these typological scenes of human endeavor with the unique heroic deeds of the *Iliad* itself. Virgil, by contrast, offers excerpts from an extraordinary shield that in its decoration encompassed all of Roman history. Its content is a linear projection into the near and distant future of the saga of the *Aeneid* itself. But its repetitions within itself and its echoes of the text within which it is located again remind us that we are dealing with a round implement and thus also with circularities, in this case with history which is at once

INTRODUCTION

a series of evolving novelties and a tale of humanity's constant replication of itself.

But the Virgilian divergence from Homer that has most occupied critics since the eighteenth century is the fact that the Greek poet allows us to share in the actual making of the shield, whereas Virgil, though he reminds us regularly that the shield has been crafted for Aeneas by Vulcan, places his ekphrasis at the moment of reception by the hero, not of manufacture by the god. Immediacy both of subject matter and of construction are replaced by topics only the student of the ekphrasis, not the receiver of the shield, can understand, and by presentation of the artifact sometime after it was produced. Perhaps a certain spontaneity is lost in such a mutation, but Virgil, by privileging ignorant recipient and omniscient reader over divinity in the act of creation, asks us not only to observe closely the moment of Aeneas' response but also to reflect on the meaning of the ekphrasis and on the importance of its position in the poem as a whole.

Interplay with earlier descriptions is also vital, though the scale is smaller, in the Ganymede and Daedalus ekphrases. For the former, both object and content urge us to compare the cloak, described in book 1 of Apollonius Rhodius' *Argonautica,* which Athena herself weaves for Jason. The emphasis its vignettes give to art and artistry spills over into our reading of the figuration of Ganymede and into any consequent pondering of the relation the craft of its particular story has to the meaning of the epic as a whole.

The Daedalus ekphrasis is more complex. In both its introductory lines and in the ekphrasis proper Virgil is thinking back to the sixty-fourth poem of Catullus and its more expansive look, first, at the initiation of the journey of the *Argo,* then at the story of Theseus and Ariadne as detailed in the ekphrasis telling of the decoration of the coverlet on the marriage bed of Peleus and Thetis which takes up nearly half the poem. There is overlap in the stories themselves as we deal with the heroism of Theseus. The *inobservabilis error* of Catullus' labyrinth becomes Daedalus-Virgil's *inextricabilis error,*[10] and Ariadne, in Catullus' description, "directing [Theseus'] wandering feet with slender thread" (*errabunda regens tenui vestigia filo*) blends into Daedalus himself helping both lovers and "directing the blind tracks [of the Labyrinth] with a thread" (*caeca regens filo vestigia*).[11]

But if Catullus turns from *Argo* to ekphrasis and its misfortunate lovers, Virgil dwells solely on Daedalus who in his daring, as he swims birdlike through the air, echoes the courage of the initial sailors swimming through the sea on the way to capture the golden fleece, and who in his artisanship undoes the products of his own imagination and fails from sorrow (*dolor*) to finish his own work. Where Catullus is expansive, and allows the verbal aspects of ekphrasis to have full sway,[12] Virgil opts for a compression that centers particularly on artists and artistry. He thus again urges a comparison between Daedalus, the artist recreating his autobiography, and the poet himself, between the daring of the Daedalian enterprise and that of the *Aeneid* as a whole, where the epic hero's final action, instigated through *dolor,* leaves so much unfinished and so many questions unanswered.

The close connection between the opening of *Aeneid* 6 and Catullus 64 raises another issue concerning Virgil's use of ekphrasis. Ekphrasis, as we have seen, tends in Virgil to occur at moments of friction—between narrative modes, say, or at instances where the plot is readied for a dramatic turn of events. Creative friction can also occur, as in the cases of the shield and Ganymede ekphrases, by comparison with earlier, parallel descriptions in the epics of Homer and Apollonius, on which Virgil cast a close eye as he worked. But Catullus 64, though the longest of his poems, written in hexameters and often given the label epyllion, or "little epic," is a very different work from the *Iliad* and the *Argonautica.* It tells not so much of great adventures unfolding over time, of the clash before Troy, or of the exploits of Jason and his followers during their voyage of exploration, as of human sufferings in the immediacy of present experience.

Though not technically a lyric, the sixty-fourth poem shares a great deal in tone and content with the shorter verses which give Catullus his reputation. More than one-third of its length, for instance, is devoted to soliloquy or spoken song: to Ariadne's lament at her deception, to Aegeus' prayer to his son (who betrays his plea), and to the marriage hymn of the Fates at the wedding of Peleus and Thetis, a hymn which pivots on a vision of the brutality of their child, Achilles. This pervasive emotionality is the stamp of a Catullus who is as much master of the whole as is Virgil, creator of Daedalus as heroic voyager and then as autobiographical sculptor whose passional side not only undoes the trickery of his art but causes it finally to fail.

The Daedalus ekphrasis, with its allegiance to Catullus, suggests then tangentially a complementarity with lyric. In the subsequent chapters I will look closely at two other instances where the creative challenge between ekphrasis and nonepic poetic genres becomes a major source of meaning for the Virgilian texts. The first is the episode of Silvia's stag, where Virgil's allusions to Propertius and to the tonality of Latin subjective elegy play a crucial role in enhancing our perceptions of the eroticism and, in particular, of the humanizing of the tamed animal, which serves as counterpoint to the growing bestiality fostered by the Trojan arrival in Latium.

The second instance, which I touched on above, is the relation of the Danaid ekphrasis to Greek tragedy. It is essential for our understanding of the *Aeneid*'s final books once more to observe the concomitant tension between epic's developmental demands and the attention which tragedy places on a character's inner anxieties and on the often deadly solution of individual ethical dilemmas. Moreover, Aeneas' violent, final thrust of the sword, as the sight of Pallas' belt brings with it the grief of bitter memories, offers no Aeschylean resolution of Furies into Eumenides. We remain caught in a web of killings which suggest reiteration of tragic suffering, not release from its very human toils.

Virgilian ekphrasis has another important sphere of interest to which the story of the Danaids on the sword belt in particular calls attention. In two instances openly, and in others in a more circumspect fashion, a comparison suggests itself between the poet's descriptions and examples of monumental art created in Augustan Rome contemporaneously with the writing of the *Aeneid*. The first clear example is the connection between the *balteus* of Pallas and the portico which Octavian (who would soon gain the title Augustus) constructed adjacent to his temple of Apollo, vowed in 36 B.C.E., while he was campaigning against Sextus Pompeius, and dedicated on October 9, 28 B.C.E.[13] As adornment in its intercolumniations it sported statues of Danaus with sword raised and of his progeny presumably in an equally belligerent posture. To superpose the idea of vendetta on the Danaid cluster allows still for a variety of interpretations of their role as a major component of the iconology of one of Augustus' architectural masterpieces. The women's husbands, the sons of Aegyptus, were both foreigners and cousins and could therefore, as we saw, stand as symbolic representations for both foreign and civil wars, for the need for retribution in either case, and perhaps even for the problematics of the final conflict leading to Actium and its aftermath, where Antony stands for a Roman antagonist, Cleopatra for an alien foe.

Great art, as here, must be open to a variety of explanations, often overlapping and mutually supportive. But in this instance the correlation between Augustus' public accomplishment in the plastic arts and the poetic ekphrasis by which Virgil imagines some forty-nine murders compressed into being raises special challenges for the student of both. The poet makes it clear, by his pointed use of *foede* ("foully") to qualify the massacre of the victims, that the killings were treacherous and therefore, to him at least, immoral, as the unsuspecting, helpless male quarry were duped by their perfidious brides. Virgil leaves unmentioned what Horace, writing in the same years, makes the subject of a powerful ode: the sparing of her husband, Lynceus, by the Danaid Hypermestra.[14] Though Virgil does not refer to this striking example of *clementia*, I suspect that any reader of the *Aeneid* who recalls the exhortation of Anchises in the Underworld to his son, as incorporation of future Roman heroism, to spare the beaten and war down the proud, would think of the virtue's conspicuous absence in the actions of the epic as it runs its final course.

The other instance where Augustan monumentality and Virgilian ekphrasis find a direct parallel is the connection between the shield of Aeneas and the golden shield which the senate and people bestowed on the emperor in the year 27 B.C.E. and which was set up on display in the Curia.[15] The conferral was made in token of his *virtus, iustitia, pietas*, and *clementia*, and these significant abstracts found as clear an expression on the *clupeus aureus* as they were deemed salient in the Augustus' ethical life. What complementarity exists between the senate's gift and the poet's imagined vision of Roman history must be left to the reader to decide. There is no doubt that we can discover exemplifications of

Augustus' broadcast virtues in the deeds of earlier Roman history, as crafted by Vulcan and written by Virgil, and find therein a compliment to the emperor, who incorporates the characteristics that have led Rome to the pitch of greatness that Vulcan's artifact displays climactically in the glorious days of Actium and beyond. Certainly *virtus* is ever-present in figures like Cocles and Cloelia; Cato giving laws illustrates *iustitia;* and we may find *pietas* in Manlius Torquatus as he stands before the temple of Jupiter, in the behavior of the mothers after the Gallic siege, and, writ large, in Octavianus Caesar himself as he leads his gods into battle against Egypt's theroid divinities. But the shield ekphrasis presents a far more complicated, ambiguous, mystifying entity than one that would rest comfortably in the confines of a eulogistic, quadripartite, public allegory.

The same holds true for two other ekphrases that, in a more general way, may be partially meant to echo Augustan monumentality. It is, after all, on the doors of a temple to Apollo, dedicated to the god after a difficult period of transition, that Daedalus sculpts salient moments in his aesthetic life. Augustus, too, makes a parallel offering to his protecting divinity, likewise after a time of challenge. On the doors of the Palatine shrine Augustus ordered to be sculpted two acts of revenge on the god's part, against Niobe for her boastfulness toward Leto and against Brennus for his destructive incursion against the god's sacred precinct at Delphi. For Augustus the theme of vengeance continues on, reinforcing the propagandistic, in some respects unidimensional, aspects of the Danaid portico. Virgil, by contrast, allows us a glimpse into the origins and feelings not only of the craftsman himself, of the power given to the creative artist, but of his emotional life as well and its sufferings and fallibilities.

Something similar can be said for the ekphrasis of the murals in Dido's temple to Juno. Again we may be meant to think specifically of Augustus' temple to Apollo. We have preserved, for instance, two large terra-cotta plaques that formed part of its decoration, one devoted to Apollo and Diana, the other depicting a wrestling match between the god and Hercules. In drawing a comparison here, we must paint in broader strokes. Dido and Augustus have this much in common: each is founding or refounding a city and initiating or enhancing its monumentality. For Augustus, Apollo and his genius, with the bow of war and the lyre of poetry as his attributes, complement two of the emperor's conspicuous qualities, as political mastermind and as *fautor* of the arts. Virgil's murals serve a far different purpose, but their place near the opening of the epic, as part of a burgeoning urban aesthetic design, would not be wholly foreign to certain of Augustus' own goals and achievements.

We can summarize many of these points about Virgilian descriptions by looking briefly in conclusion at the one notional ekphrasis to which I have not devoted a separate chapter. This occurs toward the end of book 7 where we are told of the armor of Turnus. Aeneas' chief opponent wears a helmet surmounted by a flame-spouting Chimera,

> at levem clipeum sublatis cornibus Io
> auro insignibat, iam saetis obsita, iam bos,
> argumentum ingens, et custos virginis Argus,
> caelataque amnem fundens pater Inachus urna.[16]

But Io in gold, her horns upraised, was represented on the smooth shield, now beset with bristles, now a cow, a mighty sign, and Argus, guardian of the maiden, and father Inachus, pouring water from a carved ewer.

Again we are reminded that we are seeing an artifact. The shield, after all, has a *signum* on it which is made of gold, and the river-god Inachus is properly emblematized by holding an urn that could be carved either on the shield or in the reality of the story the shield depicts. But this "sign," as so often in Virgil, is also miraculously alive. The still artifact is in motion, and the stoppage of time for the depiction of a work of art is paradoxically challenged by the continuance of the action which the ekphrasis portrays. However distant temporally or topographically remains the myth to which it alludes, the shield shows the event as still occurring. Io is even yet in the process of turning into a cow, and Inachus stays continually pouring water from his urn.

We have before us an *argumentum* in several senses. It is at once the inert embellishment on a shield and a moment in myth that is very alive before our eyes. It is also animate in another sense, as part of a tale in progress. We are witnessing an extraordinarily palpable crisis in the tale of Io, as the virgin princess appears in the process of metamorphosing into a cow, an event which is only part of a larger story with a before and after of Io's adventures.

This varied activity in the ekphrasis is what distinguishes it, in this instance, from a simile. However enriching it is for other contexts for us to see Turnus as a huge tiger among helpless sheep (as he holds sway within the Latin camp and now "sends gleaming lightning flashes" from the shield we have just seen for the first time)[17] or as the sufferer of a nightmare in which, as we noted, he cannot move despite his best efforts (as Aeneas approaches for the final clash), his shield ekphrasis reaches even more widely into its intellectual setting. First, it forms the climactic occurrence of a motif which permeates book 7, the metamorphosis of human into beast, and of calm into violence, as war begins in Latium. We begin the book observing the animals that Circe has made out of her human victims, among them bristle-bearing pigs (*saetigeri sues*), bears, and wolves. The Trojans apparently escape her transforming spells, but their arrival triggers the change of allegiance from pruning hook and plow to sword that both typifies the landscape's newly rearoused martiality and leads inevitably to Turnus as animal (and virgin warrior) and, finally, to Camilla, a woman playing a man's role, who, in the book's final line, carries as weapon a pastoral myrtle, emblem of Venus and peace, with a spear point affixed to its top.

There is activity of another sort in the ekphrasis. The implicit equation of Turnus with Io brings with it further intellectual baggage. We know from earlier words of Amata to Latinus of Turnus' Argive roots:

> "et Turno, si prima domus repetatur origo,
> Inachus Acrisiusque patres mediaeque Mycenae."[18]

> "and for Turnus, if the initial beginning of his ancestry is sought out, Inachus and Acrisius are his forebears, and the core of Mycenae."

Turnus brings with him, through his ancestor Inachus, the whole of the myth of Io which, at the point on which Virgil chooses to dwell, assumes his posture as a feminized, bestialized, tragic figure. He is the dupe and prey of Jupiter, presumably. Closer to home, and more explicit in terms of the epic plot, is the hero's connection with Juno. When in book 7 we first see the queen of the gods, "the savage wife of Jupiter" (*saeva Iovis coniunx*) is on her way "from Inachian Argos" (*Inachiis . . . ab Argis*).[19] She notices the Trojan ships safely landed in Latium and, in a clear parallel to her ruinous maneuvering that opened the first half of the poem, "transfixed by sharp resentment" (*acri fixa dolore*) she sets out on her path of renewed violence.[20] After Amata, Turnus is the second victim of the irrationality Juno brings to bear through her stooge, the Fury Allecto.

Turnus' continuing victimization by Juno suggests another aspect to the ekphrasis which reaches further into the poem. Io is the ancestress, some five generations in the past, of the Danaids.[21] The ekphrasis of Turnus' shield in book 7 thus anticipates the description of the baldric of Pallas in book 10, and for a purpose. As we noticed with the story of the Danaids, as well as with the Ganymede ekphrasis and with the comparison of Dido to the figures of Pentheus and Orestes performing their infuriate actions on the stage, there is no resolution to the tragic dilemma of Turnus-Io. There is no safe arrival in Egypt, no return to human form, no regenerative birth of a child. Just as Virgil allows no redeeming finale to the tale of the murderous Danaids, so nothing here compensates Turnus as he takes to himself the fatal metamorphosis of their Argive progenitor.

In terms of the development of the epic, then, we may see the connection of the two ekphrases as redolent of both the evolutionary and the static, just as the descriptions themselves are both motionless works of art and filled with multivalent energies that affect the text on several levels of meaning. They are evolutionary because they convey us along from book 7 to book 10, from preparations for war to the actual outbreak of conflict, just as the tales they tell draw us along in the history of a central Argive myth. But they are fixed as well, in time and space. Superficially both are connected with Turnus. He brings into battle the emblem of Io and, after his defeat of Pallas, absorbs the concentrated figuration of the Danaids as well. As an ill-fated figure who enters the fight taking as his icons a virgin turned into an animal or brides brutally murdering their incipient husbands, he stands for all warriors and all warring parties in Virgil's epic universe. No release from a cycle of repetitive savagery is suggested in the emblems of books 7 and 10 and the continuing tragedy they delineate. Nor does the ending of the poem itself hint that any change toward a more productive future is about to take place, as Aeneas kills under the influence of Junonian savagery, resentment, and anger.

Therefore, as a device that both demands of us a period of contemplation, as the narrative momentarily rests, and yet on a symbolic level propels that narrative along, the ekphrasis of Turnus' shield has much in common with other Virgilian descriptions. Its suggestive contents, however succinctly rendered, also propose reciprocity with the epic's other ekphrases, especially those of brief compass. It shares its complex eroticism with both the Ganymede and Danaid descriptions. With the latter there is the implicit, shared relationship of father and daughter(s), with the former of divine and mortal lovers, while *custos* or *custodes* look on helplessly. In this instance there is no maker named, but once again we admire an artifact that is both active and passive, a still work of art that yet remains vibrant and that contains characters that are either doers or sufferers, victimizers or victims. And in pondering the alteration from human to beast, we look back not only to a pervasive theme of book 7 but in particular to the ekphrasis of Silvia's stag, where the reverse takes place and a wild animal is not only domesticated but humanized and where eroticism also tinges the whole.

Finally, the ekphrasis of Turnus' shield has in common with virtually all other Virgilian descriptions the fact that the poet is contemplating and varying another ekphrasis from an earlier text. Here, too, a comparison can elucidate Virgil's accomplishment. The poet is thinking back to the second poem of Moschus, the "Europa," in which a twenty-line ekphrasis describes the decoration on the heroine's basket, which was made by Hephaistos for Libya, Io's granddaughter, and contained two scenes.[22] The first showed Io as a heifer, passing over the wide sea like a swimmer. In the second Io is transformed by the touch of Zeus back into a human. Beneath the rim we find Hermes, with Argus overcome and springing from his blood a peacock whose plumage fringes the whole.

For yet another time Virgil prejudices us by what he adopts and by what he omits, and again the intellectual pattern is familiar. Our poet in this case has seized for his ekphrasis on an event that takes place shortly before the time frame chosen by Moschus, namely, the actual instant of Io's dehumanization. What follows in Moschus, the seafaring adventure of Io and her return to normality in Egypt due to Zeus' intervention, is deliberately paralleled by the tale in which it is placed—where Europa makes a similar journey on the back of Zeus, for the moment in the guise of a bull, to Crete where their fruitful union is consummated.

Virgil leaves us without any of the happy fulfillments of either tale, only, in the case of *Aeneid* 7, with the animalization of Io, as Inachus and Argus look on. And again generic friction comes into play. Moschus' idyll, his "little picture," is a circumscribed entertainment, as charming in its narrative as it is emotionally unharrowing. Virgil tells another story. Epic, at least Virgilian epic, has few joyous completions, few happy roundings-off, only a steady pattern of emotional debasement typified in the career of Turnus, who begins as Io, enduring the lash of Juno's irrationality, and ends where his killer began in the first book of the epic, suffering his limbs to grow chill with cold. He is the final, passive, virginal target of a hero who in his ultimate deed betrays both the omnipotence of Jupiter and a Junonian wildness foreboding ill. It is Virgil's use of ekphrasis, here and in the examples analyzed in the pages which follow, that presents formidable signs for the reader in pursuit of meaning in that larger, ultimately "unnarratable" text which is the *Aeneid* as a whole.

I

Dido's Murals

Virgil's initial use of ekphrasis in the *Aeneid* is also his second longest and serves to educate the reader in many of the imaginative patterns the poet will follow in his subsequent descriptions. It comes halfway through the epic's first book as Aeneas views the murals which decorate Dido's inchoate temple to Juno. After a detailed critique of the verses themselves, I will turn to the influence the passage exerts on the poem as it evolves. In conclusion I will trace Virgil's originality vis-à-vis Homer and the eighth book of the *Odyssey* which serves as the Roman poet's primary model.

Of the six ekphrases of works of art scattered throughout the epic, the description of the mural paintings that Aeneas sees in the Carthaginian temple claims the reader's attention for a variety of reasons.[1] Because it stands as the initial example of the trope in the epic, it sets a pattern against which later uses will be measured. In particular, this is the first instance in ancient letters where the narrator has us "see" an artifact through the eyes of his protagonist who, moreover, takes part in one of the scenes put before us.[2] The paintings are the work of *artificum manus* (495), the "hands," literally and figuratively, "of craftsmen." But the narrator also posits Aeneas' responses as a form of artisanship, allowing the hero to add his interpretive prejudice to what he views and to influence the reader accordingly. Aeneas, as he is associated with the epic's initial ekphrasis, thus anticipates the roles of Daedalus and Vulcan in the epic's only other lengthy descriptions of art: his re-creation is parallel to their acts of origination. With Daedalus' artisanship Aeneas shares the element of autobiography, watching himself within an episode he views. In comparison with his portrayal of Vulcan at work,

Virgil scatters his initial ekphrasis with manifestations of Aeneas' emotional reaction to what he sees. These responses stand in place of words concerned with the artifact's manufacture in the shield ekphrasis, as if, in the case of Aeneas here, his inner perceptions are presumed to take an active role in the reproduction of what he contemplates and of what we review through him.

But, critics now rightly ask, in what senses do readers of Virgil's poem unduly limit themselves if they relinquish their own rights of interpretation to those of a character within the text, focal though he is? Aeneas construes the murals as evidence for two facts. First, since the eight episodes all deal with events associated with the downfall of Troy, Aeneas notes how universally celebrated such incidents were and, presumably, how worthy they and their protagonists were of immortality. This is especially so, given the fact that Dido and her artisans, not unlike Helen in *Iliad* 3 weaving her tapestry as Homer patterns his words, were selecting from a grand panorama of events the subjects for visual art to decorate her city's central temple. The pride implicit in Aeneas' reaction complements the second way Aeneas views the murals, namely, as evidence for the enormous sorrow such happenings engendered as they occurred and now arouse again at the moment of retrospection, and therefore of Dido's compassion in the face of human suffering and, in particular, of her understanding of Trojan hurt. We imagine from this, and we project into Aeneas' thinking, the shared experiences, and parallel sympathies, that might unite the two *duces* of their exiled peoples.

But Aeneas' critique of what he sees, his self-presentation as experiential witness through the narrator, need not preclude more disturbing readings of what Dido has crafted and of what Aeneas is made to contemplate.[3] Commentators, for instance, point to the disquieting fact that the murals decorate an edifice exalting the goddess who, the poem's opening lines remind us, is the archenemy of the Trojans and whose temple is dominant over a city whose future includes an intense struggle with Trojan Rome for control of the Mediterranean basin.[4] Moreover, we sense from the moment of the Trojans' landing on the Carthaginian shore, where threatening woods and black rocks form a backdrop (*scaena*, 164) against which evolving action will be performed, that tragedy, stemming from a chain of events riddled with instances of deception, will be a major concomitant of that action.[5]

Presuming, then, levels of intent in Virgil's ekphrasis more profound and troubling than what Aeneas seems to experience, I will first look at the description in detail. By examining the ways by which Virgil tropes visual art into verbal narrative, I will trace the strands of symbolism that run climactically through the ekphrasis. I will then pursue those themes that connect it with what follows in the epic. I will attend, nearer to hand, to Aeneas' subsequent narrative which directly continues the forward momentum of the ekphrasis, then to the reappearance of Dido in book 6, where Virgil uses language from the ekphrasis to reempower her after her suicide, and to the final four books, where especially the behavior of Aeneas and its consequences are highlighted by a series of references back to what he "sees," and soon figuratively becomes, in book 1.

Finally, I will turn back to Virgil's primary model for the sequence that takes us from the murals to Iopas' song of entertainment at Dido's banquet and thence to Aeneas' tale of doom and exile, namely, the three songs of Demodocus in *Odyssey* 8 followed by Odysseus' four-book chronicle of his adventures. My purpose is to search for the later poet's originality and especially for the heightened possibilities of meaning in an ekphrasis which forces the reader to pause not only to examine closely Aeneas' responses to what he views but also, relying on knowledge given to neither Dido nor Aeneas, to glean from the time-bound narration of timeless art matters which Aeneas himself cannot perceive. What may be an "empty picture" (*pictura inani*, 464) to the remembering hero, or even to the mindful queen behind its creation, with art standing in for life and reproduction for immediate experience, will take on further signification for the reader who is alert to the poem as a whole and to Virgil's propensity for layered meanings.[6] Virgilian ekphrasis both brings time to a standstill and energizes its context.

In addition to the novelty of having the reader closely observe Aeneas' responses and of making the hero for a moment a part of the action itself, the ekphrasis is unusual in that Virgil first offers us a summary of the whole and then a brief reaction by Aeneas to one aspect of what he sees before proceeding to the description as a whole. First the summary (456–58):

> . . . videt Iliacas ex ordine pugnas
> bellaque iam fama totum vulgata per orbem,
> Atridas Priamumque et saevum ambobus Achillem.

he sees in order the battles at Troy and the warfare now known by reputation throughout the whole world, the sons of Atreus, and Priam and Achilles fierce to both.

Aeneas, in the précis, sees two things shortly to be elaborated. He first takes note of the scenes of battle in a row and of the universality of such warring, the smaller spacings of Carthaginian art (*ordo*) taking their restricted place in the grander sphere (*orbis*) of what humankind as a whole knows. *Hic etiam,* here too, Aeneas shortly announces, there is reward for heroic prowess as well as acknowledgment of life's trials. As we prepare for the intense emotionality of the episode, the particular setting stands as synecdoche for the larger reaches of human endeavor, much as Virgilian poetry itself at every turn brilliantly combines excellence in the details of craftsmanship with cosmic implications. But it is to the worldwide repute that Aeneas immediately responds, noting the universality of Trojan suffering (*labor*).

The second focus of Aeneas' summary is on the figure of Achilles and on another variation of comprehensiveness, his ferocity to friend and foe alike. Catholicity of Trojan *labor* is complemented by catholicity of Greek *saevitia*. We will see both at work in detail in the ekphrasis proper. Here it is well to ask if the adjective *saevus* results from the narrator's perception of Achilles' emotionality or from Aeneas' or from both. We remain uncertain whether the hero observes what we certainly do—that is, not merely pictorial details but an inner characteristic given to a figure particularized climactically at the end of the summary. Does Aeneas, as he watches the ubiquity of Trojan *labor* further extended by the immortalizing *labor* (455) of Dido's craftsmen and martial exploits centered finally on one individual warrior, do what the reader must and pry into deeper meanings of the scenes' validity?

One brief phrase that intervenes between summary and detailed exposition also forms an important introductory note—*en Priamus* (461). Aeneas' exclamation comes partway through his address to Achates and divides it into two segments, the first an interrogative exclamation concerned with Trojan *labor,* the second a statement of assurance that *fama* brings reputation and that reputation fosters empathy of sufficient strength to formalize such esteem in art, to touch the mind even with matters worthy of tears (to rephrase one of the poem's most famous lines). For a brief moment, Priam is the special focus of Aeneas' own empathy which will be confirmed by his prominence in the larger ekphrastic design.

In discussing the ekphrasis proper I will have as a general goal to trace how we are made to admire the figuration of art through the figurations of language. We are at the mercy of a master deployer of words who manipulates what we see by what we read, fomenting a conspiracy between the reading eye and the seeing eye and proving, at least for the ekphrastic moment, the complementarity between the dimensionality of tangible art and the spatial quality of writing. In particular, Virgil uses various devices, including signposts for space and time, the interspersion of Aeneas' responses, and the tenses of verbs, to build toward a climax which at the end, however, exposes the failure of any idealizing aspect of ekphrasis in its effort to stop time. In the final scene, ekphrasis prepares to burst into narrative as stilled, timeless art sheds its static nature for the reality of immediate (narrative) experience.[7] The fact that the episodes are out of chronological order (the second episode, for instance, is based on events described in *Iliad* 10 while the third is pre-Iliadic) prepares the reader for divining that Virgil's purpose is more than the mere exposition of historical detail.

The first scene is devoted to general fighting (466–68):

> namque videbat uti bellantes Pergama circum
> hac fugerent Grai, premeret Troiana
>   iuventus;
> hac Phryges, instaret curru cristatus Achilles.

for he was seeing how, as they battled around Troy, here the Greeks were in flight, the Trojan youth were in pursuit; here the

Trojans were in flight, plumed Achilles was tracking [them] in his chariot.

The essential rhetorical figure here is chiasmus. We have, in order, Greeks, Trojans, Trojans, and Greeks, with the repetition of *hac* emphasizing the duality. Our eye follows from one side of the fighting to the other (twice represented) and then returns to the first side. It is forced to travel back and forth by verbal play in order to design what one critic, of another context, calls the "spatialization of synchronic tension."[8] Yet the lines also build to a climax. We have already seen Achilles characterized as *saevus* (458). Here our act of visualization also traces in the mural a growing sense of particularity as we contemplate a still more specified Achilles. Abstract leads to concrete as we observe the hero in his glory: *instaret curru cristatus Achilles*. Assonance and alliteration, figures of sound in service of a presumably visual impact, help lead our eye as it follows from chariot to the terrifying crest of the warrior's helmet. (The participial adjective gains particular stress for being Virgil's only use of a word which he may have invented.) Aeneas merely continues to gaze (*videbat*), and spatiality is insisted upon by the repetition of *hac*.

Centrality is the narrator's concern in the second episode (469–73):

> nec procul hinc Rhesi niveis tentoria velis
> agnoscit lacrimans, primo quae prodita somno
> Tydides multa vastabat caede cruentus,
> ardentisque avertit equos in castra prius quam
> pabula gustassent Troiae Xanthumque bibissent.

not far from here he recognizes, in tears, the snow-white canvas of the tents of Rhesus which, betrayed in their first sleep, Diomedes was laying waste with much slaughter, and turned the eager horses away into the camp before they could taste the fodder of Troy or drink of the Xanthus.

The five-line vignette focuses around its median line. This is itself golden, with noun, adjective, noun, adjective, in ABBA grammatical order, the whole pivoting around the central verb *vastabat*. The line is also ear-catching for the slow spondees in the first four feet and, once more, for the alliteration which links *caede* and *cruentus,* and the assonance that, among other effects, draws *Tydides* and *caede* together. Again verbal figuration forces the inner eye to follow a pattern which words dispose, toward an axis telling of a continuity of slaughter, but here, more than elsewhere in the ekphrasis and as a further aid to seeing, Virgil attends in particular to color vocabulary. There is the light-dark contrast between the snowy sheen of the tents and the (implicit) nocturnal background of the events, as well as the red-white contrast, so beloved of the Romans, between *niveis velis* and *caede cruentus.* We have the hint of yellow in the name of the river Xanthus and perhaps of yellow again or green through the mention of *pabula.*

The episode is carefully placed spatially (*nec procul hinc*), and its narration draws attention to Aeneas' empathetic reaction, both recognizing and weeping. The tense change between *vastabat* and *avertit* emphasizes what one sees, namely, the persistence of gratuitous slaughter occurring prior to what the viewer-reader must know from memory: the unique event which sparked the night raid in the first place. Both Aeneas and the reader must comprehend the larger circumstances of the episode.[9]

We will return to their importance later. Here we should note that this is the only incident among the murals devoted directly to Diomedes (he is implicit in the fourth episode, to come). As I noted before, it is out of order temporally with what follows; thus a pattern based on something other than chronology is crucial for our appreciation of the ekphrasis as a whole.

In the third episode we turn away from centrality and its complementary circularity to directionality as an organizing principle (474–78):

> parte alia fugiens amissis Troilus armis,
> infelix puer atque impar congressus Achilli,
> fertur equis curruque haeret resupinus inani,
> lora tenens tamen; huic cervixque comaeque trahuntur
> per terram, et versa pulvis inscribitur hasta.

Elsewhere Troilus, in flight, his weapons lost, unfortunate youth and ill-matched to clash with Achilles, is carried along by his horses and, fallen backward, clings to his empty chariot, yet clutching the reins. His neck and hair are dragged over the ground, and the dust is inscribed by his reversed spear.

The language of this vignette stresses the difference between the present, which in this case rules the episode so that we share in its immediacy, and a past which we must know about (*amissis armis, congressus*) in order to make the horror of the present more vivid. Complementing this distinction are the categories of active and passive, singular and plural, life and death. We begin with the juxtaposition of *fugiens* and *amissis*, continue with *congressus* contrasting with *fertur, haeret,* and *tenens,* and conclude with two present passives, *trahuntur* and *inscribitur,* which form part of a duet of concluding lines that sharply contrast briskness (477) with slow finality (478). Again, aural and visual aspects of the description conspire to collocate the fast dragging of Troilus' head with the more measured act of inscribing which brings the episode to an end.

There is a growing particularity as we move from horses, chariot, body drawn on its back (*resupinus*), and reins to neck, hair, earth, dust, and spear. From one vantage point, our seeing-reading eye follows the line of motion forward with the march of hexameter lines mimicking the onrushing speed of chariot and horses. From another, we look in the opposite direction as our vision works backward, from animals and vehicle out front, to reins and supine body (whether alive or dead is left to our imagination), to neck and hair, and, still further behind, to spear. In the final moment of particularity we turn from bluntness to pointedness. This change is supported by paronomasia on the word *versa.* We behold the action of writing as the culmination of a series of verses describing both forward impetus and backward inversion, a combination emanating from the tension which Virgil again builds between the seeing and the reading eye, between the multidimensionality of notional ekphrasis and the unforgiving drive of narrative.

More than the two previous episodes, therefore, the description of Troilus illustrates the tension inherent in ekphrasis between dynamic and static, between the verbal aspects of ekphrasis which the momentum of narrative necessitates and the inherent immobility of the visible art that we are meant to imagine. It is as if Virgil, in his first recourse to ekphrasis in the epic, were experimenting with it as a point of friction between various aspects of narrativity in epic and testing the possibilities available to him.

Concomitant with this creative tension is the irony lodged in perusing verbal description about an act of writing located in painting. Useless "writing" is inscribed climactically in brilliant words about art, as if to underscore the inseparable union in ekphrasis between what is seen and the medium through which sight is imagined. Ekphrasis here fosters such a collusion, of writing in war and writing of war, of dust and permanence, of the "turns" on which linear writing depends that also both mimic the reversals, and therefore portend the ultimate moment of mortality, which fate brings even to the young.[10]

Though the episode is placed graphically (*parte alia*) vis-à-vis the other murals, there is no response from Aeneas to the scene. The resultant shift from first-person perspective to third person objectivity combines with the immediacy of description to give the episode a universal, atemporal quality. One *infelix puer* and his tragedy, depicted in the presentness of art, anticipate, as paradigm, the several ill-fated youths, from Marcellus to Turnus, whose misfortunes mark the epic's course.

We move in the fourth episode from the rhetorical characteristics of the first three scenes, that is, chiasmus, centrality combined with circularity, and the challenge between the linear thrust of verse and an inner eye working against that thrust, to repetition as a unifying feature (479–82):

> interea ad templum non aequae Palladis ibant
> crinibus Iliades passis peplumque ferebant
> suppliciter, tristes et tunsae pectora palmis;
> diva solo fixos oculos aversa tenebat.

Meanwhile, the Trojan women were making their way to the temple of unjust Pallas, their hair loosened, and in suppliant fashion they were carrying a peplos, sad, their breasts beaten by the palms of their hands. Turned away, the goddess was holding her eyes fixed on the ground.

The scene consists of four lines, three of which end in a verb in the imperfect tense (*ibant, ferebant, tenebat*). What abets the atemporality of ekphrasis here, and runs in counterpoint to narrative, is multivalent repetition, where rhyming verbs in the same tense suggest unchanging continuity within the same temporal framework. The resultant stichic, measured quality complements the stateliness and majesty of the event itself. In breaking this pattern, line 481 receives particular emphasis. It begins with *suppliciter*, enjambed and at a sense pause, and continues in highly alliterative fashion with repeated *p*'s and *t*'s which both co-opt the sounds of the preceding line (*passis peplumque*) and reinforce those of *suppliciter*.[11] This burst of emotionality contrasts with the subsequent, concluding line, where Athena's lack of response is paramount. Hence we trace a chiastic pattern from Pallas in the opening line to *diva* in the last, with the expanded emotionality of the Trojan women intervening. Rhyme and repeated, final imperfect verbs overlay and confirm the effect of this balance. They take us back in the concluding line to the processional order of the initial two and offer the appearance of controlling emotionality and with it, for a moment, the course of events through the deployment of words. The circularity of chiasmus conjures up a picture's framed wholeness, while repetition aims, however futilely, to stop time. On this occasion a word of temporality (*interea*) replaces one of space to designate the relationship between scenes, reminding us that, however much ekphrasis may subscribe to a posture of temporal fixity, differentiation of time would exist between the events depicted in the paintings themselves, just as it takes the eye time to pass from one frame to the next.[12] The narrator here allots no response to Aeneas, one reason perhaps being that *interea* itself pinpoints the onlooker within the ekphrasis as he moves along.

In the fifth episode we see Priam in the prayerful process of ransoming the body of Hector which Aeneas, and we, know to have been dragged around Troy's walls (483–87):

> ter circum Iliacos raptaverat Hectora muros
> exanimumque auro corpus vendebat Achilles.
> tum vero ingentem gemitum dat pectore ab imo,

> ut spolia, ut currus, utque ipsum corpus amici
> tendentemque manus Priamum conspexit inermis.

Three times had Achilles dragged Hector around the walls of Troy and was selling his lifeless body for gold. Then indeed from the bottom of his heart he gives a mighty groan when he saw the spoils, the chariot, the very corpse of his friend, and Priam stretching forth his weaponless hands.

Once more, as in the second episode, there is a central line (485) whose axial position is staged for us by the repetition of the word *corpus* in the adjacent, bounding lines (*exanimumque auro corpus*, 484; *ipsum corpus*, 486). We are made carefully to contemplate one body as it affects three men, mistreated by one, prayerfully bought back by another, and witnessed through art's retrospective present by yet a third, Aeneas, who is the viewer within the narrative. The power of the hero's reappearance as spectator is especially evident here. He becomes central to the description, being allotted the entire pivotal verse and a verb of recognition in the last line, a more emphatic entrance than at 470 (*agnoscit lacrimans*), the only other instance in the ekphrasis where the responsive immediacy of Aeneas as viewer is also strongly felt.

We honor here a virtuoso five-line compression of major events of books 22 and 24 of the *Iliad*. Once again verbal rhetoric serves as metaphor for spatial deployment, designing a circularity that focuses the reading eye as if it were also actively seeing. Hence the reader of the text and viewer in the narrative here tend to become one and the same. In this case the Aeneas who knows all aspects of Hector's death, in particular the circumstances of how he had been mutilated before he was ransomed, is paralleled by a reader alert to the fact that Virgil is following a post-Homeric source for the setting of the mutilation. Scanning Virgil's text arouses in us a sense of recognition and commiseration akin to what seeing the mural brings to Aeneas. For the first time in the ekphrasis proper the painting remains unlocated in relation to its neighbors. This absence makes the appearance of Aeneas and his placement one of the major foci for the reader's eye as it surveys the scene.

The participant shares pride of place with the events themselves in our minds as we read Virgil's text.

I will return in a moment to one further detail, namely, what is intimated by the progress of verbs from *raptaverat* to *vendebat* and *dat* in adjacent lines. As a whole, this powerful reintroduction of Aeneas as viewer, after his absence in the poignant third episode, also prepares for his own unexpected entry into the pictures themselves which occurs in the first of the two brisk, subsequent designs (488–89):

> se quoque principibus permixtum agnovit Achivis,
> Eoasque acies et nigri Memnonis arma.

> Himself also he recognized mingled among the chiefs of the Achaeans, and the Eastern ranks and the weapons of dark Memnon.

As we enter a post-Iliadic world from here until the end of the ekphrasis, we find the pictures once again placed (*quoque*), and we observe Aeneas watching (*agnovit*), but here and in what follows Aeneas displays no empathy toward the scenes themselves. Likewise, in the change from *agnoscit lacrimans* (470) to *agnovit*, we experience a lessening of intensity as we turn from the hero's immediate, emotional acceptance of what he sees to an act of mere cognition. The restitution of the perfect tense to the narrative is a deliberate change from the present tenses that have hitherto characterized Aeneas' responses and from the imperfect tenses that have generally ruled the narrative. The effect is to give distance and historical perspective to both Aeneas and the reader. The turn away from actuality causes a conflation of the two viewers through mutual acts of recognition. Aeneas recognized himself at a remove from the events in which he once shared, now become an object of aesthetic interest, and the reader has a parallel sense of perspective in the belated act of contemplation and understanding.

Last we have the portrait of Penthesilea (490–93):

> ducit Amazonidum lunatis agmina peltis
> Penthesilea furens mediisque in milibus ardet,
> aurea subnectens exsertae cingula mammae
> bellatrix, audetque viris concurrere virgo.

Penthesilea in fury leads the forces of the Amazons with their crescent shields and flames in the middle of the thousands, a warrior, binding a golden belt beneath her naked breast, and she dares, a virgin, to clash with men.

Of the eight temple murals whose descriptions the ekphrasis comprises, the depiction of Penthesilea, at once conclusion and climax, is the only scene that lacks any locating word (in this it matches the Hector episode) and any reaction from Aeneas (here the Troilus vignette alone is parallel). It is likewise narrated completely in the present tense with only active verbs. There is no allusion to past events, as in the cases of Troilus or Hector, or of action to come (the situation of Diomedes soon to turn Rhesus' horses away from the fields of Troy) which the reader as seer must recollect for full comprehension of a painting. In this respect any comparison with the presentness of the Troilus episode breaks down. Troilus suffers as much as acts. Penthesilea, by contrast, is inspiring, not enduring, events which appear to be still happening before our eyes.

Hitherto we had been urged to share Aeneas' perceptions and, on two occasions, his spiritual involvement with what he saw. We now for the first time in the ekphrasis both observe a character's actions directly and enter into her emotionality. We have imagined the psychic reasons at the basis of the prayers of the Trojan women to Athena or behind Priam's gesture of supplication to Achilles. In the case of Penthesilea we are made, through words, both to see exterior and to intuit interior circumstances. The vividness of her visual appearance is complemented by a number of verbal novelties unprecedented in the previous episodes. The words *lunatis, peltis,* and *subnectens* are used here for the first time in Latin letters. We are urged to contemplate a woman who not only leads but rages, burns, and is filled with a daring that, in the poet's sonic play, pits *virgo* against *viri.*

The immediacy that first allows us to visualize the scene without the interruptions of spatial placement or of response on the part of Aeneas, as participant viewer, is complemented by an astonishing lack of the rhetorical devices that, in the first five episodes, co-opted the power of verbal artistry in such a way as to have the reading eye mimic the seeing eye. As we share in both the superficial and profound characteristics of the episode's cynosure, we are also experiencing the disintegration of a major aspect of ekphrasis, or at least this particular description as Virgil has hitherto prejudiced us to interpret it.

Such is the poet's extraordinary sleight-of-hand in the creation and placement of his final episode that the unspoken boundary between ekphrasis and narrative, between apparently timeless visual art under scrutiny (projected by brilliant rhetoric that forces the reader again and again to pause for atemporal contemplation) and the time-ridden world of epic narrative tends to break down. The inescapably narrational aspect of ekphrasis, which by definition as a figure it must seek to minimize, takes control as the ending of the description blends into the resumption of the story line. Ekphrasis and narrative begin finally to merge, and with good purpose. The energy only implicit in the inert picture suddenly is activated as it works its way into the epic tale itself. Penthesilea, envisioned fighting for Troy in the painting's graphic present, yields to Dido alive and right before us in all her bravery; we, understanding spectators of the whole scenario, need no additional ekphrastic representations of time and space.[13]

Virgil furthers the connection by linking the Penthesilea vignette to the simile that follows in four lines, after Dido has made her way to the temple. The Carthaginian queen is compared to Diana, keeping busy her choral dancers (498–502):

> qualis in Eurotae ripis aut per iuga Cynthi
> exercet Diana choros, quam mille secutae
> hinc atque hinc glomerantur Oreades; illa pharetram
> fert umero gradiensque deas supereminet omnis
> (Latonae tacitum pertemptant gaudia pectus).

Even as on the banks of the Eurotas or along the heights of Cynthus, Diana urges on her dancers, around whom a thousand mountain nymphs swarm on this side and on that. She carries a quiver on her shoulder and as she strides she towers over all the goddesses (gladness excites Latona's silent breast).

The linkage from *virgo* to Dido to Diana is forthright.[14] The thousands among whom Penthesilea burns for battle become the thousand Oreades who cluster around the goddess, and the Amazon's weaponry and exposed breast blend easily into the quiver which the huntress slings over her shoulder. The ekphrastic moment and subsequent simile serve parallel purposes here, and each aims to complement Dido, who metaphorically possesses the martial capabilities of Penthesilea and shares in aspects of the divinity of Diana, whose activities center on the dance and the chase. But the equation of Dido with two *virgines,* one heroic, the other immortal, has its ominous side. As long as she remains a virgin, which in her case means as long as she refrains from sexual involvement, she can retain her quasi-divine stance of power. Eroticism, we soon learn, will bring her only misadventure.

The search for deeper significance in Aeneas' relation to the ekphrasis must begin with one of the more salient aspects of the description, namely, the overriding presence of the figure of Achilles. He appears, we remember, at the climax of the initial summary (458), so we are not surprised to find him a constant in the ekphrasis proper. He is explicitly mentioned in episodes 1, 3, and 5 and his force is implicit in 7 and 8. (Only the episodes that directly or indirectly include Diomedes, numbers 2 and 4, and the single line devoted to Aeneas' recognition of himself among the Greeks lack any reference to him.) As critics duly note, Virgil has us attend particularly to the hero's brutality.[15] The summary dwells on his *saevitia,* and this ferocity takes vivid form in his treatments of Troilus and Hector, which have their similarities. The first, ambushed and forced into unequal combat, is towed, moribund, behind his chariot. The second, before the scene of ransom, had been dragged three times around Troy's walls, a dramatic change from the *Iliad,* where he is drawn only around the bier of Patroclus.

As the presence of Achilles alters from explicit to implicit, his victims change from dying or dead (Troilus, Hector) to alive (Memnon, presumably, and Penthesilea). It is crucial that at this moment in the paintings' "narrative," during the brief episode 6, Aeneas is presented for the only time in the ekphrasis, which is to say that at the moment Achilles disappears, Aeneas briskly but strikingly takes center stage. The insinuation is tellingly accomplished. The Aeneas who in the epic's final triad of books is regularly compared to the Greek warrior through the poet's allusiveness is already at work here. In the poem's final scene Aeneas faces a Turnus who is both Priam, as he stretches forth his hands to Achilles in prayer, and Hector, as he prepares to meet his doom. The reader at the epic's conclusion thinks back to the prophetic power of the complementary vignette in the ekphrasis. But Aeneas-Achilles is still nearer to hand. Achilles may lurk in the reader's mind, poised to kill Memnon and Penthesilea, after the events of the ekphrasis have concluded, but it is Aeneas who, for whatever reason, causes the demise of the latter's surrogate, Dido, not much later as the narrative proper resumes and takes its tragic course.

To help adumbrate an equation of Aeneas with Achilles in the reader's mind is a major reason for the extraordinary sequence of verbs in lines 483–85. Achilles is the subject of the first two, which take us from pluperfect, looking to the long-past mutilation of Hector, to imperfect, describing the act of ransoming still in progress during a past the spectator-reader must imagine. As we turn to the narration's immediate present, with the verb *dat*, Aeneas, the responsive beholder, is of course the subject, but the logic of the list of verbs, one per line in a temporal sequence from distant past to present, and the fact that no subject is directly named, both urge the reader at first to infer that Achilles, who in *Iliad* 24 grieves along with Priam, continues as subject of the final verb in the sequence. Such a hint supports what I have already suggested. Aeneas begins to merge with Achilles at a moment in the ekphrasis when the Greek hero becomes a background figure and when Aeneas turns from being the immediate viewer of the pictures to participant in their "action." As this action becomes dramatized fully in present time and as the poet prepares to project us from ekphrasis back to the narrative of Dido and Aeneas, Memnon and Penthesilea are still alive, and so is their killer.

As Penthesilea becomes Dido, past yields to present and ekphrasis is replaced by narration as the figured rhetoric of a presumably atemporal description of art gives way to a renewal of epic time. But the ekphrasis also continues to exert influence on reaches of the epic both near and far. As we trace this influence, we will be dealing, not unexpectedly for a poet of Virgil's complexity, with acts of anticipation, of repetition, and, in turn, of retrospection. Let us first look at its continuum with book 1 as the narrative resumes.

In terms of plot development, as we have seen, Virgil manages a smooth transition from Penthesilea to Dido. In terms of the rhetoric of ekphrasis, in this case as a device to look at time past through the fixity of art, as well as in terms of the story line itself, the murals anticipate the narrative of Aeneas which takes up the entirety of books 2 and 3. Even with the arrival of Memnon and Penthesilea, after Hector's death Troy is in its final moments, and it is to the downfall of Troy that the first segment of Aeneas' tale is devoted. Likewise, merely as an act of narration which stops epic time to tell, again in this case, of past Trojan events, Aeneas' first-person recitation has much in common with the murals' description. The results of Dido's *manus* and Aeneas' reportorial skills are richly complementary.

Virgil prepares the transition in several ways. One is through the figure of Priam. The aged king's presence is felt more strongly than that of any other individual save Achilles during the whole episode before the murals. Priam shares in the initial summary (458), receives a singular address from Aeneas (*en Priamus,* 461), and, of course, appears prominently in the ekphrasis proper (487). He is the first principal in the fall of Troy of whom we hear Dido later asking (*multa super Priamo rogitans,* 750) as she retabulates the major protagonists of the ekphrasis prior to the commencement of Aeneas' narrative. And the old man's death remains a climactic moment within that narration.

Another important link between the ekphrasis and Aeneas' narrative involves the talismans connected with Troy's fall. Three elements, in fact—the loss of the Palladium (the small statue of Pallas Athena stolen by Ulysses and Diomedes from her shrine on Troy's citadel), the death of Troilus, and "the tearing up of the lintel of the Phrygian gate" (which is to say the entrance of the wooden horse into the city)—do come together in Plautus' *Bacchides.*[16] Virgil begins his series of references with an event not mentioned by Plautus but one which forms an implicit subject of the second episode of the ekphrasis, namely, the turning away of the horses of Rhesus before they could crop the grassland of Troy. He continues with Achilles' killing of Priam's youthful son

Troilus, who by both name and genealogy stands as emblem for the city itself. Though Virgil would have known from art and literature scenes involving fallen warriors, there are no specific models, either literary or artistic, for the Troilus episode. It is therefore up to the reader to decipher its message. Part of Virgil's point, given the contiguity of the tale of Rhesus, is its iconic quality as a symbol of Troy's collapse.[17]

Such an emblematic, nonhistorical *ordo* of events in the ekphrasis, which is to say in the way Aeneas is made to view the murals, continues implicitly in the two episodes that follow.[18] It is presumably a monumental cult statue which, enlivened by the poet's rhetoric to personify the goddess herself, fails to be appeased by the gift of a peplos from the suppliant Trojan women. But the reader who has absorbed a deeper significance in the preceding two episodes might well make the passage from grand temple adornment to the smaller Palladium on whose stability the safety of Troy depends. Turning to the Hector episode with this sequence in mind, the reader is not surprised to find Virgil's non-Homeric emphasis on the walls of Troy, which replace the bier of Patroclus as the locale for Achilles' mutilation of Hector's body. The death of Troy's major hero, another son of Priam, and Achilles' flaunting of this accomplishment before the walls of the dead hero's city proleptically announce the demise of the city itself and the uselessness of its protective bastions.

What is implicit in the ekphrasis becomes explicit in Aeneas' narrative. Aeneas' entry into the ekphrasis, which concisely calls attention to his presence during Troy's last moments, breaks the chain of talismans whose representation also prepares us for the city's end. This combination makes the reader all the more eager to watch what happens when another aspect of the ekphrasis comes alive, this time in book 2. Aeneas' narration will tell us in detail what the ekphrasis only hints at—his actions during Troy's final hours. It is to a purpose that its first several hundred lines concern themselves directly with the two talismans that remain only adumbrated in the ekphrasis. We learn from Sinon's quoted speech what happens (or at least what he wanted his hearers to think happened) when Diomedes and Ulysses stole the Palladium from Athena's temple. But the central focus of Aeneas' initial words, indeed of the first half of the second book, is on the wooden horse. It is the ceremonial breaching of the city's walls, as Aeneas tells us, to allow the monstrous creature's entry that prepares the way for the immediate arrival of the Greeks and for Troy's doom.[19]

The ekphrasis, then, reaches out in anticipation to what follows, to become "enlivened" in two significant ways, through the association of Dido with Penthesilea and of Aeneas with Achilles, and through Aeneas' narration, which picks up the tale of Troy's fate. This double continuum has a distinctly sinister side which leads us directly into book 4.

When, at the end of the banquet which brings *Aeneid* 1 to a conclusion, Dido asks Aeneas of Priam, Hector, Memnon, the horses of Diomedes and Achilles, then, in direct speech, of Greek treachery and his own wanderings (750–56), she is pressing the transition from what she knows to what is apparently unknown (or, in Virgil's rhetorical usage, from ekphrasis to first-person narrative). But the narrative proper has already told us something of the queen's psychic state as she makes these requests (749): *infelix Dido longumque bibebat amorem* (and unfortunate Dido was drinking in long love). We have been prepared for Dido's tragedy to unfold by a number of factors, not least the military language Virgil had earlier allotted to Venus, who plots how she will "seize her by trickery and gird her with flames," and to Amor, who "seeks" the queen as if she were an enemy and "occupies" her, again as if she were conquered territory.[20]

Dido's destruction, which is limned here metaphorically and had been suggested symbolically in her identification with Penthesilea, continues through and then beyond Aeneas' narration. Dido's initial solicitation, at the end of book 1, is echoed toward the beginning of book 4:

> nunc eadem labente die convivia quaerit,
> Iliacosque iterum demens audire labores
> exposcit pendetque iterum narrantis ab ore.[21]

now, as day wanes, in her madness she seeks the same banquet and again prays to hear the sufferings of Troy and hangs again on the lips of the recounter.

Dido's world now shares a crucial characteristic with the ekphrasis and first-person narrative that have introduced the final act of her drama. Epic action of itself now comes to a stop in the renewal of banquets and in the reiteration of words that accompany them. It is no accident that the splendid phrase Virgil gives to Aeneas as he begins his tale to describe the complicity of stars and sleep (*suadentque cadentia sidera somnos*) is repeated in the story line of book 4, line 81. Original narration and its setting are carefully reintegrated in book 4 as Dido's life takes its catastrophic final turn.[22]

The murals of the ekphrasis may betoken for Aeneas the fame of Troy and Dido's empathy for suffering and sufferers. By the time we reach the initial lines of book 4 we realize that the ekphrasis forms the initial segment of a deeper narrative, of which Aeneas' own first-person exposition forms the next significant stage, preparing for Dido's death. Artistic implications of Troy's ruin lead to metaphorical adumbration of Dido as city in the process of being devastated. These in turn anticipate Aeneas' narrative of Troy's collapse which, as Dido hears it, abets her own downfall. When her death finally comes it is compared, in simile, to the fall of Tyre or Carthage.[23] She herself endures that which her murals foretell and what her paramour describes. And Aeneas is the cause, witting or otherwise, of this suffering.

This gradual change from Dido, creator of murals and thus performer of an act which stands as synecdoche for the establishment of a city in all its grandeur, to Dido, source of her own self-destruction, raises certain paradoxes about the ekphrasis and its relation to what follows. It is often the case that ekphrasis is treated in such a way that the viewer-narrator-re-creator plays a masculine role while that which is viewed, and therefore passive and reimagined, is seen, as feminine.[24] This distinction, which privileges the word—that is to say literature— over image and visual art, would at first appear to be reversed vis-à-vis the mural ekphrasis. Aeneas at Carthage watches a monument to his vanquished countrymen, an elegiac memorial that induces mourning. He who was once an active participant in a scene the ekphrasis portrays is now the passive sufferer of what he sees, yielding to a protracted display of grief. Dido, by contrast, not only causes the murals to be fashioned but seizes the opportunity to design a series of studies of brutality and venality which eliminate the compassionate side of Achilles that we find in *Iliad* 24 and serve to offer subtle homage to the violent Juno we have already come to know in the *Aeneid*.

But the reader watches another aspect of this change at work in the ekphrasis. The subtext of the murals is the metamorphosis of Aeneas, from victim in a shared defeat and lamenter upon viewing its stabilization in art, first into the once and future hero which the paintings postulate, but also more particularly into the vanquisher of someone nearer to hand. Dido, dynamic fashioner of New City, may at first seem in league with Juno as the embodiment of the destructive potential of those in power and as harbinger of Carthaginian hatred of Rome.[25] But the Roman enemy is already psychically within the gates. He who suffers his city's literal defeat and is a voyeur of its aged leader's ugly death metaphorically becomes the killer of another city's ruler and the destroyer of the city itself.

The change can be formulated also in terms of artisanship. We watch in the ekphrasis a moment where Dido is in power and Aeneas is the emotional responder. With the narrative of books 2 and 3, Aeneas is the craftsman of words and Dido the one who yields to destructive passion. The linkage from the horses of Rhesus and death of Troilus to the wooden horse is strongly forged. The talismans of Troy's downfall help conjoin ekphrasis and narrative into one continuous tale of defeat. But the percipient viewer-hearer observes a different pattern of cohesion between these exempla of visual and verbal rhetoric. As Aeneas takes the place of Achilles in the postekphrasis narrative, so as narrator himself he extends and confirms the parallel, telling of one city's defeat while becoming the symbolic conqueror of another. With Aeneas' mutation into a destructive Greek, Dido's civilizing act comes to an end along with her life. But the emblematic posture that Virgil allots his hero stays with us until the epic's final book where, among other incidents which look to his narration to Dido, Aeneas prepares to destroy the city of Latinus. It is not fortuitous that Virgil there describes Aeneas' destructive impulses using vocabulary similar to that of Aeneas in book 2 as he tells of the violent entry of Achilles' son Pyrrhus into Priam's palace and of his slaughter of the king.[26] Dido is the first, symbolic victim of this aspect of Aeneas.

The story of Dido continues on, first in book 4, with her desertion by Aeneas and death, then with her reappearance in book 6 when he finds her among the suicides, newly reunited with her former husband, Sychaeus. Aeneas addresses her, wondering out loud if he were the cause of her death. She scorns his excuses and his attempts at consolation:

> illa solo fixos oculos aversa tenebat
> nec magis incepto vultum sermone movetur
> quam si dura silex aut stet Marpesia cautes.[27]

Turned away, she was holding her eyes fixed on the ground, nor is she any more moved in her features than if hard flint or a Marpessian cliff were to stand [there].

Virgil means us to recall Dido's final speech in book 4 where she accuses Aeneas, because of his treachery and, to her at least, unresponsiveness, of being the offspring not of a goddess and a Trojan but of a mountain and tigresses:

> . . . sed duris genuit te cautibus horrens
> Caucasus Hyrcanaeque admorunt ubera tigres.[28]

but the Caucasus, bristling with its hard cliffs, bore you and Hyrcanian tigers offered [you] their teats.

Matters are now reversed. It is Dido who takes on the characteristic of hard flint or of a glimmering, Parian crag. But her reempowerment is depicted even more dramatically through line 469 which, with the sole change from *diva* to *illa*, reflects exactly line 482 of the ekphrasis where Athena scorns the peplos offered her by the Trojan women.

But to change here is also to confirm. Dido, who was compared to Diana in the first simile allotted her, is once again *diva* with the originating, active potency she possessed in book 1 restored to her. Nor does any disastrous liaison loom now in her future, no Aeneas as divinized Apollo, his weapons resounding on his shoulders.[29] In death her earlier marriage is restored. As for Aeneas, Virgil has him give way to tears during the episode.[30] He, too, for his final moment of association with Dido, takes on the feminine part he had assumed in his reaction to the murals. As a segment of the ekphrasis comes alive again in book 6, the two protagonists reassert their original roles, and Dido, for her last direct appearance in the epic, once again assumes the masculine posture of full command.

The topoi of the ekphrasis live on, also, in the poem's last four books in both specific and general ways, as if to say that what we witness and contemplate in the ekphrasis is the stuff of history with patterns that ever recur no matter how changed the detail, in Virgilian epic or even human destiny.[31] I will take the episodes of the ekphrasis in the order they are originally described. Diomedes' nocturnal slaughter of sleeping warriors, unaware of danger, looks ahead, first, to the happenings of Troy's last night, when the Greeks arrive to release their confreres from the wooden horse and wreak havoc in the city, and second, to book 9 and the night adventure of Nisus and Euryalus whose unnecessary violence leads to their own undoing. The graphic death of Troilus anticipates the several occasions in the final battles where a less experienced and usually younger warrior contends with one more powerful. We think of the combats of Pallas and Turnus and of Lausus and Aeneas in book 10, but Virgil's vocabulary draws us still more closely to the final duel of Turnus and Aeneas. Virgil's only two uses of the adjective *impar* in the nominative occur at book 1, line 475, describing Troilus as he faced Achilles, and at book 12, line 216, glossing how the Rutulians view the combat about to commence between their leader and Aeneas. Concomitant emphasis on the youth of Turnus—we hear of his "boyish face and the paleness of his youthful person" (*pubentes . . . genae et iuvenali in corpore pallor,* 221)—is another link with Troilus. The wider contexts also are conjoined by Virgil's choice of the adverb *suppliciter* to qualify Turnus as he approaches the altar in prayer (220) and the Trojan women as they make their supplication to Athena in the next scene of the ekphrasis (again, these are the only two occasions on which the poet employs the word).

A version of the Athena episode is replayed in the epic's eleventh book as queen Amata and her fellow matrons make their way "to the temple and highest citadel of Pallas" (*ad templum summasque ad Palladis arces,* 477). Their gifts and subsequent petition will have as little effect against the Trojan onslaught as do the prayers of the Trojan women against the Greeks, according to Homer's account in *Iliad* 6 and its recasting in Virgil's ekphrasis. Aspects of the Hector-Priam episode are replicated at several later moments in the epic but never more cogently, as I suggested earlier, than in the epic's final lines where we find Turnus, in the narrator's phrasing, "stretching forth his right hand in prayer" (*dextram . . . precantem/protendens*), a gesture reconfirmed in words allotted to Turnus himself and addressed to Aeneas: "You have conquered and the Ausonians have seen me, conquered, stretch forth my hands" (*vicisti et victum tendere palmas/Ausonii videre*).[32] The ekphrastic episode summarizes books 22 and 24 of the *Iliad*, asking us to ponder Hector's past mutilation and to "see" Priam's ransoming of his body. Turnus' supplication before Aeneas resumes aspects of both Iliadic moments. As far as Turnus is concerned, it reminds us of Hector's prayers before his death. In the case of Aeneas, we ponder Achilles' compassion for Priam, a reaction not shared by his latter-day refiguration.

Finally we have Penthesilea, whom Virgil carefully links by simile (11.659–63) with the virgin warrior Camilla, whose *aristeia* dominates the second half of book 11. We first hear of her at the end of book 7 where she is styled a *bellatrix* (805), the only other figure in the epic besides Penthesilea in the ekphrasis (1.493) to receive that designation. The parallels between the two, and also with Dido, are obvious enough not to need further explication, but a reminder of how Virgil deliberately links the deaths of Camilla and Turnus, by appropriating 11.831 as the last line of the poem, is relevant. Heroic as are all three characters (and the similarities are purposefully wrought), nevertheless, all must die, victims of fate and of its unstoppable instrument whom they are powerless to oppose.

Certain patterns come clear, even from this brief overview of how details of the ekphrasis resonate in the last quartet of books. In general terms, as we behold art becoming life, and as rhetoric that figures and freezes the visual melds into the closure of epic's grand narrative, we sense most saliently that history repeats itself. The last chapters of the *Aeneid* both continue and reiterate the contents and meaning of the ekphrasis, which becomes a synecdoche for the poem as a whole, suggesting *in parvo*, in a fashion typical of Virgilian poetics, the intellectual schemata of the larger entity. On the surface at least, names, dates, and places may change, but deeper symbols remain constant. In essence, this grander continuum reasserts what the intimacy of the ekphrasis with Dido and books 2–4 taught us: that the adventures of heroes have much in common. There are murderous nocturnal sorties, young warriors doomed to die in combat with their betters, goddesses obdurate to the entreaties of their worshippers, ancient kings whose cities share their own agonies, virgin women who play the part of heroic men.

But we must be still more specific. Our study of the ekphrasis showed two Aeneases, one the passive resufferer of Troy's demise now taken visual shape, who gains hope from the celebrity of his past and from Dido's empathy for its tribulations, the other a literal Trojan become symbolic Greek, an Achilles whose son, in Aeneas' narrative, brings about the actual destruction of Troy but who himself not only fails to heed Dido's prayers and emblematically destroys her city but, as the epic comes to a close, begins the actual devastation of Latinus' city and kills a series of young warriors, one of whom prays for mercy as the poem ends. In book 11 the Latin women see their enemy, against whom they implore Athena for help, as a Paris, a Phrygian robber (*Phrygii praedonis,* 484), echoing the sentiments of Juno and Amata in the seventh book who find a parallel for his behavior in a past Trojan act of rape.[33] But the ekphrasis proposes a more violent mutation. Instead of changing roles within a Trojan perspective, Aeneas becomes a Diomedes (*Aeneid* 11 repeating *Iliad* 6) or, at the conclusion, an Achilles who forgets his *pietas* toward paternal ethics based on *clementia* and acts, like the focal figure of the ekphrasis, with a brutality which in Aeneas' case is abetted by anger and the Furies' fire.

I would like to conclude with a comparison of the ekphrasis and its larger poetic setting to its primary model, the three songs of Demodocus before the Phaeacian court in *Odyssey* 8, followed by Odysseus' narrative of his adventures (*Odyssey* 9–12).[34] Demodocus' first song serves as entertainment at a banquet, and the narrator tells its contents, namely, a quarrel between Odysseus and Achilles and the pleasure it gave Agamemnon for presumably predicting in its early stage a positive outcome for the Trojan war (72–82).[35] The second, which Demodocus chants as accompaniment to dancers and is recounted by Homer at much greater length with the inclusion of several first-person speeches, is devoted to the adulterous affair between Ares and Aphrodite and to their capture by Hephaistos (266–366). Demodocus' third song which, as his first, likewise accompanies a feast, concerns the entrance of the wooden horse into Troy and the ruination that results (499–520).

Virgil alters this pattern in several salient respects. He replaces Demodocus' first song and its hint of Troy's future demise with the ekphrasis of Dido's murals and their detailed presentation of events precursorial to Troy's final collapse. A brief *De Rerum Natura,* sung by Iopas at Dido's banquet, stands as substitute for Demodocus' more expansive tale of erotic escapades among the gods (742–46):

> hic canit errantem lunam solisque labores,
> unde hominum genus et pecudes, unde imber et ignes,
> Arcturum pluviasque Hyadas geminosque Triones,
> quid tantum Oceano properent se tingere soles
> hiberni, vel quae tardis mora noctibus obstet; . . .

He sings of the wandering moon and the efforts of the sun, whence the race of humankind and beasts, whence rain and fire, Arcturus and the rainy Hyades and the twin Bears, why winter suns make such haste to dip themselves in the Ocean, or what delay holds back slow nights.

Finally, the chronicle of the wooden horse and the results of its induction into Troy anticipates directly Aeneas' first-person elaboration of the same events. Yet Aeneas, by rehearsing his own tale, also merges with Odysseus so that he becomes both blind bard and picaresque hero, entertainer at a grand repast, apparently uninvolved with what he sings, and valiant participant in that same story line. By placing such emphasis on alterations to his Homeric model, Virgil asks his reader to examine these changes for their part in explicating the later poet's intellectual designs.

One point of departure is to watch audience reaction to what it hears or, in the case of the ekphrasis, sees. To all three of Demodocus' songs the Phaeacians respond with pleasure. They take only aesthetic delight in what they hear for, in the case of the first and third songs (which deal with the initiation and conclusion of the Trojan conflict), their utopian existence has kept them immune from war and hence from the ability to empathize with those who have endured its horrors. Odysseus, to be sure, shares the response of his fellow hearers to the second song which, rich though it may be in meaning, does not recount a situation with which any of Demodocus' listeners, including their foreign visitor, could be expected to identify. But upon listening to the first and third songs, Odysseus weeps uncontrollably yet manages to hide his reaction from everyone else in the audience save king Alcinous.[36]

Virgil reverses this distinction between public and private, and this reversal may help to explain why the Roman poet chose to expand the matter of Demodocus' first song (one episode at the start of the Trojan war) into a series of vignettes connected with Troy's fall, whose order is independent of chronology, and to honor them with the figuration of ekphrasis which has no equivalent in Homer. What is private in the *Odyssey*, namely, Odysseus' sorrow because he had experienced the events of which Demodocus sings and now reendures them in a way his fellow hearers cannot share, becomes public in the *Aeneid*. Aeneas feels no qualms about openly weeping (459, 465, 470) and groaning (465, 485) as he stares at the murals, and, in one of the epic's more memorable lines, he finds in them evidence of *lacrimae rerum* (462), "tears for things."[37] The scenes are sorrowful in themselves and are of such poignancy that mere knowledge of the events, from whatever source, could cause Dido to create the murals in the first place. The empathy that impels the Carthaginian queen to imagine the suffering of others in sufficient depth to actuate their permanence in art is paralleled in the tears which Aeneas sheds in response to this double aspect of the murals.

This means that what is public in the *Odyssey*, the enjoyment of art for art's sake, especially for its value as entertainment, is replaced by what is private in the *Aeneid*, but in a profound, particularly Virgilian way, abetted by the poet's brilliant recourse to ekphrasis. Aeneas sees the surface meaning of the murals, namely, the sorrow, which is brought to himself by the events they picture and which can be shared by others. But it is the reader who, through the ekphrasis, has the opportunity of making the leap from the empathy that superficial viewing allows to the deeper understanding that description fosters. The frozen figuration of ekphrasis demands of the reader a pause for the contemplation of art. This in turn permits the connotational aspects of what is described to register along with, and often in contradistinction to, what it readily denoted. The reader in the *Aeneid* becomes what Dido and, in part, Aeneas are not permitted to be, a type of knowing Odysseus, harboring knowledge to himself and meditating upon what the immediate responder in the narrative cannot observe. No doubt there is also a certain equivalence between the reader, contemplating at leisure, and the perceptions of an Odysseus or an Aeneas, responding emotionally to what he hears or sees. They, too, not only were participants in the events in whose artistic reproduction they share but also now have a temporal distance between the occurrences and the present moment, which gives the past a deeper resonance in the memories of each hero.

Ekphrasis offers the reader the challenge, as well as the privilege, of contemplating not art but words about art. The reader replaces Aeneas to become a spectator by imagination, an inner evaluator of art. Should he choose or be able to take advantage of the situation, he is allowed, by repeated contemplation in the mind's eye, to generate meaning for art which the uninitiated audience, experiencing only a surface response, is not allowed to share. On the immediate level the poet replaces bardic performance with painting, aural with visual art, hearing with seeing. But Virgilian ekphrasis, by putting the final onus of interpretation on the scrutiny of visual images as it turns external into internal seeing, adds a dimension absent in Homer and prepares the reader to expect a more complicated outcome to events subsequent to the ekphrasis than viewers within the text are capable of realizing. The ekphrasis of Dido's murals is no exception to a general rule about notional ekphrasis: just as the art described seemingly freezes time in a permanent visual image, so ekphrastic narrative about such images likewise aims at atemporality. And this very atemporality allows the reader the leisure to shape opinions that characters within the text are unable to form. Confronting the timeless murals Virgil describes ekphrastically in a text that is neither totally outside of time nor totally within it, the time-bound hero must pass limited judgment, as in book 1, or move on before deeper meanings might become clear (the situation of Aeneas in book 6, facing the sculptures of Daedalus), or marvel in ignorance before Vulcan's astonishing shield.

Finally, replacement of Demodocus' first song by Dido's decorative art might also be seen as a particularly Augustan gesture on the part of Virgil. Instead of oral poetry repeating past epic adventures as bardic entertainment within a palace, we have the public monumentalizing of art. A reader of Virgil's time who had seen Augustus' grand monument to Apollo (dedicated in 28 B.C.E.) and pondered the meanings of its decoration, whether interior statuary, door panels, or terra-cotta embellishments, would not find the poet's description foreign to his or her intellectual milieu.

The relation of the song of Iopas to the second song of Demodocus, indeed, its appropriateness in the first place, was debated in antiquity. Macrobius felt that to chant *de sapientia* at a banquet, whether among the Phaeacians or the Carthaginians, would bring laughter down on the performer. Servius, in clear answer, counters that a "song concerned with philosophy" (*philosophica cantilena*) was perfectly suitable as part of a *convivium* for the queen while she is "still chaste" (*adhuc castae*).[38] Servius is on the mark, especially when we think of the generic conflict which the Roman poets themselves encourage between love-elegy and didactic poetry concerned "with the nature of things." When Tibullus' speaker wants the help of the Muses to regain his girl's affection, he will not sing of war

> nec refero Solisque vias et qualis, ubi orbem
> complevit, versis Luna recurrit equis.[39]

> nor do I tell the ways of the Sun or what the Moon is like when she has completed her circuit and runs back [on her path] with her horses turned.

Propertius looks forward to learning the *naturae mores,* but only after age has called a halt to his involvement with Venus.[40]

But Servius' comment also helps point up the rich irony in the situation Virgil is developing. Dido may still be chaste, in the commentator's phrase, but she is already the victim of Amor (the narrator styles her *misera* already at 719) before the banquet begins, and we have seen how, three lines after the song's conclusion, "she was drinking in her long love" (*longum . . . bibebat amorem*). An impersonal celebration, in traditionally dispassionate verse, of the patterns nature imposes on the physical universe would be an appropriate complement to a human world that was equally graced with order, balance, and control.[41] Since such is no longer the case with Dido's psychic state, Virgil sets up a tension between song as entertainment and the queen's erotic situation.

This tension is reinforced for the reader pursuing Virgil's elaborate dialogue with the Homer of *Odyssey* 8.[42] Virgil's narrator may tell of a bard's chanting *de rerum natura,* but we are expecting to hear something parallel to Demodocus' extended tale of the adulterous union of Ares and Aphrodite and their imprisonment in the toils of Hephaestus. Whatever the actuality of Iopas' song, the reader tends to overlay it with a version of Homer's story of corrupt eroticism. And in fact it is a more serious version of Demodocus' divertissement that Virgil's story line fashions, leading first from Dido's infidelity to the memory of her husband, then to her suicide.

But Iopas' song may not be as out of place, or as deliberately contrastive, as it at first seems. The "nature" of which the bard tells is not unproblematic. The matter of the first line (742) is a case in point: *hic canit errantem lunam solisque labores.* Virgil is modifying a verse drawn from his extended bow to Lucretius in the second *georgic* (478) where he tells of *defectus solis varios lunaeque labores* (the different withdrawals of the sun and the efforts of the moon). To the *labores,* attached now to the sun, Virgil in the *Aeneid* adds the notion of wandering, which has become the moon's lot. It is not long before both these characteristics recur in the narrative. Dido will soon ask Aeneas to tell of his wanderings (*errores tuos*) and of how seven years carried him wandering (*errantem*) over sea and land.[43] We have long since heard of the *labor* or *labores* of the Trojans and the Carthaginians.[44] But the content of Iopas' song anticipates both Aeneas' incipient narrative, which will tell of Troy's "final labor" (*supremum laborem*) and of Dido's frenzied request, at the start of book 4, to hear him recount once again "the labors of Troy" (*Iliacos labores*), as she renews her banqueting.[45]

Iopas thus symbolically anticipates both Aeneas and his tale that tells of wandering and struggles. Taken simply as singer of a *de rerum natura,* he merely entertains. Seen as precursor of Aeneas' subsequent narrative, and as replacement for Demodocus' second song of adultery surprised, Iopas' song appears as a logical next step in the progression that began with the ekphrasis of the murals. In each case Aeneas is deeply involved, and each part of the sequence looks to the destructive eroticism that the Trojan hero will bring to Dido's world, first as murderous Achilles, then as narrator of a tale of misery that brings to his Carthaginian listener the ultimate suffering of death.

This intimacy of Iopas and Aeneas, along with the ambiguities attached to each bard's subject matter and performance, leads directly to the final parallel between Virgil and Homer, namely, the merger of Demodocus, through his last song on the wooden horse, and Odysseus, for his subsequent extensive narrative, into the single figure of Aeneas himself.[46] Aeneas becomes twice over a performer, diverting his audience as did both Demodocus and Odysseus. But the combination also further underlines the doubleness we have already seen Virgil encourage us to see in Aeneas from the earlier ekphrasis. He is both a continuator of the art he enlivens (ekphrasis become narrative) and participant in that "art," both entertainer in words and sufferer of the events he describes. But as Odysseus redivivus he becomes Greek as well as Trojan and in particular a Greek who is master of a rhetorical subterfuge that could deceive at the same time as it enthralls.[47]

By means of the comparison of Dido to Diana we noted earlier, among other links, Virgil is at pains to draw a connection between the ruler of Carthage and Nausicaa who, in the simile at *Odyssey* 6.102–109 (which served as model for *Aeneid* 1.498–502) is likened by Homer to Artemis.[48] But to move from the virgin princess to Dido, from the Eden of Phaeacia to the hard realities of Carthage, is to shift from a young girl's gossamer existence and its erotic suggestiveness to the incipient tragedy of the infatuated queen. In the process Aeneas becomes not only Odysseus engrossing Dido as a type of Alcinous who could listen "until bright dawn," so enchanted is he by what he hears, but a duplicitous lover as well, whose narration expands the ambivalent role that he must play throughout his liaison with Dido.[49]

Let me return, in conclusion, to my initial discussion of Aeneas as both viewer and object of view, of the hero as "artist" who both reacts and explains. Why does Virgil place Aeneas in this privileged role as contemplative and critic, especially at the challenging moment when the poet is experimenting for the first time with ekphrasis and with the tension in narrative techniques its embedding in epic engenders? Why at this particular instant is he both a passive figure, pondering his own active past frozen in art, and yet dynamic, beholding for a moment his own passivity but responding as well? One answer lies in the ambiguous potential of Virgilian ekphrasis, at once both bringing the immediate plot to a rest and enhancing its ongoing concerns. Here at least, through the pause ekphrasis necessitates, Aeneas is allowed the complementary occasion for self-reflectivity and for the demonstration of empathy toward self and others. At the start of the epic, the reader, for an instant becoming Aeneas by watching him watching, absorbs at least one extraordinary set of circumstances where its hero is allowed to choose meditation over action.[50]

The differences between how Aeneas sees the murals and how the reader understands the ekphrasis that describes them are therefore crucial for appreciation of what follows, both immediately and in the epic's longer distance. The ekphrasis furthers the several reversals that come Dido's way, from active to passive, male to female, as control is gradually wrenched from her and given to her absconding lover. It is thus typical of all the other descriptions of art in the *Aeneid,* claiming the reader's contemplative attention, as the narrative appears to stop, to the nexus of multiple meanings which it harbors. As he rivals Homer for one of the most extensive stretches of his epic, Virgil also exerts his originality, turning Demodocus' brief first song into one of the singular moments in the poem, where sight and insight converge.

2

The Cloak of Cloanthus

We turn now to the first of the poem's three shorter examples of ekphrasis. It deals with the tale of Ganymede woven on the cloak given by Aeneas as prize to Cloanthus, victor in the boat race of book 5.[1] After first analyzing the ekphrasis in detail, I will place it in its various contexts, in the history of the Ganymede myth, in the ekphrastic tradition of embroidery on cloaks, and above all in the nearer setting of book 5, which in turn has ramifications extending toward the meaning of the poem as a whole. My thesis is that here, as well as with the grander ekphrases, Virgil is offering a paradigm for his poem as a whole and that the spatial design of the artifact, however limited in compass, offers us a way to reformulate major concerns of the host poem in which it is embedded. Its "story," under the pretense of a topos which aims for the stoppage of time, helps us revoice larger unifying patterns of cohesion and unity which typify the epic's structuring and, going against the temporality of history's narrative, give the poem, too, the appearance of an artifact's wholeness.

Here are the verses themselves with their two-line introduction (5.250–57):

> victori chlamydem auratam, quam plurima circum
> purpura meandro duplici Meliboea cucurrit,
> intextusque puer frondosa regius Ida
> velocis iaculo cervos cursuque fatigat
> acer, anhelanti similis, quem praepes ab Ida
> sublimem pedibus rapuit Iovis armiger uncis;
> longaevi palmas nequiquam ad sidera tendunt
> custodes, saevitque canum latratus in auras.

to the winner a cloak with gold, around which ran deep Meliboean purple in double waving line; inwoven thereon the royal boy, with javelin and speedy foot, on leafy Ida tires fleet stags, eager, like someone panting, whom Jove's swift armorbearer has caught up aloft from Ida in his hooked talons; his aged guardians in vain stretch their hands to the stars, and the barking of dogs rages against the breezes.

In the arc of one sentence covering six lines Virgil takes us across chronological space that covers three events in the life of the Trojan youth: his hunting in the forests of Ida, his capture by the eagle, the reactions to his loss by guardians and hounds.[2] In the initial segment of the actual description we are twice reminded that through words we are witnessing a work of art. The boy is, at the first, *intextus*, the passive subject of two weavers, of cloth and of language, fabricated on a cloak whose structuring is mimicked in the elaborate intertwinings of the Latin phraseology. He is also, as the brief opening episode comes to a close, "like to someone panting" (*anhelanti similis*). Just as the initial word of the ekphrasis proper stressed his artificiality, so we are now to imagine him not as acting but merely as seeming to act, alive only in appearance. This double passivity, this enclosing reminder that Ganymede is being shaped, extends by grammar into the second episode, conveyed in a relative clause whose ten words offer him as the object of the eagle's grasping onrush and of desire.

But, though *similis* for a moment abstracts us from action, *anhelanti* has the opposite effect. From the generalized hunting scene sketched in the preceding lines, the phrase *acer, anhelanti similis* forces our attention directly on to the youth himself. It takes us, via an intense, compressing asyndeton, from his mindset, as shrewd (*acer*) tracker of deer, to our thoughts which assert the vigor of his physical and emotional presence (*anhelanti*). And this climactic imagining of corporality, as Ganymede pants from the force of exertion that mimics his desire, carefully anticipates his immediate metamorphosis from hunter to hunted, from a predator of animals to the prey of a creature used to handling the thunderbolt of Jupiter. Though a separate event in the poet's tripartite scheme, the new episode is treated, as we saw, in a subordinate manner grammatically, through the relative construction which turns the energetic youth into the goal of the bird's quest and of Jove's presumed yearning, which we must supply but which the poem conspicuously refuses.

Until we hear otherwise—and we never do in Virgil's version of the myth—Ganymede would only seem to suffer change from human to another version of the eagle's ordinary quarry in the animal world, weaker creature in the clutches of stronger, readying his victim for death.[3] For all we are told, Jove's (unstated) erotic will, as executed by his emissary and construed by the willful poet and by his complicitous reader in the boy's grammatical passivity, betokens for Ganymede only mutation down to bestiality and presumed death. As our eye first rests on Ida and then soars heavenward again from it, the poet does not draw either his protagonist, or the thoughts of his readers, toward apotheosis or even erotic fulfillment. The ascent from mountain to heaven leads not to a vision of transcendence but only to a return to earthbound dissatisfaction.

The greed of winged servant and of master is elaborated, lexically, in the false prolepsis of the attribute *praepes* ("well-omened," but more essentially "forward-seeking") and, figurally, in the alliteration between *praepes* and *pedibus,* the instrument whereby the beloved youth is captured. The particular capability of these claws is stressed through the placement of the word's adjective, *uncis* (hooked), at the conclusion of the line which also brings completion to the phrase. If, at the end of the first moment, our eye is made to rest on the eager boy, it is on the curve of the eagle's talons, and on the amalgamation of desire and destruction, that we attend as the second vignette comes to a close. We are arrested at the talons of the eagle, which substitute for any pleasure on Jove's part, and returned to a world of absence and unfulfillment.

The third episode finds its protagonists on earth but expands our visual horizon to embrace the vertical axis suggested by the relative clause, now on a still grander scale. Its poles are presented to us twice, with guardians stretching their hands to the stars and with howls of canine anger hurled against the breezes. Each group—humans ordered in prayer, animals venting their bestiality through rage—aims its vain, vanishing desire toward an apparently unresponsive world above.

Our reading thus takes us, temporally, across the visual space of events also occurring over time, but narrative time in Virgil's craft initiates a countermovement as well. The grammar of the three episodes effects a chiastic balance between direct statement, relative clause, and direct statement that is reflected in the alternation of tenses from present to perfect and then back to present. The continuity of hunting, the regularity of a youthful pursuit that in an adolescent's ordinary experience would lead to the responsibilities of manhood, is broken by a unique moment of pastness which lends to the myth of Ganymede its specialness at the same time as it removes him from our quotidian expectations. This singular event compels the expectation that Ganymede has been whisked into a position where youthfulness remains invulnerable to the demands of growing up, not to speak of the importunities of mortality.

What remains, thereafter and finally, for Virgil's readers is to dwell on a second, complementary moment in the world of ongoing humanity where those whose lives Ganymede particularly touched, the elders who served as his guardians and the dogs who were essential accompaniments to his hunting, react continually to his loss. Whatever the particularities of the two central verses that press forward a story line, the framing pairs, by their careful balance, where parallels in grammar complement the terrestrial presentness of the protagonists, give a sense of wholeness to the description which belies the loss of which it tells. They also exemplify for us, through this circularity and repetitiveness, the impossible but inescapable goal of spatial atemporality toward which poetic ekphrasis vainly strives.[4]

In dealing with this or any poetic ekphrasis, we should remember the irony that enargeia, the vividness of description that is a crucial complement to ekphrasis, presumes. Because we are not literally seeing but only visualizing a scene created for the mind's eye, we join in a complicity with the poet and his words which maneuver our imaginings. A phrase like *puer frondosa regius Ida,* with its complex interplay of ABBA and ABAB order, is a case in point. Its very artistry is open to the poet alone, illustrating through syntax how slightly such descriptions are in fact ekphrastic and how dependent they remain on the molding power of words. The superficial aim of ekphrasis is verisimilitude, but semantic history and the figurations of language intersect this manifest purpose in a radical way. The poet gains his particular force from construing and from teaching us to infer, not from any unwonted ability to make his readers behold a tangible object. Only a poet can suggest, through a syntactic determinacy that challenges an artifact's pictorial limitations, that we "see" the impossible, such as Ganymede panting and heaven's breezes, or that we apprehend a triptych founded on a circle, which is the structural mystery of this particular ekphrasis.

This circularity reminds us of what Virgil chooses to emphasize and to suppress in his concentrated version of the Ganymede tale. When we combine previous literary references with what we possess or know of artistic representations of the myth before Virgil, the full range of events in the history of Ganymede is covered and would have been available to the reader and hence to the poet for his manipulation. He would know from Homer of the gods' abduction of the boy because of his beauty, from Troy to Olympus to be Zeus' wine-pourer.[5] Later sources place the abduction on Mount Ida, as the boy harried its animals, and name its perpetrator not as some vague "gods" but as the king of the immortals or his thunderbolt-bearing eagle (with claws that either hurt or tenderly grasp),[6] or the former in the guise of the latter. Finally, they view Ganymede about his heavenly task, even to the point of offering goblets to his feathered captor.

If we look in particular to his main literary predecessors, Homer and Apollonius, and to his immediate successor, Ovid, we find a striking omission to which Virgil would have us attend. In the *Iliad* the poet, as we noted, places Ganymede on Olympus as Zeus' wine steward. The Homeric *Hymn to Aphrodite* (202-206) is explicit that Zeus did the abducting and more detailed in looking at the red nectar which the youth draws from a golden bowl. Apollonius, assuming his audience's detailed grasp of the story, wittily shows the boy playing dice with Eros in Zeus' flourishing orchard,[7] while Ovid has Orpheus initiate his list of *pueri dilecti* with Ganymede, carried to heaven by Jupiter as eagle and now become the pourer of the god's wine in spite of Juno's unwillingness.[8]

It is the last episode, the conclusion, however varied, of Ganymede's tale with a presumably fortunate ending, which locates him on Olympus, ever youthful, ever the erotic plaything of Jupiter, that Virgil calculatedly suppresses. After the moment our eye, already on Ida, follows the boy carried aloft (*sublimem*) from the same mountain, we turn first to his holder's curved claws and then back to the earth and the longings of its inhabitants projected against the heavens. The unique instant of rape brings no pleasurable completions with it. Jove's desire, or perhaps even Ganymede's, is suppressed along with any fulfillment the reader might sense from a happy rounding-off of the tale. We are graced with no apocalyptic vision of mortal become divine, no banquets favored with the constant presence of an ever-young *minister*. Had the poet shown the eagle as a metamorphosed Jupiter he could thereby at least have indirectly lent a touch of immediate emotion to his central scene, but he did not. There is nothing triumphant or in any sense truly sublimating to Virgil's Ganymede ekphrasis. What he offers us, as a merely transitional moment, is the triumph of immortal beast over mortal man, of strong over weak, followed by a brief study of earthbound loss and frustration wherein the guardians give vent to their longing and the dogs, in Virgil's astonishing presentation, to their rage. Unfulfilled, futile prayers and instincts thwarted are the essence of the final present moment of the ekphrasis. This is tragedy's mundane stuff, not the celestial integrations which are often typical of comedy.

Before commenting on the expanding contexts of the ekphrasis, I would like to pause once again on the phrase *anhelanti similis* (254). It is, I think, meant to recall the juxtaposition *simul anhelans* at Catullus 63.31, along with its whole setting which finds Attis, athlete turned emasculate devotee of Cybele, leading his entourage of Gallae up the slopes of Ida.[9] The special effect of the allusion will be apparent in a minute. Here I want only to emphasize the self-consciousness that it gives to the poet as craftsman. We have already seen something similar in Virgil's turning of what had been narrative material in Homer and Apollonius into implicit paradigm through its reuse in ekphrasis. Allusion, too, breaks narrative flow and, by suggesting analogy with past poetic performance and community of reference, enhances the static quality to which ekphrasis ascribes and its position as self-contained figuration that in fact, as we will see, multifariously refigures the whole of which it is part.

In turning from text to context, it is important first to observe how closely the contents of the ekphrasis, the adventures of the boy woven into the chlamys, are correlated with the border that edges it and therefore frames the story textured within. The cloak's purple and gold are symbolically suitable for the regal youth whose tale is woven on it, but there are a series of particular links as well. The place-names *meandro* (river become emblem of design) and Meliboea blend smoothly into the double mention of Mount Ida. The alliterative and assonantal connection between *plurima* and *purpura* leads directly to the *puer* of the ekphrasis, while the border that runs its sinuous path around the images (*cucurrit*) seems directly to prepare for the first woven episode of a hunter tiring his prey with weaponry as he rushes after them on the run (*cursu*).[10]

This connection between external decoration and internal scenography is for a purpose. If the (imagined) visual artistry of ekphrasis helps us better to "read" the poem for which it stands as synecdoche, then the compatibility between border and bordered should not surprise us. We are reminded that poems, like the ekphrases of which they often tell, are the products of verbal texturing, and that the enmeshing of designs into a frame is but a smaller version of that larger artistic entity we call an epic. The careful description of the entwined, patterned filigree which graces the cloak's edge only further calls attention to the poet as maker, to the act of crafting as well as to the object-artifact that exercises our mind's eye as words boldly attempt to reify visual artistry.

But there is a more specific reason why frame and framed are here so tightly interlocked which will take us back for a moment into literary history. The cloak "around which ran deep Meliboean purple in double waving line" (*quam plurima circum/purpura m͵ ˈndro duplici Meliboea cucurrit*) has a noble past within those very acts of literary craftsmanship which most stimulated Virgil's imagination as he composed the *Aeneid*, namely, the epics of Homer and Apollonius Rhodius. By comparison with the four examples of cloaks in the *Iliad, Odyssey,* and *Argonautica*, Virgil makes two significant changes in his act of co-option. Homer and Apollonius always speak of a δίπλαξ πορφυρέη, a purple cloak that is capable of being folded double or perhaps is of double thickness. Virgil, by transferring both color and doubleness from type of cloak to the decoration adorning it, twice over privileges artistry before utility, the beautiful instead of the practical. As if contemplating a mosaic, our inner eye passes through a thickly purple zone of two intertangled stripes before it reaches the scenes which the band presumably fringed roundabout. Perhaps here, too, as we traverse the weaver's bright meander, we are passing through a mazelike moment not dissimilar to labyrinth or to the circular, equally decorative patternings of dolphins which grace the shields of Hercules and Aeneas. The encompassing meander motif reminds us yet again of the wholeness toward which ekphrasis of art lays claim, and, at this moment of duplicity, we likewise remember that purple is the color of death as well as of royalty.

These alterations only invite further scrutiny of the objects themselves which Virgil would have us recall from previous epic. In three out of the four earlier cases, the cloak was embellished, and in all these instances we are told something of the contents of the ornamentation. One, in fact, elicits a full-scale ekphrasis. Only in the case of *Odyssey* 19.241–42, where Odysseus, disguised as a beggar, tells Penelope of a cloak which he has once given her husband, is no decoration mentioned.

The most elaborate survey of content is, reasonably enough, the ekphrasis which forms part of Apollonius' description of the cloak woven by the goddess Athena for Jason, leader of the Argonauts. The unitary meaning of its seven events and their relationship to the epic as a whole has been much debated, a recent interpretation being that Apollonius, through the varied viewpoints of its episodes, "incorporated an artistic perspective and aesthetic standards reflecting the major concerns and interests of Late Classical and Early Hellenistic painters and sculptors."[11]

No such detail nor such consequent problematics greet us as we work back to the *Iliad*'s two examples of double, purple cloaks. The first occurs as we directly meet Helen for the first time:

> . . . ἡ δὲ μέγαν ἱστὸν ὕφαινε,
> δίπλακα πορφυρέην, πολέας δ' ἐνέπασσεν ἀέθλους
> Τρώων θ' ἱπποδάμων καὶ Ἀχαιῶν χαλκοχιτώνων,
> οὕς ἕθεν εἵνεκ' ἔπασχον ὑπ' Ἄρηος παλαμάων.[12]

She was weaving a mighty web, double, purple, and was embroidering on it many exploits of the horse-taming Trojans and brazen-chitoned Achaeans which they suffered on account of her at the hands of Ares.

The second finds Andromache weaving flowers into a cloak during the time that Hector fights with and loses his life to Achilles:

> ἀλλ' ἥ γ' ἱστὸν ὕφαινε μυχῷ δόμου ὑψηλοῖο
> δίπλακα πορφυρέην, ἐν δὲ θρόνα ποικίλ' ἔπασσε.[13]

But in the inner chamber of her lofty dwelling she was weaving a web, double, purple, and on it was embroidering variegated flowers.

The two episodes clearly reflect and balance each other, the realist Helen self-consciously reproducing the war of which she is the cause, Andromache in the recesses of her home naively re-creating flowers or love charms while her husband is being done to death on the field of battle.

But there is a further level to the portrait of Helen which did not escape Virgil's sensibility. From the ancient scholiasts on, it has been observed that, through the instrument of Helen, Homer is re-creating an archetype of his own poem. Not only are life and art somehow continuous for her, but she also becomes another Homer inside his imagined world, representing in visual form the text itself. She is at once the trigger of action and the reconceiver of that action, an object of memory in Homer's poem who in her own art equally memorializes the same fictions.

In referring us back, through his own usage, to instances in his poetic heritage where purple and doubleness are also associated with weavings, three of which were adorned with figuration, Virgil has something to tell us of the equally brilliant, multivalent quality of his own work. We learn especially from Apollonius and from Homer's Helen. From reading/viewing Jason's cloak we ponder the importance of art to enhance art, for in the seven vignettes illustrated thereon, art's reproduction of art is a major theme.

The first episode deals with Cyclopes forging Zeus' thunderbolt; the second finds Amphion with his music magically conducting boulders together to form the walls of Thebes; the third shows Aphrodite wielding the shield of Ares in such a way that, Helen-like, her image is reflected in it. The fourth event, depicting a fight between Taphian pirates and the sons of Electryon over the latter's cattle, while itself containing no reference to art, nevertheless closely looks back to two episodes in Homer's most famous ekphrasis, the shield of Achilles. In the fifth we watch the two chariots of Pelops and Oenomaus, and the seventh, dealing with Phrixus and the talking ram, carefully transports us from ekphrasis to the story of the *Argonautica* itself, one art form anticipating another. Only the sixth, in which the very young Apollo defends his mother against the advances of Tityus, lacks, within itself or by allusion, reference to a form of craftsmanship. Yet even this incident is artistic in the widest sense, for, like the second episode (to which it may serve as balance), it speaks to the triumph of order over violence and of civilization over earth's brutishness.

Apollonius' ekphrasis helps us see how art not only reflects and contains other art but anticipates visually the verbal story in which it is contained. Homer's vision of Helen at her tapestry, weaving her version of the *Iliad,* tells us of art's magical ability infinitely to reproduce and reimagine itself. In the Ganymede ekphrasis Virgil forgoes all mention of the artisan—no Helen or Athena is put before us as maker. But maybe this omission has its own form of creative duplicitousness. It forces the reader to fill in the blank with the most plausible inscription, namely, Virgil himself, here the unmediated crafter of his own ekphrasis. He is not, as a Helen, literally reproducing his poem nor is he, at least in this instance, leading us directly into its artistry or commenting more generally on art itself. Rather, in a deeper act of allegoresis, he is offering a brief poem in the form of art that comments significantly on the content and meaning—which is to say on the imaginative brilliance—of its parent masterpiece.

It is time, then, to expand our sights out into the poem itself. As we do so we must ask why Virgil replaces Helen's self-reflective weavings of battle, Andromache's love charms, and the covert meditation on Alexandrian aesthetics by which Apollonius graces Jason's cloak with a condensed version of the story of Ganymede, especially one which dispenses with any happy ending on Olympus and returns our inner vision to earth and to the contemplation of two studies of yearning and rage which his loss entails. Circularity abets the ideal aim of ekphrasis (the instantaneous revelation of a visual object), but what does it signify that Virgil's version of the Ganymede tale serves as analogy for epic rather than some figuration more apparently appropriate to a linear narrative whose telos is climactic accomplishment? More particularly, what does it mean for a *victor* to carry with him such an ominous image as the ekphrasis conveys?[14]

A preliminary answer to this final question can be posited by noting two ways in which details of the ekphrasis reach out into the story line of book 5. The first is the phrase *palmas . . . ad sidera tendunt*, given in the ekphrasis to Ganymede's aged guardians who pray vainly to heaven, presumably for the safe return of their charge. Virgil is deliberately looking back some twenty lines to the moment when Cloanthus, rowing in a dead heat with his rival Mnestheus, prays to the gods for victory, *palmas ponto tendens utrasque* (233). After he promises to make offering of a bull and throw its entrails into the sea, the marine divinities grant his wish which in turn soon brings him the cloak as reward. Prayer and victory prize are interrelated in a particularly Virgilian manner. In the world of game-playing, ordinary animal sacrifice brings the goodwill of the gods. In the larger sphere of the realities of epic endeavor, as the Ganymede ekphrasis suggests, victory brings with it human victimization and loss, as the victor absorbs the consequence of his enterprise. We can observe within book 5 variations in this pattern ranging from the bull which the boxer Entellus offers instead of taking the life of his opponent Dares to Aeneas' helmsman Palinurus, demanded as victim by Neptune and hence real-life equivalent of the helmsman Menoetes who survived after a dunking during the boat race.[15] Many other examples of such victimization precede and follow in the epic, but it is the conclusion of the poem which we will find offering the final, most disturbing analogy for the victor-Ganymede complex.

A second detail within the ekphrasis also reaches out into book 5 and into the poem as a whole. I noted before how the phrase *anhelanti similis* recalled Catullus 63 and how the allusion helped draw a parallel between Ganymede and Attis, the one immortalized by Jupiter's desire into a perpetual *puer delicatus*, the other self-effeminized so as to remain man-woman priest of the Great Mother. Virgil capitalizes on the connection at lines 568–69 with a double example of *figura etymologica* when he lists among the companions of Iulus-Ascanius, during the performance of the *lusus Troiae, Atys, genus unde Atii duxere Latini,/ parvus Atys pueroque puer dilectus Iulo* (Atys, whence the Latin Atii have drawn their race, little Atys, boy beloved of the boy Iulus). Not only do the future Atii draw their name (in Virgil's imagining) from his invented Atys, but the latter keeps alive the resonance of both Attis and, through him, Ganymede.[16]

Virgil emphasizes the erotic point of the interconnections of Iulus, Atys, and Attis by immediately describing Iulus as *forma . . . ante omnis pulcher* (570), but, when the linkage with Ganymede is made, there once again arises a series of resonances also for the epic as a whole. The forces of mythic history dictate that Iulus must survive the events of the epic, and when he momentarily suffers metamorphosis from leader of cavalry games, in book 5, or boy-hunter, in books 4 and 7, to killer of Remulus Numanus in book 9, his brief career as warrior with human prey is immediately thwarted by Apollo's intervention.[17] The same cannot be said for the sequence of young soldiers, such as Pallas, Euryalus, and Lausus, whose early deaths, not to speak of their emotional bonding with others which Virgil is at pains to develop, lend particular poignancy to the epic's final books. The case of Turnus is special and I will take it up shortly. When applied to the rest and to those many others whose lives the epic's final battling cuts short, the linkage between the Ganymede myth and victor is consequential. Victory, especially when the less devastating defeats of game have yielded to the harsher killings of war, brings with it the implications of Jupiter's intervention in the career of Ganymede. The *eros* of the omnipotent king of the gods is analogical to the fatal *eris* of war. Like the aspiration of ekphrasis itself, each stops time, the one by freezing youth at the liminal stage of development before the *puer dilectus* makes the expected change from sexual indeterminacy to heterosexuality, from the blossoming of adolescence to full virility, the other by killing the virginal warrior at a moment before life's normal developments can come into complete play.

But it is not so much the devastating, Jovian gains of victory to which the Ganymede ekphrasis and the *Aeneid* give permanence as the idea of loss and the combination of pleading and rage which are concomitant with it. We think, again, of the procession of androgynous youths whose flowerlike beauty is cut down by war, but the point has particular bearing on the death of Turnus and on the whole concluding episode of the poem.

Aside from its appearances in book 5, the stretching forth of hands in prayer has a rich history in Virgil's texts. In the *Georgics* we find Eurydice, drawn back into the underworld, addressing her lover, "and, alas no longer yours, outstretching strengthless hands to you" (*invalidasque tibi tendens, heu non tua, palmas*).[18] The first instance in the *Aeneid* comes at 1.93 where Aeneas, helpless like his model, Odysseus, before the buffets of nature and "stretching forth both his hands to the stars" (*duplicis tendens ad sidera palmas*), exclaims on how much better it would have been to die an active hero's death at Troy than passively to suffer shipwreck.[19] The sequence of parallels leads climactically, and with no little irony, to the epic's final scene and Turnus' gesture of petition to Aeneas. The narrative shows him *dextram . . . precantem/protendens,* and he himself, praying for clemency, addresses Aeneas: *vicisti et victum tendere palmas/Ausonii videre* (You have conquered and the Ausonians have seen me, conquered, stretch forth my hands).[20] The double prayer, where narrative is reinforced by the suppliant's first-person plea, is unexampled elsewhere in the poem. It comes at a point, neatly balancing the epic's opening, where Aeneas is now in full control of events. His spear is *fatale.* It carries fate with it and bears comparison with the thunderbolt of Jupiter.[21] When Turnus lifts his palms, it is not toward some aloof, careless stars that he prays but to a hero who, as he triumphs over his enemy, takes on the combined force of Jupiter and of nature itself.

The guardians, beseeching the heavens at the end of the Ganymede ekphrasis, find their counterpart, at the epic's conclusion, in Turnus begging his all-powerful opponent to spare his life. The accompanying image of the personified barking of the dogs that rages (*saevit*) in frustration against the breezes (*in auras*) is also paralleled in a series of other Virgilian moments where lover loses beloved. Once again Eurydice initiates the *exempla,* withdrawing from Orpheus "like smoke mixed into thin breezes" (*ceu fumus in auras/commixtus tenuis*).[22] Virgil adopts the simile into his story line in *Aeneid* 2 where Creusa's wraith deserted her husband "and withdrew into thin breezes" (*tenuisque recessit in auras*).[23] There are no disappearing breezes at the end of the poem—Pallas has already been many days dead—but there is rage, the fury stemming from Aeneas' memory of his fierce resentment (*saevi monimenta doloris*) which the young warrior's sword belt, worn by his killer Turnus, now brings back. So far the analogy with Ganymede is direct. A youth as beautiful as Venus' star (8.589–91) has been torn from someone closely committed to him, rousing a combination of grief and anger in the person bereft.

But Virgil now performs an extraordinary variation on his theme. As the epic closes, two youths are involved, not one, as in the Ganymede tale, and Aeneas places this second youth, the suppliant Turnus, in the position to receive the vengeance of the first: *Pallas te hoc vulnere, Pallas/immolat et poenam scelerato ex sanguine sumit*[24] (Pallas sacrifices you, Pallas, with this wound, and extracts punishment from your criminal blood). Aeneas in his own wild thinking becomes Pallas restored, reincorporated in Aeneas himself and an excuse for the infuriate violence on which he embarks as his epic ends.[25]

One detail of the ekphrasis stays with us as we watch its analogy evolve toward this conclusion, and that is the baying of the hounds whose rage concludes the picture (*saevit . . . canum latratus*). The last simile Virgil allots his hero in the poem (12.749–55) finds Turnus in the position of a stag, hemmed in by a stream and by colored feathers, pursued by the dog Aeneas who has encountered him: *venator cursu canis et latratibus instat* (the hunter hound presses after [him] in the chase, with barks). Virgil means us directly to recall a parallel simile at *Iliad* 22.189–92 where Hector is compared to the fawn of a deer whom the hound Achilles has started from its mountain covert. The poet's many alterations to Homer give his simile a special vitality and urgency, but in its context and placement he makes us look not only to his Homeric model but to a particular imagistic history he has allotted to Aeneas the hunter.

We first find him in this role in the epic's opening book where he routs a herd of deer, "driving [them] with his weapons" (*agens telis*) and killing seven to equal the apparent number of ships saved from Aeolus' storm.[26] In book 4 he is both literal and figurative hunter. He literally sets out with Dido on the chase that ends in their mock marriage, but Virgil has not long previously compared him to a shepherd who, "driving [her] with his weapons" (*agens telis*), has in ignorance wounded Dido, the unwary doe.[27] At the end, bestialized for the third time in the epic, Aeneas remains the hunter but now suffers metamorphosis into a dog who is about to grasp his prey and who does so, in a fatal frenzy, as the epic ends.[28] The dogs of Ganymede, finally, in their rage have not retrieved their master. Nevertheless, in the person of Aeneas, they have gained in place of Ganymede a victim whose death can bring satisfaction for loss and resentment. For Ganymede's hounds, rage is for loss just as his guardians' prayers are in vain. Turnus' prayers, too, are bootless, but this new Ganymede, replacing one whom Jupiter's minions had grasped (*rapuit*) aloft in hooked claws, is not this time to be so easily disposed of. This is Aeneas' shout: "*tune hinc spoliis indute meorum/eripiare mihi?*" (Are you, clothed in the spoils of my own, to be snatched hence from me?) This time the hound has grasped his quarry, and the victim, who can compensate for the loss of someone previously snatched hence, will not in his turn be seized away by some external force (in the case of Aeneas we might call it the invisible tug of a father, preaching *clementia* toward a suppliant).

Anger finds its outlet, but Aeneas' final action suggests an interminable continuity of the same linkage of cause and effect, of loss, rage, and a new victim taken. The poem itself, in its final deed, makes permanent not only the presence of loss, as the Ganymede ekphrasis suggests, but the constancy as well of vendetta. The victim from whom revenge can be extracted is ever available. One beautiful youth may be torn away forever in death, but another is always at hand against which to apply physical force. It is to the point that the *Aeneid*, like the Ganymede ekphrasis—or all other ekphrases, for that matter, which attempt to suggest the wholeness of visual art through circularity—bends back in on itself at its conclusion. Turnus' limbs, in the epic's next-to-last line, are undone with cold just as are Aeneas', as he endures the storm of the opening book, and we have already seen how Turnus at the end repeats Aeneas' initial gesture of prayer.[29] There is a difference: Aeneas survives and Turnus dies. But it is the similarity of the episodes that advances the notion of epic history, as Virgil imagines it, not so much as a teleological narrative than as an ever-repeated cycle with only mutation of superficial details. We begin with Juno's anger and we end with that of Aeneas, and the episodes which this anger charges are both built around jealousy and the need for vengeance and for savagery of response. And this leads us back to the figure of Ganymede for one final time. We return to him via Macrobius.

On one occasion where the fourth-century scholar is commenting on the position of the *Aeneid* as generic successor to the *Iliad* and the *Odyssey*, and consequently on the particularities of this instance of tradition versus originality in Virgil's poetic enterprise, he makes the following remarks:

> Nullam commemorationem de iudicio Paridis Homerus admittit. Idem vates Ganymedem non ut Iunonis paelicem a Iove raptum sed Iovalium poculorum ministrum in caelum a dis ascitum refert velut θεοπεπωσ. Vergilius tantam deam, quod cuivis de honestis feminae deforme est, velut specie victam Paride iudicante doluisse, et propter Catamiti paelicatum totam gentem eius vexasse commemorat.[30]

> Moreover, Homer does not make any mention of the judgment of Paris, and he refers to Ganymede not as Juno's rival carried off by Jupiter but as Jupiter's cupbearer received into heaven by the gods as worthy of their company. Virgil, however, tells of Juno, great goddess though she was, as having resented the adverse judgment of Paris on her beauty—conduct unbecoming any honorable woman—and as having harassed his whole race for the sake of the wanton Ganymede.

The reference is, of course, to the opening of the epic itself where the narrator details the sources of Juno's continuing resentment toward the Trojans, an inner wrath soon to take external shape in the storm she rouses against her enemies (1.25–28)

> necdum etiam causae irarum saevique dolores
> exciderant animo; manet alta mente repostum

> iudicium Paridis spretaeque iniuria formae
> et genus invisum et rapti Ganymedis honores.

not yet, too, had the cause of her wrath and her bitter sorrows faded from her mind; deep in her heart lie stored the judgment of Paris and her slighted beauty's wrong, her hatred of the [Trojan] race and the honors paid to ravished Ganymede.

Two aspects of origination and emulation are at work here. The first is Virgil's rivalry with Homer. As Macrobius reviews the matter, it is through his specific emphases given to the Ganymede legend—that is, by seeing Ganymede not as ever-youthful cupbearer to the gods, as does Homer, but rather as the rival of Juno whose jealousy spurs her to action—that Virgil stakes out his own imaginative territory. The second aspect is implicit in the first. If meditation on the Ganymede tale elicited from Virgil a calculated act of differentiation from Homer, poet provoking poet, the focus of that differentiation, the anger of Juno, is the initial motivating force for the contents of the poem itself, an important generating impulse behind what follows.

Yet even this anger helps designate a major direct challenge that Virgil offers the poet of the *Iliad*. While *ira* and *dolor* characterize the initial reactions of Jupiter's angry wife, Μῆνιν is Homer's first word. The wrath of Achilles becomes, in Virgil, the wrath of Juno. But the Roman poet's careful modifications are again crucial. Achilles' emotionality is centered on the loss of a woman given him as a prize. Resentment for her loss drives him first to nonheroic inaction, then to the arming of Patroclus as surrogate, and finally to his own *aristeia* against Hector and its richly textured consummation. The wrath of Juno, which opens the *Aeneid*, derives, by contrast with Achilles' rage, from sexual jealousy over a youth given preference to her by Jupiter. It is an emotion which she seems to renounce at the end of the epic.

Nevertheless, Virgil gives his poem its extraordinary final twist, as we have seen, by imputing to Aeneas, as he prepares to kill Turnus, emotionality parallel to that he ascribes to Juno as the epic commenced and couched in similar language. As matters come full circle, her initial *ira* (4, 11, 25), *dolor* (9, 25), and *saevitia* (4, 25), about to be violently manifested in the storm that nearly proves the Trojans' undoing, suffer metamorphosis, first into Aeneas' recollection of the *saevus dolor* he had experienced at the death of Pallas, then into fury when, *furiis accensus et ira terribilis,* he buries his sword under his opponent's chest as the epic ends. It is no accident that when we are first introduced to Turnus he is "before all others the most beautiful" (*ante alios pulcherrimus omnis*), and that, as we noted, Pallas preparing to march forth to battle is compared to Venus' morning star.[31] The death of one beautiful youth arouses such resentment in the poem's hero that, in a surge of vindictiveness, he kills the youth's killer whose indignation in turn concludes the poem.

Here too, then, a major element of the Ganymede legend plays so formidable a part as doubly to rule the poem. Juno's initial jealousy over the preferment of Ganymede is transmuted into Aeneas' final fury at the killing of the beautiful Pallas. Since the queen of the gods cannot succeed, despite repeated attempts, either to do away with Aeneas or to abort the Trojans' mission to establish Rome, she apparently allows her anger to pass. Rome's founding hero, by contrast, not only acts in anger as the epic ends but succeeds in his deadly act of vengeance. His anger reiterates Juno's but operates with greater potency.

The Ganymede legend, therefore, plays a duplex role for the reader who both watches Virgil as poet of the *Aeneid* vying with his Homeric past and examines the plotline of the poem itself. We may review this powerful presence from another angle by pondering the role of memory at the same two crucial junctures of the poem, the beginning and the end. Within a brief stretch in the epic's opening paragraph we hear of two acts of memory—the "remembering wrath" (*memorem iram*) of Juno which sets the story going and the speaker's prayer to the muse to recall this very wrath (1.8–11):

> Musa, mihi causas memora, quo numine laeso
> quidve dolens regina deum tot volvere casus
> insignem pietate virum, tot adire labores
> impulerit. tantaene animis caelestibus irae?

Tell me, O Muse, the cause, wherein thwarted in will or why angered, did the queen of heaven drive a man, splendid in his goodness, to traverse so many perils, to face so many toils. Can resentment so fierce dwell in heavenly breasts?

The poet's memory is a major attribute of his creative enterprise, whether it be discerned by comparison with the past history that his genius is roused to re-create or by the past performances that challenge this genius, with both aspects putting stress on the power of intertextual referentiality. It is here tightly conjoined with the remembering emotionality of his own creature, the destructive goddess whose anger is also twice over signaled within these very lines. It is no accident that, as the epic ends and we are made by Virgil's language to rehear Juno in Aeneas, it is an act of memory—*saevi monimenta doloris*—that urges Aeneas toward his final deed. And we, Virgil's readers, are decisively implicated as well. Our memories follow the clues that unite beginning and end. Through them we create for the poem its special wholeness as we share in the suggestion that memory and anger will symbiotically live on in a future peppered with repeated, unresolved killings, not with acts of clemency that might finally satisfy at once the exigencies of plot and moral justice.[32] These deaths, too, will be the spur to poetic imaginations yet to come.

The only resolution, the only triumph, is in the work of art, be it the ekphrasis itself or the *Aeneid,* the all-encompassing poem. The texturing of Ganymede takes multiform shape in the composition of the epic itself. The smaller "artifact" offers analogy for the larger whole of which it is a minuscule but exemplary part. The author himself pursues the active Jovian role to which Ganymede, *intextus,* and we, admirers of Virgil's *tessitura,* capitulate. Only through reading can we experience a form of true consummation from which the poet excludes the protagonists of both artifact and poem. The ekphrastic moment within a poem is a stretching toward the unreachable. Art cannot ever be displayed in words nor Ganymede ever be fully *intextus,* statically encased on a dark cloak, interwoven for the mind's vision alone. But in looking at Virgil's uses of ekphrases, here and elsewhere, at their deliberate unfulfillments and their pondered circularities, we come close, but only as close as the limitations of ekphrasis itself as metaphor will allow, to understanding the genesis and meaning of the poem itself. As for the Ganymede ekphrasis in particular, a small act of inner seeing makes us read again the story of loss, prayer, and rage which Virgil weaves as a fundamental pattern in his larger design.

3

Daedalus' Sculptures

We turn now to the opening of book 6 and to the ekphrasis of highlights from the life of Daedalus.[1] Aeneas confronts this tale on reaching Cumae in search of the Sibyl. It is told in a series of tableaus on the doors of a temple dedicated to Apollo by the artisan-sculptor himself after his safe arrival in Italy. This is the only occasion in ancient literature where an artist is described as constructing his literal—which in this case is also to say his spiritual, or psychic—biography. As such I take it as a metaphor for the progress of any artist, for his imaginative diary, as it were. My thesis will be that in certain essential ways the tale of Daedalus, crafted by himself, sets up a typology that is mirrored in the ethical artistry practiced by Aeneas from standards set him by his father toward the end of the same book. After parading before his son a host of future Roman heroes, most of them distinguished for their military prowess, Anchises summarizes what he foresees as Rome's special genius. It will lie not in any unique brilliance as sculptors in bronze or stone, or as orators or astronomers, but in their accomplishment as governing warriors, in their moral usage of political power:

> "tu regere imperio populos, Romane, memento
> (hae tibi erunt artes), pacique imponere morem,
> parcere subiectis et debellare superbos."[2]

"Remember, Roman, to rule peoples with might (these will be your arts), to impose upon them a custom for peace, to spare the humbled and war down the proud."

This is the Roman "artistry" set up for Aeneas to model himself against in the epic's second half.

But I would go still further in drawing analogies from the *vita* of Daedalus and suggest that it reveals something, first, of the narrator's spirit as he outlines Aeneas' progress, and then also of the intelligence of the poet Virgil working with the demands of a strict generic tradition. Aeneas who has himself, like Daedalus, just completed an extraordinary journey, is not allowed by the Sibyl to meditate on even the most simplistic parallels between himself and the Cretan inventor. She brusquely whisks her charge away from what she styles *spectacula*, sights presumably purveying only aesthetic delight. But Virgil's readers, with their privileged, unheroic leisure for contemplation, are under the obligation to respond not only to the sculptured encapsulation of an artist's life—as Aeneas might have—but to what Aeneas does not know, to the emotions of the artist in the crafting and of the narrator in the telling.

Here is the story as told by Virgil at *Aeneid* 6.14-37:

> Daedalus, ut fama est, fugiens Minoia regna
> praepetibus pennis ausus se credere caelo   15
> insuetum per iter gelidas enavit ad Arctos,
> Chalcidicaque levis tandem super astitit arce.
> redditus his primum terris tibi, Phoebe, sacravit
> remigium alarum posuitque immania templa.
> in foribus letum Androgeo; tum pendere poenas   20
> Cecropidae iussi (miserum!) septena quotannis
> corpora natorum; stat ductis sortibus urna.
> contra elata mari respondet Cnosia tellus:
> hic crudelis amor tauri suppostaque furto
> Pasiphae mixtumque genus prolesque biformis   25
> Minotaurus inest, Veneris monimenta nefandae,
> hic labor ille domus et inextricabilis error;
> magnum reginae sed enim miseratus amorem
> Daedalus ipse dolos tecti ambagesque resolvit,
> caeca regens filo vestigia. tu quoque magnam   30
> partem opere in tanto, sineret dolor, Icare, haberes.
> bis conatus erat casus effingere in auro,

bis patriae cecidere manus. quin protinus omnia
perlegerent oculis, ni iam praemissus Achates
adforet atque una Phoebi Triviaeque sacerdos,   35
Deiphobe Glauci, fatur quae talia regi:
"non hoc ista sibi tempus spectacula poscit; . . ."

As tradition has it, Daedalus, fleeing from the kingdom of Minos and having dared to entrust himself to the sky on swift wings, swam on his strange way to the cold Bears and at last nimbly rested above the Chalcidian hill. Restored here first to earth, he dedicated to you, Phoebus, the oarage of his wings and built a huge temple. On the doors [is] the death of Androgeos; then the offspring of Cecrops, ordered, sad deed, to pay each year as penalty seven bodies of their sons; there the urn stands with the lots drawn. Opposite, rising from the sea, faces the land of Crete: here is the cruel love for the bull, Pasiphaë mated by craft and the Minotaur, a mongrel breed and two-formed offspring, record of forbidden love. Here that house of toil and inextricable maze; but, having taken pity on the princess' deep love, Daedalus himself unwound the deceits and tangles of the palace, guiding the blind tracks with a thread. You also, Icarus, would have a large share in such a work, were grief to allow; twice he attempted to fashion your fall in gold, twice fell the father's hands. Indeed, they would have scanned everything with their eyes had not Achates, sent on ahead, now returned and together with him the priestess of Phoebus and Trivia, Deiphobe the daughter of Glaucus, who speaks thus to the king: "The moment does not demand for itself these sights."

The story divides itself into five parts: introduction (Daedalus' arrival in Italy), first segment of sculpture devoted to events at Athens, counterbalancing Cretan exploits, the story of Ariadne, and the address to Icarus. There is a climactic heightening of emotion on the part of both the artist and the narrator of his tale as the story progresses, leading in the final episode to the artist's inability to create. Let us watch this happening by examining each section in more detail.

At the start, through the phrase *ut fama est,* the narrator seems hyperconscious of putting things before us. By re-creating someone else's report and not, it would seem, inventing his own version of the Daedalus story, he distances us in time while apparently disclaiming any direct involvement on his part in the telling.[3] Yet even in this introduction the narrator betrays a certain empathy with his version of Daedalus which suggests a deep understanding of his subject's imaginative ways. Daedalus, as the Cretan vignette makes clear, is a dealer in duplicity, an inventor of hybrid objects that cater to the furtive in their recipients and in their turn create further hybrids—a fake beast enclosing a true human (Pasiphaë inside the replica of a cow) that begets a man-animal, the Minotaur. The narrator anticipates this proclivity even now in his own poetic inventiveness. He replaces visual duplicity with verbal contrivance, exchanging the craftsman's double-natured artifact with the poet's ambiguous metaphor by seeing Daedalus, the human aviator, as swimmer through the heavens. The terrestrial creature, though airborne, is made poetically to deal (like Aeneas for much of the preceding story of his epic) with a watery element, and dedicate on return to earth the oarage of his wings.[4]

The narrator is a discerning critic of Daedalus' adventures in two other ways. One is a simple matter of rhetoric. By apostrophizing Apollo he, as it were, mimics Daedalus, claiming himself to share the emotion Daedalus felt on safe return to earth and voiced in gesture of thanks to Phoebus Apollo. But address to the god as Phoebus proves the narrator privy to the myth of Daedalus on a deeper level. Daedalus ends his adventuring on a spot sacred to Apollo, where Aeneas will hear prophecy of his, and Rome's, future through the god's mouthpiece, Deiphobe, the Sibyl. But Apollo the sun god played an important role in Daedalus' recent life. By steering a course toward the chill Bears, Daedalus saved himself from the fate of Icarus, whose wings melted as he drew too near the sun's heat. The artisan of hybrids, who turns himself and his offspring into men-birds, loses his son in the process of artistic experimentation.

But there is also a hint, in the verb *enavit* and the phrase *gelidas Arctos,* of a certain insouciance on the part of Daedalus. By swimming free of danger toward northern cold he followed the proper procedures for survival, but his child, Icarus, either was not taught, or at least was not able to practice them.[5] To put it another way, both Daedalus within this initial segment of the narrative and the narrator expounding his tale seem in different senses careless—and leave the reader thus far unaware—that more than one person was involved in this strange itinerary. Because there is no mention of Icarus and no hint of Daedalus' role as father, the reader remains with the impression, which the narrator's metaphors abet, that Daedalus thinks largely of his invention and the clever manipulation of it, not of its human consequences.

The narrator therefore gives us a forecast of circularity in his rendering of the tale, preparing us for the address to Icarus at the end. But neither at the start nor at the conclusion of the episode is the actual death of Icarus mentioned, a fact which invites the reader to fill in the text, to exercise his own imagination by re-creating and contemplating the most poignant incident in Daedalus' biography. In his role as father Daedalus may have been lacking in understanding of his son. As an artist he is a double failure, first incapable of completely imitating nature, then unable to mime the disastrous results of this inadequacy.

Though they now forthrightly continue the theme of sons killed or sacrificed, the initial sculptures proper (20–22), devoted to events in Athens, are treated as matters of fact, save in one respect. There is no word for the act of crafting, and the only object mentioned, the urn, was not of Daedalus' making. The exception is the exclamation *miserum* (alas! dreadful!). From its placement in the middle of line 21 and therefore at the center of the three lines, it serves as emotional commentary on the whole segment. But to whom the emotion is imputed remains ambiguous. Is it that experienced by the suffering Athenians? Is it Daedalus' response as he contemplates the results of his handiwork (or, in his mind's eye, the events themselves), or Aeneas', examining the sculpture? Is it the reaction of the narrator sharing the same sensations, or of the reader being taught them in his turn? For one verbal moment, even in the most "detached" segment of Daedalus' tale, narrator, characters, and audience are united in empathy.[6]

The first Cretan segment is even more nominal, but now the list of characters and emotions concentrates specifically on Daedalus' art (23–27). His is an inventiveness which articulates subterfuge and doubleness, tangibly fosters sexual perversity, and harbors its results, a man-bull, in a labyrinthine dwelling that is both *labor* and *error*.[7] It exemplifies the intensity of craftsmanship that imprisons the misformed product of human-animal passion in a maze symbolizing, like its inhabitant, the troubling results of a "wandering" of the emotions. Pasiphaë's double "error" receives its artistic complement from Daedalus' tricky fabrication.[8] Thus far in his tale, Daedalus' art is dangerous only for its recipients.

The second Cretan scene brings a series of abrupt changes (28–30). Though the Labyrinth remains an essential part of the plot, we turn from one queen, Pasiphaë, to another, her unnamed daughter, Ariadne, and from a cruel love to another labeled simply "mighty." But the viewer-reader is also appropriately disoriented. We know from what follows that the Ariadne episode is part of the tableaus of sculptural reliefs. But Daedalus has suddenly, and Virgil brilliantly, led us from his curriculum vitae as guileful artisan to his role as apparently dispassionate reappraiser of the effects of that art. He becomes the undoer of his own trickery, an undoing we can hear in the sound of line 29: *Daedalus ipse dolos tecti ambagesque resolvit*. Daedalus, who reprojects his artistic self through *se dolos*, the labyrinth's wiliness, now straightens its windings and lightens its darkening ways. But dispassionate is too mild a word. Through poetry's magic Daedalus seems actually to become Ariadne. She is the *regina* and she it was who, through Daedalus' gift of thread, directed the steps of Theseus out from the maze after killing the Minotaur.[9] Yet according to Virgil-Daedalus, we find him *regens*, taking her emotional and physical role by linguistic sleight of hand. The reason for this empathy, as the artist unwinds his own artistry and forgoes his own self-made heritage of deception, is pity. Pity is the response that transforms the apparently aloof artistic deceiver into the emotional resolver of his own deceits. It is this response in himself that he would now monumentalize.[10]

His own poet-monumentalizer is equally forward. He puts no word of crafting into his own presentation. Nothing intervenes to prevent the reader from the stated actuality of Daedalus' experience.[11] By contrast to the preceding episode, then, this tableau is *vivant*. Frozen re-presentation yields to active experience, as we are made to share directly in the artist's suffering. We are Daedalus but, because he is one with his protagonist, we are Virgil as well, uttering through the power of words what cannot be expressed in sculpture.

Finally, we leave the triply fictive world of poet imagining artist crafting himself in art to look more simply at the artist's inability to create (30–33). We find him unable to bring to aesthetic completion the delineation in sculpture of an event which in itself, to the artist as experiencer, remained a subject of sorrow, rousing emotion unsatisfied and therefore incomplete. As an interested third party, Daedalus could be shown to share in Ariadne's feelings, ruling with her out of pity her lover's steps. The death of Icarus is a deeper matter. It is the death of a son from the misuses of his father's artistry and for which the father's artistic but duplicitous heroizing must bear some responsibility. As he did in the case of Ariadne, the narrator draws a lexical connection between artist and subject. But the artist who there rules the queen he depicts (*regina-regens*) now fails in his vocation. Because of Icarus' attempt to emulate his father as man-bird, he suffered a mortal fall, and the contemplation of this mischance (the Latin *casus* plays on both literal and figurative senses) caused his father's hands twice to fall as he attempted to monumentalize it.[12]

Here the empathy of the narrator, which has been building from the opening segment, is most fully expressed. As in the initial apostrophe to Phoebus Apollo, he seems to adopt the voice of Daedalus. There his cry was in thanksgiving. Here his words are uttered in sorrow. But in fact so strong is the narrator's involvement that he replaces Daedalus entirely so as to address Icarus directly in explanation of his father's artistic failure. In replacing the sculptor-father, the poet's narrator becomes a Daedalian figure, bringing Icarus and his father's frustrating grief before us in the permanence of words.

We have, therefore, in one of Virgil's richest poetic moments, a study in artistic incompletion that is extraordinarily complete as a poetic act. The incompletion, the tale within the tale, is Daedalus', and it results from a gradual heightening of his emotional participation. In the last three episodes of Daedalus' story as Virgil tells it, the only ones where the artisan is directly involved, we watch him first as aloof artificer of duplicity, constructing monsters to create further monsters. His empathy grows, and his characterization as artist disappears, as he shows himself (and is shown) pitying Ariadne and as a result unraveling his own artistic stratagems (which, I take it, is not only to show himself powerful over his own art but also, perhaps, even to admit fallibilities in that art). Finally, he becomes the victim of *dolor,* of the spasm of grief for his lost son, and this distress results in his inability to create at all. Death renders this artist artless. Daedalus' final honesty, his deepest response to natural feelings, brings artistic barrenness as well as a final powerlessness. But this very gesture of unfulfillment becomes, through Virgil's narration of it, the perfecting element of a poet's holistic enterprise. One artist's failure through passion is the subject of another's successful finishing of his art.

My thesis is that this treatment by one artist of the spiritual biography of another serves as paradigm of the Virgilian career and of the equally tripartite division of the *Aeneid* as a poetic entity, and that it is particularly enlightening for the reader probing the meaning of the epic's conclusion. It is important for my argument to remember that the *Aeneid* begins and ends with acts sparked by *dolor.* At line 9 of the first book, Juno, Aeneas' divine archenemy and emblem of irrationality, is *dolens,* aggrieved, as she launches this hero, noteworthy for his *pietas,* into a sea of troubles. Sixteen lines later we are told in greater detail of the *causae irarum saevique dolores,* the sources of her wrath and fierce anguish that now spur her on to violence. In balance, eight lines from the epic's conclusion we learn of the *saevus dolor,* the fierce anguish which Aeneas experienced at the death of Pallas. Recollection of this event, aroused by sight of the belt Pallas had worn, now on the suppliant Turnus, who had killed him earlier in battle, drives Aeneas to a frenzy of rage (he is described as "set aflame by furies and terrible in his wrath"). In this paroxysm he slays his antagonist whose soul flees under the shades as the epic comes to its abrupt end. I have proposed elsewhere, from several angles, that Aeneas' final deed turns him into a Juno figure—that he becomes a personification, not of his much touted *pietas* based on his father's injunction to *clementia* for the beaten down, but of its opposite, Junonian anger.[13] The subsequent pages will further defend this contention.

First, we must trace Daedalus and the Virgilian career, and Daedalus and the structure of the *Aeneid*. In two cryptic lines near the start of the second book of his *Georgics*, Virgil in his own voice addresses his patron Maecenas: *non hic te carmine ficto/atque per ambages et longa exorsa tenebo*[14] (I will not detain you here with made-up song, and through meanderings and long preambles). This definition of casuistic poetry may apply to work Virgil anticipates for his later career, but more likely it is his way of looking back to his first work, the *Eclogues*. Certainly no other poems in Latin, given the *Eclogues'* many layers of symbolism and multivalent masquerades, could more justly claim the epithets fictive and ambiguous. The rich later history of pastoral poetry as a vehicle for necessary indirection of statement looks back in honor to its primarily Virgilian source.

As Virgil, Daedalus-like, leads his poetry out of the *ambages* of pastoral and into the greater openness and practicality of didactic, his poetic voice moves from playful to serious and he shifts from poet as implicit deceiver to poet as explicit pitier. His opening prayer to Augustus asks Caesar to nod approval to his bold beginnings: *ignarosque viae mecum miseratus agrestis/ingredere*[15] (and, pitying with me the farmers who do not know their way, enter [on your worship]). Pity creates poetry with the Daedalian power of Ariadne's thread, capable, through teaching, of directing those unsure of the path they tread. The immediate result, as the poet and his farmer set out on their interactive labors, is that spring arrives, snow melts, and "the crumbling clod has broken itself up" (*resolvit*) under the power of the west wind.[16] Pity's poetry has also Daedalus' power to resolve nature's seasonal dilemmas and set the farmer firmly on his arduous road.

Last in the Virgilian career comes the poetry of *dolor*. The *Aeneid* seems the impersonal epic of one man's pious journey toward accomplishment, mirroring in smaller compass the future achievements of imperial Rome as it rises to unparalleled greatness under Augustus. But it is also, as we have seen and will further observe, a passion-ridden poem whose final deed of violence stemming from anguish and anger leaves open as many questions as it answers. It leaves dissatisfied the reader's expectations of praise for Aeneas' most memorable action as model for Rome's glorious enterprise to come, and instead completes a cycle based on *dolor*, that is, on an emotion founded in discontent and battening on deprivation. Like Virgil's history of Daedalus it is a brilliantly complete poem ending on premonitions of artistic incompletion.

For the *Aeneid* itself also has the rhythms of a Daedalian undertaking. As one of the most highly ordered of poems, it offers numerous possibilities for imaginative structuring. We gain pleasure, as we approach the epic in linear fashion, from sensing books grouped as pairs or trios, or from savoring a balance between the epic's halves, as they open out in clear echoes of book 1 in book 7. We may also acknowledge Virgil's grand chiasmus, where opening anticipates closure. We then focus centrally on the powerful linkage between books 6 and 7 which begins with the address to Caieta, Aeneas' nurse—another in the host of those, especially prominent in the preceding book, who gain real death and dubious immortality for being in Aeneas' entourage.

I would like here to reconsider what has long been observed as the *Aeneid*'s tripartite division.[17] We could distinguish the three movements as follows: books 1–4, which take us topographically and temporally from Troy to Carthage and revolve on Aeneas' meeting with Dido; books 5–8, which move from Sicily to Cumae, to Tiber-mouth, which contain Aeneas' two great revelations of the future, from his father in the Underworld and on the shield of Vulcan; books 9–12, which deal primarily with the war for supremacy in Latium and, in particular, with Aeneas' confrontation with Turnus.

After the pattern Virgil has Daedalus establish for himself, the first segment of the *Aeneid* is rich with exemplification of deceit. As recreated for us in Aeneas' words, the wooden horse, Troy's equivalent of Pasiphaë's cow, is, save for the shield of Aeneas, the single most memorable artifact in the *Aeneid*, notable for its Daedalian duplicity and duality.[18] It is at once alive and dead, a wooden object, fashioned as an animal, pregnant with a human brood. As objects, both cow and horse are marvelous on the outside, deceptive on the inside. They can, even should, be viewed as Virgil's epic can be read. Past a veneer of artificial charm—in regard to the *Aeneid* the veneer is partially manufactured of our idealizing expectations—lie, in all cases, terrible truths. The second part of Aeneas' narrative is also riddled with the monstral and the biform, with a plant that drips with human blood, Harpies who are at once birds or maidens or goddesses, Scylla (part human, part fish, part wolf), the man-mountain Etna, and the mountain-man Polyphemus. But it is the story of Aeneas, especially as it merges with Dido's, to which I want to call attention.[19] Venus, divinity of love and mother of Aeneas, arrives on the scene in the disguise of the virgin-goddess Diana. She soon hides her son in a cloud as he makes his way into Carthage, and his beauty is said to be his mother's artifice (grace added by craftsmen to ivory is the poet's simile, gold embellishing silver or marble) as he bursts from its enclosure. But counterfeiting is once again her province, her "new arts" (*novas artis*) in the narrator's words, as she replaces Ascanius with Cupid in preparation for the temptation of Dido.

The pretendings of Aeneas, as orchestrated by Virgil, are more elaborate. The most patent example is his gift-giving. He offers to Dido Helen's cloak and the scepter of Ilione, which is to say his presence brings her, from Helen, illicit love leading to her city's symbolic razing by fire, and from Ilione, suicide. His relation to the sculptures on Juno's temple which he sees in Carthage's midst is more subtle. As we have seen, they depict scenes from Troy's fall which summarize Homer or intervene between the story line of the *Iliad* and Aeneas' own tale. Aeneas and Achates take them as evidence of Dido's sympathy for human suffering. The reader, aware of their connection with Juno and her vengeful proclivities, looks at them in other ways. Their great figure is Achilles, who appears directly in three of their episodes, indirectly in three others, primarily as a killer, of Troilus, Hector, Memnon, and Penthesilea. By the end of the epic, Aeneas will become in part an Achilles, pitilessly killing his Latin Hector, Turnus. The equation here is more understated. By continuing on the tale of Troy in his narrative to Dido, Aeneas becomes active as well as passive, a participant in events but their passionate recaller as well. His verbal artisanship, in other words, takes up where the sculptures left off yet also becomes part of the seduction of Dido.[20] The destruction of Troy, which he suffers as a character within his narrative, leads inevitably to the destruction of Dido which his very act of narration helps to cause.

The lexical, symbolic, or imagistic continuum from the end of book 1, through Aeneas' narrative, to the masterful delineation of Dido's downfall in the fourth book needs only brief documentation. Cupid's fake words (*simulata verba*, 1.710) lead directly to the faking of the wooden horse (*simulant*, 2.17), which in turn anticipates Aeneas' attempts at dissimulation (*dissimulant*, 4.291) which Dido unmasks in her first words addressed to him after his decision to depart: *"dissimulare etiam sperasti, perfide, tantum/posse nefas?"*[21] ("Did you also expect, treacherous man, that you could hide so great a wrong?"). It is an easy transition from the *doli*, the wiles of Venus and Cupid, in book 1, to the deceits of the Greeks in book 2 as executed by Sinon and the horse, to the deception of Aeneas which Dido uncloaks. The symbolic flames with which Venus plans to gird Dido become the destructive arson of Troy and then the triple fires of book 4—the metaphoric ardor of her love, her literal burning on the pyre which, as we have seen, is visualized as the burning of Carthage, the queen as city demolished by a concatenation of circumstances.

It is not necessary to argue yet again the moral fine points of a tragic adventure where ignorance and knowledge play intermeshed roles, and human weaknesses make its characters easy prey for divine machinations as well as self-deceptions. I want only to suggest that in detail and in general the constancy of deceit in the story line of *Aeneid* 1-4 finds its parallel in the exploits of Daedalus as artificer. The particularities and their consequences press the connection between Pasiphaë and Dido. Pasiphaë's love is *crudelis,* and this is the adjective Dido twice applies to her absconding lover. Just as the Cretan queen's erotic adventure is based on a stratagem which is also a hiding (*furto*), so also, in the narrator's words, Dido ponders a furtive love (*furtivum amorem*), and it is against accusations of trickery (*furto*) from her that Aeneas must defend himself. Finally, the Minotaur, symbol of Pasiphaë's "unspeakable passion" (*Veneris monimenta nefandae*) has its more tangible counterpart in Aeneas' trappings and their marriage, "all the reminders of that unspeakable man" (*nefandi/cuncta viri monimenta*) which Dido will set aflame along with herself.

The generalities, on the other hand, center, as we have seen, on the artificers rather than on their products. They define Aeneas, and the narrator of his tale, as Daedalus figures. Both particular points of contact and more broad equations persist in the second segment of Virgil's scheme. Critics have remarked on the abruptness with which Ariadne is introduced into the narrative at line 28. She is not named, and, though she was a princess, she was certainly not, at least not at that moment in her eventful life, a *regina*. This apparent discontinuity, however, is actually a brilliant transition when we pursue our projection of the plot of Daedalus' psychological progress onto the *Aeneid*'s triple divisions. For, if in the life of Daedalus we move from Pasiphaë to Ariadne, in the artistic development of the *Aeneid* we stay with Dido, who need not be renamed and who remains the poem's great *regina*.[22] The difference is that, in the second movement of the *Aeneid*, her *crudelis amor* (now become *magnum amorem*) is resolved. When Aeneas sees her in the Underworld, in the company of those "whom harsh love has gnawed through with cruel wasting" (*quos durus amor crudeli tabe peredit*), she scorns him, fleeing into a shady grove *coniunx ubi pristinus illi/respondit curis aequatque Sychaeus amorem*[23] (where her former husband Sychaeus responds to her sufferings and returns equal love). Differentiation leading to suicide has yielded, in book 6, to reciprocation and balance.

Yet we have been readied for this denouement earlier. At the conclusion of book 4, as we prepare to leave the epic's initial third for its central articulation, we have Virgil's first, enormously moving example of pity for suffering leading to its resolution. The moment is Dido's death:

> Tum Iuno omnipotens longum miserata dolorem
> difficilisque obitus Irim demisit Olympo
> quae luctantem animam nexosque resolveret artus.[24]

> Then all-powerful Juno, who pitied her long-suffering and difficult death, sent down Iris from Olympus to release her struggling soul and her entwined limbs.

At the end, pity releases the troubled queen from her enmeshed body, which is to say from the deceits of what Anchises is soon to call the blind prison which confines us within the toils of our destructive emotions.[25]

There is another Daedalian resolution, centering on book 6, that belongs more exactly to Aeneas. The literal labyrinth of Daedalus' manufacture (*hic labor ille domus*) becomes now symbolic, but equally present, in the hero's effortful life as he faces the prospect of descending, alive, into the world of the dead and returning whence he came. *Hoc opus, hic labor est* ("this the task, this the effort"), says the Sibyl.[26] As preparation for this undertaking, Aeneas must attend to the *horrendas ambages,* the fearful enigmas of the seeress' utterances, which correspond to the palpable but no less devious windings (*ambages*) of the Minotaur's dwelling. The Daedalian "threads" that bring resolutions to Aeneas' quandary are manifold. They consist not only in a growing clarity to the Sibyl's words but in the person of the Sibyl herself, who will serve as guide through the Underworld's paths. He is, however, given further assistance by a series of talismans: first, the birds of his mother, then the golden bough—a very Daedalian object, serving now to open out rather than close in, to undeceive instead of dupe—his chief passport, to which the birds direct his traces. Finally, we have the words of the poet Musaeus to whom the priestess turns for help in the search for Anchises.

If deceit is the chief impulse behind Daedalus' initial fabrications, pity rules him in their undoing. Though Aeneas does address Dido in his first words to her as the only person to have taken pity on the Trojans' sufferings, it is a virtue noticeably absent from the first four books. Yet here once more our changing viewpoint on the figure of Dido helps us make the transition from segment to segment. At 4.369–70 she speaks to her former lover as if he were already absent:

"num fletu ingemuit nostro? num lumina flexit?
num lacrimas victus dedit aut miseratus amantem
   est?"[27]

"Did he groan because of my tears? Did he bend his eyes toward me? Vanquished, did he shed tears or take pity on the one who loves him?"

This, we remember, is exactly what Aeneas does here in the Underworld, though she refuses to respond to his plea for words: *prosequitur lacrimis longe et miseratur euntem*[28] (Weeping, he pursues her for a distance and pities her as she goes). Aeneas has now performed the great act of which Dido had earlier found him negligent. He himself has—at last, and too late—also pitied the queen's love (*reginae . . . miseratus amorem*).

He had come to this emotion for the first time in the epic in the fifth book, which opens the *Aeneid*'s second of three divisions. There, at the end of the footrace, Aeneas pities the unfortunate Salius, who had slipped during the competition.[29] It is an emotion that he must receive as much as offer during this middle segment of the epic. He pities the unburied, who are forced to wait at length before crossing the Styx. Yet he is also himself subject to three notable acts of pity during these books: from Jupiter, who saves his fleet; from the Sibyl and her inspirer, to both of whom he must pray; and from the Tiber in book 8. For this reach of the epic is Aeneas' most extended period of dependence, which proves at the same time to initiate him, and the reader of his saga, into the most elaborate revelations of the future. Pity of Sibyl and of river-god lead him, on the one hand, to his father, and on the other, to the site of future Rome. Anchises parades before him future Roman heroic greats and gives him his ethical commission. Evander's tour of Pallanteum anticipates the grand city to come, and the shield, which Venus brings to Aeneas at Caere, concludes book 8 with another series of visions into heroic action, the *non ennarrabile textum* of Roman history.

In details, then, and from a larger viewpoint, during the second segment of the epic, Virgil has his hero put behind him the deceitful, artifice-ridden atmosphere of the initial quartet of books. He replaces it with a portrait of the artisan-hero as pitier. Aeneas undoes his own dissimulations, or those thrust upon him, while the mazy mysteries that lead him to Rome's future are tantalizingly unraveled for him by others, who offer him their rich solace in turn.

The last third of the epic can be treated more briefly. Its plot is the war in Latium, but the narrator tells a singularly purposeless tale. The omniscient reader knows from occasional prophecies that Aeneas will become overlord of Latium and marry Lavinia. But the fullness of the narrative dwells on the relentless futility and unceasing loss that war engenders. It furnishes a catalogue of deaths, especially those of the young. We think immediately of Nisus and Euryalus, of Pallas and Lausus, of Camilla, and finally of Turnus. The rampage of slaughter that Aeneas embarks on after Pallas' death, in which he kills with equal indiscrimination suppliant and priest, takes its last victim in his primary antagonist who is wearing Pallas' belt. Yet for all his *violentia* and pride, our sympathies lie at the end with Turnus, not with Aeneas, with Turnus beaten down by Jupiter's minion Fury and by the inner furies which set Aeneas at the last ablaze.

One of the framing emotions of this last quartet of books, as it is of the epic as a whole, is *dolor.* We find Turnus near the opening of book 9 as he casts a greedy eye on the leaderless Trojans penned within their camp: *ignescunt irae, duris dolor ossibus ardet*[30] (His anger flames up, and resentment burns in his hardened bones). Or, soon again, in a speech of exhortation to his colleagues:

" . . . sunt et mea contra
fata mihi, ferro sceleratam excindere gentem
coniuge praerepta; nec solos tangit Atrides
iste dolor, solisque licet capere arma Mycenis." . . . [31]

"I also have my fate against theirs, with the sword to cut down a criminal race who snatched away my bride; this resentment does not touch the sons of Atreus alone, nor is it allowed Mycenae alone to take up arms."

It is remarkable how much of the same language recurs in the counterbalancing moment of anger with which the epic concludes. Aeneas, in his final words, accuses Turnus of possessing *scelerato sanguine,* criminal blood. The reader could presume that a variation of the reason Turnus gives for his own *dolor*—that Lavinia, his Helen, has been torn from him—is applicable also now to Aeneas, poised to kill because of the *dolor* aroused by the death of Pallas. In any case, though the last appearance of *dolor* doubly brings the epic to a splendid rhetorical and psychological moment of closure, it is, in senses that transcend mere personal feelings, an extraordinarily unfulfilling, not to say devastating, emotion. Turnus asks for pity, and Aeneas hesitates, as if he were preparing to respond with sympathy and practice *clementia.*[32] For Aeneas to grant pity through clemency, though it might appear an unheroic act by Homeric standards, would be for Virgil to round out the poem spiritually. He does not—cannot, perhaps—allow himself the luxury.[33]

I would like, in conclusion, to look in more detail at reasons why *dolor* leaves Aeneas-Daedalus-Virgil with his (their, if you prefer) heroic-artistic-poetic fabrication unfinished. First, Aeneas-Daedalus. The ethical artistry imposed on Roman might, pursuing its political ends, was summarized, as we have seen, by Anchises to his son near the end of their meeting in the Underworld. The nub of his command, which he addresses to Aeneas as *Romane,* ancestor of and paradigm for his distinguished race, is to remember to spare the suppliant and war down the proud. By the end of the poem, proud Turnus has been battled into abject submission, but, for whatever deep-seated reason, Aeneas does not spare him. He fails, finally, to recall his father's admonition. Instead, in the narrator's words, he drank in the reminders of his fierce grief (*saevi monimenta doloris*) and, in an access of fury and rage, buries his sword in his opponent's chest. *Dolor* initiates Aeneas' final act. In so doing it gives the lie to Roman pretensions toward clemency, toward an artistic morality that reincorporates an antagonist, abased but alive, into the civic community. Aeneas' attack of *dolor* proves the impossibility of realizing in fact Anchises' exhortation. In this case, to complete is to idealize, and to idealize is to dream untruths.[34]

Second, we must pursue the analogy of Virgil, the creator of the *Aeneid,* and Daedalus. We are now concerned not with Aeneas' emotions as they undermine Roman political artisanship but with the imagination that shapes such an ending. My thesis is that Virgil deliberately leaves his poem incomplete vis-à-vis the epic genre as he inherited it, as if the *Aeneid* were to serve as one final, magnificent metaphor—one masterful artistic symbol—for the incompletions in Roman (which is to say human) life. Let me illustrate my point with brief reminders of the plot endings of four other epics of which three (the *Iliad,* the *Odyssey,* and the *Argonautica* of Apollonius Rhodius) precede the *Aeneid,* while the other, Statius' *Thebaid,* follows.

Turning first to the *Iliad,* we find the bulk of its last book is taken up with the reconciliation scene between Priam and Achilles, but its last moments are devoted to the aftermath of the burning of Hector's body:

> And when they [the people of Troy] were assembled together, first they quenched with flaming wine all the pyre, so far as the fire's might had come upon it, and thereafter his brethren and his comrades gathered the white bones, mourning, and large tears

flowed over down their cheeks. The bones they took and placed in a golden urn, covering them over with soft purple robes, and quickly laid the urn in a hollow grave, and covered it over with great close-set stones. Then with speed heaped they the mound, and round about were watchers set on every side, lest the well-greaved Achaeans should set upon them before the time. And when they had piled the barrow they went back, and gathering together duly feasted a glorious feast in the palace of Priam, the king fostered of Zeus. On this wise held they the funeral for horse-taming Hector.

The completion of a life demarcates the completion of a poem. The careful rituals of burial and feast that bring the funeral of Hector to conclusion with communal ceremony are complemented by the perfection of the epic that describes them, by poetry's own exacting ritual.

The twenty-fourth book of the *Odyssey* finds its hero taking revenge with bloody slaughter on the suitors of Penelope. But the ending turns this thirst for vengeance around. Zeus says to Athena in heaven: "Now that goodly Odysseus has taken vengeance on the wooers, let them swear a solemn oath, and let him be king all his days, and let us on our part bring about a forgetting of the slaying of their sons and brothers; and let them love one another as before, and let wealth and peace abound." Thus, as Odysseus is preparing to kill the suitors' relatives, who are bent, in their turn, on revenge, Athena speaks to him, bringing the epic to end:

"Son of Laertes, sprung from Zeus, Odysseus of many devices, stay your hand, and make the strife of equal war to cease, lest haply the son of Cronos be wroth with you, even Zeus, whose voice is borne afar."

So spoke Athena, and he obeyed, and was glad at heart. Then for all time to come a solemn covenant between the two was made by Pallas Athena, daughter of Zeus, who bears the aegis, in the likeness of Mentor both in form and in voice.

Forgiveness, reconciliation, a commitment to peace, and a statement by the narrator of an eternal pact to ensure it—these are the gestures with which the *Odyssey* ends. Reintegration of society betokens poetic wholeness, and vice versa. Content and imagination are one.[35]

The ending of the *Argonautica* is simpler still as the singer speaks in his own voice: "For now I have come to the glorious end of your toils; for no adventure befell you as you came home from Aegina, and no tempest of wind opposed you; but quietly did you skirt the Cecropian land and Aulis inside of Euboea and the Opuntian cities of the Locrians, and gladly did you step forth upon the beach of Pagasae." Just as the Argonauts bring their journey to completion by returning whence they started, so the singer, proclaiming direct control over the matter of his verse, brings his own poetic voyage to a parallel stop.

Unfortunately, we lack the final lines of any pre-Virgilian Latin epics. We must therefore jump in our survey to silver Latin and in particular to Statius who, at the end of his only completed epic, the *Thebaid,* directly acknowledges his indebtedness to Virgil. He finishes with an address to his own book:

> vive, precor; nec tu divinam Aeneida tempta,
> sed longe sequere et vestigia semper adora.
> mox, tibi si quis adhuc praetendit nubila livor,
> occidet, et meriti post me referentur honores.[36]

> Live, I pray you: and do not put the divine *Aeneid* to the test, but follow it at a distance and always adore its traces. Soon, if some dark envy still stretches a cloud over you, it will perish, and deserved honors will be offered you after my time.

The ending of the narrative proper, which precedes the speaker's *sphragis,* is equally important for our purposes. After the hideous carnage of civil strife and Theseus' killing of Creon (the equivalent moment to the end of the *Aeneid*), who had refused to allow the dead to be buried, the warring factions forge a treaty as the women rejoice in the Athenian leader's calming presence. The epic's plot ends with due display of mourning for the fallen and with some of Statius' most beautiful (and most Virgilian) lines. I could not tell, says the speaker, even if I had a hundred voices, of all the cries of grief:

> Arcada quo planctu genetrix Erymanthia clamet,
> Arcada, consumpto servantem sanguine vultus,
> Arcada, quem geminae pariter flevere cohortes.
> vix novus ista furor veniensque implesset Apollo,
> et mea iam longo meruit ratis aequore portum.[37]

> With what lament the Erymanthian mother mourns the Arcadian, who keeps his beauty though all his blood is lost, the Arcadian for whom the twin hosts equally wept. Scarcely would new inspiration or Apollo's presence complete the task, and my far-voyaging bark now deserves its haven.

Though he gives them new turns, especially in his elaboration of the autobiographical "seal," Statius essentially clings to the closure patterns of his generic inheritance. In fact, he combines elements from the endings of all three Greek epics—the *Iliad's* ceremonies of lamentation, the *Odyssey's* call for forgiveness and reconciliation, and Apollonius Rhodius' self-projection as traveler, appropriately completing at once his poetic journey and the heroic voyage of which it had sung.

It is important to notice not so much how influential Greek epic remains upon Statius' conclusion but how clearly the *Aeneid*'s finale is absent as an imaginative force on this most Virgilian of poets while he wrote his envoi. In terms of its Greek epic past and its Roman poetic progeny, Virgil's *Aeneid* is a strikingly incomplete poem.[38] Its ending is equivalent to Achilles' killing of Hector, to the death of the suitors in the *Odyssey* or of Creon in the *Thebaid*. No Iliadic mourning breaks the spell of Aeneas' inexorable blood-lust.[39] Reconciliations akin to the *Odyssey's* are mouthed in heaven but form no part of human action, as victor kills suppliant. Turning to the end of the *Argonautica,* which has its spiritual kinship to the *Odyssey's* conclusion, we do not find in the *Aeneid* any equivalent satisfactions. No wife is given Aeneas in a marriage ceremony that might give the epic's quasi-tragic ending a comic twist. Nor is there a speaking "I," proud of his accomplishment, who could at least abstract us at the end from the experiential violence his story tells into the imagination that fostered it.

We will never know what Daedalian *dolor* within Virgil caused him to leave his epic so generically incomplete. (The ancient lives tell us that at his death Virgil had failed only to apply his *ultima manus,* his finishing touch, to the poem, not that it remained deficient in any substantial way.) But I have a suggestion. Critics have long since, and quite correctly, sensed a parallel between Icarus and the many people who die as they follow in the wake of Aeneas. I listed earlier the most prominent losses in the last quarter of books, and it is well to remember that books 2 through 5 all end with deaths, of Creusa, Anchises, Dido, and Palinurus. The clearest parallel structurally, however, is with the death of Marcellus, the son of Augustus' sister and his adopted heir, whose funeral is described at the end of the sixth book.[40] It is as if the poet were saying that the Roman mission cannot go forward without loss of life, that the reality of death ever looms as a counterbalance to progress.

What critics have not stressed is the concomitant parallel between Aeneas and Daedalus. To do so is to turn from deaths suffered as the price of empire to place responsibility for those deaths.[41] The artisan loses his son as a consequence of his overreaching. Aeneas loses Pallas, but he also kills Turnus. These deaths receive the final emphasis which is on causes as much as on results, on perpetrator as much as on victim.

The conclusion of the *Aeneid,* then, doubly uncloaks the deceptiveness of art. Aeneas cannot fulfill his father's idealizing, and therefore deceptive, vision of Rome, and Virgil, the artisan of his tale, cannot show him as so doing. Aeneas' killing of Turnus differs from Daedalus' loss of Icarus essentially for being active instead of passive. Each demonstrates nature's final, Pyrrhic triumph over art.

We may be meant to think that, as he crafted the *Aeneid,* in the process of writing, of practicing his own art, Virgil followed his own voyage of self-discovery and came with full assurance to see *dolor,* the immediacy of suffering, frustration, resentment, as an overriding presence in human life and therefore in his creative life. His plotline, which mimes and reproduces the artist's growing inwardness, suggests a paradox: when in the course of his experience an artist forgoes his natural role as trickster and relieves his art of duplicity in favor of truth of expression, his artifact, as his life's work, is an apparent failure. To idealize is to envision wholeness in self and society, to claim consistency in their patternings. It is to twist the tragic divisiveness of life's irrationality into comic returns, reconciliations, renewals. But Virgil, by ending his epic with two consequential acts of resentment, the one resulting in violence, the other owing to acceptance of that violence, does not finally idealize. His final artifice is the sham of forgoing art.

In sum, Virgil does, idiosyncratically, complete the *Aeneid,* just as he completes with growing emotion the tale of Daedalus' inability to create. This carefully, brilliantly flawed wholeness is perhaps his passionate way of saying that art's feigned orderings do not—and cannot—claim to control the uncontrollable. For a poet of consummate honesty, the truths of nature, Virgil would seem to say, are ever triumphant over the soothing trickery of art's order, however seductively its practitioners pattern their wares. For the art that supplants deceit with honesty, that composes life's imperfections, that unthreads its own labyrinthine text, no piety, or even pity, is possible, only the final, perfecting deficiencies of anger and sorrow.[42]

4
Silvia's Stag

In the preceding chapters we have examined the initial three "notional" ekphrases in the poem.[1] All have direct bearing on the meaning of the poem as a whole; in fact, in my view, all are to whatever degree metaphoric in sometimes astonishing ways for the text in which they are embedded. But there is also a series of other ekphrases which punctuate the epic. The majority of these are centered on landscape. We have, for instance, the magic harbor at Carthage which receives Aeneas and his battered ships after the initial storm but whose menacing backdrop—Virgil calls it a *scaena*—prepares us for the tragic dimension of, and allusions to tragedy within, the subsequent story of Dido. Then there is the brief account of the island of Tenedos near the beginning of book 2. The Greeks bury themselves there (*condunt* is Virgil's word), just as they also hide in the wooden horse, and both landmass and animal soon release their destructive energies on the city of Troy. Or we have the astonishing first sighting of martial Italy in book 3, with turreted rocks and twin walls given it by nature, and an omen of four horses, white like those of a Roman triumph, and, nearer to hand, of Turnus as he enters the epic's final battle.

But there is one example of ekphrasis which is doubly special, namely, the portrayal in book 7 of Silvia's tamed stag, whose flushing by Iulus' hounds and shooting by their master is the initial cause of fighting between the Trojans and the natives of Italy. The episode is special because there is no other description of an animal elsewhere in the Virgilian corpus and because there is no parallel in the poet's primary model, the Homeric epics. It was found wanting in antiquity not for any lack of genius in the portrayal but because such a pretext for the war it details was considered trivial.[2] I would like to examine it closely, first putting it in the setting of book 7. I will then follow out the many allusions made in the episode to the *Eclogues* and *Georgics*. My point is that such a concentration of references illustrates the changes which epic's narrative of the incipient history of war brings to the spiritual worlds Virgil has created in his previous pastoral and didactic work. I will then turn to several startling parallels between the episode and its context with the initial poems of Propertius' third book of elegies. These will be seen to continue the metapoetic dialogue Virgil had previously initiated by acknowledging his own earlier poetry and to emphasize the confrontation between epic and elegy which is at the heart of the episode's distinction.

My purpose is also to speculate on the relationship between this trenchant self-consciousness and the meaning of ekphrasis. It is a productive thesis to propose that analogies exist between Virgil's descriptions of works of art and the artful poem which they embellish, as if all the notional ekphrases, that is to say, descriptions of imagined pieces of visual art, in the *Aeneid* were partial metaphors for that grand act of *descriptio* which is the poem itself. I would maintain much the same premise for the ekphrasis of Silvia's stag. The ekphrastic moment, as conjured into being by Virgil here, makes time stop for a retrospective glimpse into a concise emotional history. Through it we observe the texturing of a work of art—indeed, a multivalent symbol for aspects of poetry itself and in particular for a world of lyric-elegiac intensity. Virgil has created an extraordinary instant of reflectivity where we watch him not only reviewing himself and his own past writing but co-opting for his special purposes some of the symbolism his great contemporary Propertius imagines in order to illustrate the generic difference between elegy and epic. This, too, is a version of art looking at art, telling us much about its grandeur and also about its vast potential for failure.

We begin with the ekphrasis proper, followed by three lines that effect the transition from description to ongoing narrative (7.483–95):

> cervus erat forma praestanti et cornibus ingens,
> Tyrrhidae pueri quem matris ab ubere raptum
> nutribant Tyrrhusque pater, cui regia parent

armenta et late custodia credita campi.
adsuetum imperiis soror omni Silvia cura
mollibus intexens ornabat cornua sertis,
pectebatque ferum puroque in fonte lavabat.
ille manum patiens mensaeque adsuetus erili
errabat silvis rursusque ad limina nota
ipse domum sera quamvis se nocte ferebat.
hunc procul errantem rabidae venantis Iuli
commovere canes, fluvio cum forte secundo
deflueret ripaque aestus viridante levaret.

There was a stag of extraordinary attractiveness, with majestic antlers, whom the sons of Tyrrhus and their father, Tyrrhus, had reared, torn from his mother's teats, Tyrrhus whom the royal herds obeyed and to whom the guardianship of wide acreage was entrusted. Silvia, their sister, accustomed him to her bidding, using every care to adorn his antlers with weavings of soft garlands, combing the beast and washing him in a limpid spring. Accepting her touch and accustomed to his mistress's board, he wandered in the woods and of his own accord he once again betook himself, late at night though it be, home to the threshold he knew. The frenzied dogs of Iulus on the hunt startled him as he wandered afield, when he chanced to float down a stream and seek refuge from heat's swelter on a greening bank.

The ekphrasis proper is a study in metamorphosis. It details the story of a beautiful stag to whom violence is done by snatching him from his mother but who through the ministrations of Silvia is absorbed into an apparently motherless family and becomes gradually tame. The series of verbs in the imperfect takes us into a world of process in time past, a process that is mimicked in the iterations of the language itself. We twice take note of the beasts' horns and we are twice told that it became accustomed to Silvia and her treatment of him (*adsuetum, adsuetus*). With custom comes civilization—the combing, washing, and eating that are part of ordinary human existence, which the animal joins, sustained now not by its natural wildness but by the acculturated world of Latium.

This story of domestication takes a magical turn at the end of the description through allusion to the stag's continued spontaneity. Assimilation into a human household apparently in no way diminishes the animal's natural tendency to roam and yet return to the new source of its well-being. Civilization and freedom complement each other in this extraordinary creature. It is as if Virgil were imaging for us an embodiment of the abstractions which, according to Latinus, speaking to the Trojan emissaries, typify his people. They are, he says (7.203–204),

> Saturni gentem haud vinclo nec legibus aequam
> sponte sua veterisque dei se more tenentem.[3]

the race of Saturn righteous not by bonds nor by laws but self-controlled by its own accord and following the custom of the ancient god.

Virgil has Latinus pun on one of the ancient etymologies of *lex*, as if it were derived from *ligo*, to bind, and build his definition of justice based not on compulsion and constraint but on instinctive adherence to custom. It is for this "golden" moment of wildness become civilized, held captive in its freedom only by the tugs of proven habit, that the stag stands as emblem.

Throughout the description runs the implication that the stag has suffered metamorphosis not only from wild to tame but from animal to human, and this suggestion takes firmer shape as the subsequent episode evolves (496–502):

> ipse etiam eximiae laudis succensus amore
> Ascanius curvo derexit spicula cornu;
> nec dextrae erranti deus afuit, actaque multo
> perque uterum sonitu perque ilia venit harundo.
> saucius at quadripes nota intra tecta refugit
> successitque gemens stabulis, questuque cruentus
> atque imploranti similis tectum omne replebat.

Ascanius himself also, kindled with a love of special praise, aimed shafts from his [bow's] curved horn. Nor does the god abandon his straying hand, and the arrow, sped with loud roar, passed through his belly and through his groin. But the wounded animal fled back within the dwelling he knew and passed groaning within his steading, and, bloodied and as if in prayer, was filling the whole dwelling with his complaint.

Gemens and *questu* are regularly associated with humans, not animals, and the phrase *imploranti similis* substantiates the analogy. The stag lacks only the use of words to keep from expressing human emotion by human means. Critics are right to see Virgil formulating a parallel with Dido.[4] The stag is placed in a literal version of the figurative situation in which the poet positions the tragic queen as the denouement of her story begins to unfold in book 4. The stag is *saucius,* wounded, just as Dido is *saucia* in the book's first line, and, in the book's initial simile we find Dido as a *cerva* wounded fatally by Aeneas as unwitting shepherd whose hunting instrument is a *letalis harundo,* a deadly reed. And, as the book progresses, and metaphor becomes reality as she approaches suicide, we hear of the *questus* that she utters in soliloquy.[5] One of these complaints, that she was not allowed to pass her life *more ferae,* in the manner of a wild creature, appears somewhat less curious, given this wider context, than when it stands alone.[6] Had circumstances been otherwise and Aeneas not impinged upon her world, she might have continued through life with a type of freedom similar to that which Virgil allots both the Latins and Silvia's stag.

But there is a further aspect to the relationship between Silvia and her stag to which the analogy with Dido lends credence. The details of the episode urge us to visualize the stag not just in human terms but in the particular metaphorical role of beloved. I will return in a moment to the elegiac vocabulary that tinges the whole description. Here I would like to point to one significant detail, namely, the wounding of the animal *per uterum . . . perque ilia.*[7] Aeneas' metaphorical arrow wounds Dido in the side. Iulus' arrow passes through the genitalia of the animal, emasculating it. The implicitly erotic relationship between Silvia and her stag, animal become quasi-human lover, reaches an end with the intrusion of Iulus and his hounds, and with the advent of the more abstract "love of special praise" (*eximiae laudis amore*), which motivates him as hunt turns to war and an implicitly physical eroticism that civilizes mutates into a spiritual cupidity that destroys.[8]

In this context the phrase *imploranti similis* must enter our discussion once again. It abets the humanization of the stag, but it also continues an aspect of the ekphrastic moment into the ongoing narrative. Virgil uses similar phrases of Ganymede, *anhelanti similis,* in the brief description on the victor's prize cloak in book 5 and of Porsenna on the shield of Aeneas, *indignanti similem similemque minanti.*[9] We are watching two of the several paradoxes of ekphrasis at work. Not only does it strive to make the visual verbal; it also brings alive to the mind's eye a creature or an event, giving it dimensionality and, in the case of Silvia's stag, a continuous existence. Within the story line Silvia has created out of her pet stag something richly human, and Virgil, through the mysteries of description, has manufactured a work of art that leaps from ekphrasis into narrative, carrying with it a reminder of its intellectual birth.[10]

The scene as a whole, set (at least as Latinus envisions it) in the prelapsarian, pre-Trojan Eden of Latium, illustrates one of the few relationships in the poem that we might call positive. And in a book given to studies in metamorphosis it stands out for its affirmative quality. Book 7 begins with a vision of Circe, who turns men into beasts, and ends with two emblems—the shield of Turnus, which flaunts a depiction of Io in the process of receiving the bristles of a cow, and, in its last line, the lance of Camilla, which consists of a pastoral myrtle capped by a spear point. Both represent what has happened in the course of the book whereby the arrival of the Trojans, and the machinations of Juno and her Fury Allecto, transform an essentially peaceful landscape into one which battens on war, and the latent violence of man and nature is tugged to the surface and made the paramount motivator of events.

In this larger context the stag ekphrasis, in itself and then as it becomes an animated part of contemporary events, stands apart from the intellectual framework in which it is placed. But there are also details in the nearer setting that further the distinction which Virgil has created. We might first note the powerful use of chiasmus here, and in passing observe how the rhetorical figure complements the topos of ekphrasis, defining it, as it were, one verbal ploy abetting another to create what Joyce calls an "epiphanic moment."[11] Before the ekphrasis we learn of the "sudden madness" (*subitam rabiem*) which Allecto throws before Iulus' hounds (*canibus*), and as action recommences it is his *rabidae canes* which proceed to bay the stag.[12] To introduce the ekphrasis and its aftermath, the narrator tells us that (481-82) *quae prima laborum/causa fuit belloque animos accendit agrestis* (this was the initial provocation of the troubles and inflamed the spirits of the rustics with war). And after the ekphrasis Virgil varies the same image as the focus of action narrows on to Iulus and we learn that he pursues the hunt, and initiates the war, because he is, as we saw, "kindled with a love of special praise" (*eximiae laudis succensus amore*).[13]

There are also elements within the ekphrasis proper that help draw it into the narrative. Curiously, spontaneity and wandering figure in the characterization of both the stag and Iulus. The stag intuitively returns home in the evening,[14] and Iulus of his own accord directs his wounding arrow. The stag in its freedom roams (*errabat*) at will, and Iulus' right hand is said to be wandering (*erranti*) until guided by divine power, as if to say that there exists a communion between man and beast, hunter and hunted, that is ruptured by the intervention of a higher authority which focuses man's ambitions along with his shooting skills.[15]

There is one detail linking description and action which underscores the distinction between the past time of the ekphrasis and contemporary events, namely, Virgil's treatment of the idea of horn and its use. Twice in the ekphrasis Virgil calls attention to the antlers of the stag. They form a major aspect of his grandeur (*cornibus ingens*), and their implicit hardness, which we are presumably to accept as metonymy of his feral nature, gains suppleness, and therefore becomes graced by a form of civilization, when Silvia intertwines them with soft garlands.[16] As we move from description to narrative proper we find ourselves watching Iulus direct his arrow against the beast "from the curved horn" (*curvo cornu*) of his bow.[17] As ekphrasis merges with action, peace yields to war, life is overtaken by death, and an attribute that adorned an emblem of nature evolving into culture is turned into a means of destruction. The failed, idealizing artistry of ekphrasis, and its unique moment, becomes the practical unremitting artistry of hunting as it blends into battle.

Virgil implicates still further reaches of his context in both the particular and general aspects of his point. After she has finished the last act of her tripartite maddening of Latium and war is now assured, the Fury Allecto alights on the ridgepole of a lofty steading (513–14): *pastorale canit signum cornuque recurvo/Tartaream intendit vocem* (she sounds the shepherds' signal and directs her Tartarean voice on curved horn). An animal's horn has been put to yet another martial use, now as hunting horn serving as bugle. We are perhaps meant to make the further evolutionary change in material, via metonymy, from horn to metal, as the plot unfolds and we develop sophistication from hunting animals to fighting men, but Virgil keeps Iulus and his transitional bow before our mind with the brilliant metaphor *intendit*.[18] Allecto may be blowing a war-trumpet, but metaphorically she is stretching and aiming her voice like an arrow sped from a bow of horn, further to expand Iulus' initial, limited gesture into the whole countryside. Allecto's action takes more generalized, and final, shape later in the book during the course of a double *descriptio* depicting the customary procedure of Romans going to war, one aspect of which involves the consul's throwing open of the twin Gates of War. This time, as Roman custom is ratified, now and for the future, there is no question that horn has given place to bronze (613–15):

> . . . reserat stridentia limina consul,
> ipse vocat pugnas; sequitur tum cetera pubes,
> aereaque adsensu conspirant cornua rauco.

The consul unbars the creaking doors, he himself gives the summons to battle; then the rest of the people follow and brazen horns breathe together in shrill agreement.

Virgil makes his point through a golden line of stunning virtuosity where the force of alliteration and assonance builds toward the final two words, *cornua rauco,* whose letters repeat each other in both orderly and helter-skelter ways to abet the call to war.

Virgil's treatment of the word *cornu* and its mutation from positive use within the ekphrasis to negative outside offers a limited example of a larger intellectual schema within which the description is set. Through ekphrasis of Silvia's act of civilizing, Virgil carefully places his creation in a wider context to which it is made to appear antipathetical. Allecto attacks two victims, Amata and Turnus, before devoting her malign attentions to Iulus and his hounds, but only in the last episode is her contrivance of madness dignified with the label art (475–77):

> Dum Turnus Rutulos animis audacibus implet,
> Allecto in Teucros Stygiis se concitat alis,
> arte nova, . . .

While Turnus fills the Rutulians with a spirit of boldness, Allecto hurls herself on Stygian wings against the Trojans, in a new piece of artistry.

It is this "new art" that both spurs Iulus on his way and introduces, by contrast, the ekphrasis of the stag.[19] Such is likewise the art to which Allecto can allude when the episode is past and she can report to Juno the successful completion of her enterprise (545): "*en, perfecta tibi bello discordia tristi*" ("Behold, Discord with war's sadness, finished off for you"). The final polish has been put on the manifestations of *Discordia* that she has engendered. The artistry of war, unlike Silvia's accomplishment, battens on disjunction and perfects a fractured, violent world.

Virgil allots to Juno herself a variation of the same image as the narration takes up after her departure (572–73):

> Nec minus interea extremam Saturnia bello
> imponit regina manum.

Nor in any lesser fashion meanwhile does the Saturnian queen apply her final touch to the war.

The phrase *extremam imponit manum* combines two idioms. *Imponere manum* means "to apply oneself," while *extrema manus* carries the notion of an artist's "finishing touch."[20] The energy that Juno and her minion have expended on disrupting the Latian countryside is that of an artisan bringing to fruition an imaginative design. It is no less metaphorical than Silvia's bravura accomplishment to which it serves as both frame and foil.

The perversion of the pastoral landscape is implied both in details, such as Allecto's *pastorale signum* and the *pastoralem myrtum* of Camilla, now tipped with a spear point, and in the larger impact of Junonian chaos. Hitherto we have examined the stag ekphrasis as the antithesis of this metamorphosis by placing it in the context which the *Aeneid* itself provides. I would like now to return to the description and make use of allusion to explicate other intellectual worlds which it inhabits. To begin I will make one last bow to Juno and Allecto, this time to the start of the episode and the first words of petition which the Olympian makes to the creature she has elicited from the nether regions to do her disruptive bidding (331–32): "*hunc mihi da proprium, virgo sata Nocte, laborem, hanc operam*" ("Grant me for my own, o virgin daughter of Night, this task, this effort"). Here, too, what Juno expects of Allecto is a form of artifice-making, a series of labors that converge into one grand figuration of *Discordia*, in her practical endeavors and in the poet's verbal realizations of them. It is not long since we have heard of "clothes, the effort of the women of Ilium" (*Iliadum . . . labor vestes*) as the last of the gifts Ilioneus offers Latinus as envoy of Aeneas.[21] The *labor* which Juno asks of Allecto is a parallel metonymy, the crafting— in three episodes which make use of the "thousand arts of harming" (*mille nocendi artes*) that are at her beck—of a world at peace into a vision of war.[22]

From the beginning we anticipate the outcome of the episode. We are also lured at the start into another poetic realm of particular importance to understanding the ekphrasis of Silvia's stag, and that is the world of the *Eclogues*. Juno's words to Allecto allude to the opening line of eclogue 10, the last of the collection: *Extremum hunc, Arethusa, mihi concede laborem* (Grant me, Arethusa, this final effort). Virgil's use of *labor* at this crucial moment has its own special design. To offer the "efforts" of writing in place of the poem itself anticipates two aspects of the work to come. It warns us that what follows is to be devoted to a study of the "trials" which love brings, first to Gallus and in the end to the speaker, and of the resulting tension between elegy and pastoral which is the imaginative nub of the poem.[23] It also anticipates the transition to the *Georgics,* with their own intricate brand of *labores,* which Virgil is intent on making as the poem draws to a conclusion. In my view, the allusion from *Aeneid* 7 back to the final eclogue has a more expansive goal which we might consider emblematized in the replacement of Arethusa by Allecto, virgin daughter of Night. The muse as fountain-nymph, whose fresh water remains untainted by salt, just as she herself escaped rape as she made her way from Greece to Sicily, becomes in *Aeneid* 7 a furious figure of blackness unleashed on Latium. The opposition between pastoral and elegy or between pastoral and georgic on which eclogue 10 builds is replaced by the universal perversion of a pastoral landscape—and of pastoral ideals—which is the inspiration of Juno and her servant.

An allusion to eclogue 10 also marks the end of the Allecto episode, as it had the beginning. At line 550, five lines after her announcement of *perfecta discordia* and immediately before the goddess dismisses her back to the lower regions, the Fury enthusiastically catalogues further areas where she could put her disruptive talents to work. Among the possibilities, she proclaims (550): "*accendam . . . animos insani Martis amore*" ("I will inflame the spirits [of the neighboring cities] with a love of maddened Mars"). Virgil would have us remember the use of the final phrase that he puts on to the lips of his poet-soldier friend Gallus, envisioned about to leave the amatory life he has been made to conceive for himself within the confines of the pastoral pleasance and return to the violence of war:

> "nunc insanus amor duri me Martis in armis
> tela inter media atque adversos detinet hostis."[24]

"Now a mad love of hard Mars retains me in the midst of weapons and hostile foes."

Once more a detail from the final eclogue, this time contrasting the easeful life imagined by Gallus within the shepherds' landscape with the realities, and perverse eroticism, at large, helps define the artistic mission of Allecto.

But the most obvious contrast with Allecto's corruption of pastoral comes from the stag ekphrasis, where the presence of the *Eclogues* is most strongly felt. Let me begin with the three lines from eclogue 10 that immediately precede those I quoted earlier, still part of Gallus' dream:

> "serta mihi Phyllis legeret, cantaret Amyntas,
> hic gelidi fontes, hic mollia prata, Lycoris,
> hic nemus; hic ipso tecum consumerer aevo."

"Phyllis would pluck garlands for me, Amyntas would sing. Here are cool fountains, Lycoris, here soft meadows, here a grove; here with you I would be consumed [with love] for my whole life."

In *Aeneid* 7 the garlands which Gallus imagines being woven for him by Phyllis become those with which Silvia intertwines the horns of her stag. They absorb the epithet *mollis*, left in eclogue 10 attached to some vaguer "meadows," while the chill fountains of Gallus' whimsy become the *puro fonte* in which the stag is bathed.

But reference to the weaving of garlands allows us to reach backward in the *Eclogues* and to be still more specific. Virgil combines the verb *intexo* with the adjective *mollis* twice in the *Eclogues*, as he does when describing how Silvia adorned the stag, *mollibus intexens . . . cornua sertis*. The first occurs in eclogue 2, during Corydon's imagined seduction of Alexis into his figmented domain, where a beautiful naiad will, with protreptic symbolism, join together a series of flowers and herbs:

> tum casia atque aliis intexens suavibus herbis
> mollia luteola pingit vaccinia calta.[25]

Then she paints soft hyacinths with yellow marigold, plaiting [them] together with marjoram and other fragrant herbs.

The golden line brilliantly reifies the mingling of textures that at once allude to the senses of touch, sight, and smell and adumbrate the erotic coupling that Corydon would will for himself.

Even more germane to the ekphrasis is a line from the fifth eclogue, which concludes a catalogue of the civilizing achievements of the dead Daphnis. He taught men how to yoke wild tigers to the chariot, to introduce the dances of Bacchus *et foliis lentas intexere mollibus hastas*[26] (and to interweave hard wands with soft leaves). Much the same could be said for the accomplishment of Silvia. Daphnis' acculturating power tempered the potentially martial thyrsus, which Virgil here directly calls a spear, with leaves, mitigating hard with soft (all verbally mimicked in the entwinings of another virtually golden line). Silvia in her turn tames the rugged wildness of her stag by this gesture of enclosing the rigid with the pliable. She becomes a Daphnis and, in a sense, a Virgil, too, by her texturing.[27]

These gestures illustrate what we might call the assimilating potential of the pastoral mode, to absorb elements foreign to it, even threatening to its fragile myth, and make them part of its fabric, even though sometimes only momentarily. So Bacchus' covert violence is co-opted by Daphnis, and the complex figure of Gallus finds a fleeting haven in the shepherd-poet's realm. Another trait of pastoral which is present in the ekphrasis is its bent for spontaneity, for events occurring naturally which in other situations and in other poetic modes would come about by effort or not at all. This form of pastoral idealizing, which is imagined to manifest itself in both animal and human kinds, is condensed into the last lines of the ekphrasis proper:

> errabat silvis rursusque ad limina nota
> ipse domum sera quamvis se nocte ferebat.

The stag is the perfect pastoral animal, demonstrating in itself what in ordinary situations would be either inculcated by training or achieved by man's constant intervention. He is a transitory exemplar, located for contrast in epic's hostile environment, of what we find imagined as an eternal verity in the idealizing extravaganza of eclogue 4 where, for example, *ipsae lacte domum referent distenta capellae/ubera*[28] (of their own accord goats will bring home udders swollen with milk).

The phrase *sera nocte* also must enter our discussion. For the stag it means that, no matter how late the time, he still remembers to return home (which is to say, in elegiac parlance, that he remains faithful to his mistress).[29] But Virgil also uses the phrase in eclogue 8 as part of a simile he puts in the mouth of a witch attempting to bring her inconstant lover Daphnis back home from the city. May yearning strike him, she cries, like that of a heifer for her bull, a heifer who, distraught, wanders in her search everywhere about "nor does she remember to withdraw even late at night" (*nec serae meminit decedere nocti*). Under less distracting circumstances, the lover-animal would have remembered to return home no matter how late, but unhappy *amor,* within pastoral, breaks the ordinary pattern of spontaneous, instinctual behavior. The stag's action is therefore made to seem the result of true affection displayed in a way that reflects an ideal pastoral moment.

Other details may add to the picture. Some are positive, such as Silvia's act of adornment, which reminds us of two instances in the *Eclogues* where poets are crowned, and of the garlands of Silenus which are utilized to bind him and elicit his Protean profusion of subjects.[30] Some are negative: for example, Virgil calls attention to the wounding of the stag in several ways. One is the phrase *multo sonitu,* which is unexampled elsewhere in Virgil. Nor does he ever associate the word *harundo,* in its meaning of arrow, with sound, only with expeditious flight. The roar the weapon makes is therefore a miniature instance of parody of the pastoral song that emanates from a slender reed, a song such as the speaker plans at the opening of eclogue 6:

> agrestem tenui meditabor harundine Musam:
> non iniussa cano.[31]

I will ponder a rustic song on slender reed. I sing matters not unbidden.

In the move from ekphrasis to reality we watch yet again another instance of metamorphosis from peace to war, but this time with an added dimension. As we change from slender reed as instrument of song to the loud roar that accompanies reed become arrow and now part of the apparatus of war, we leave behind an idealized world of the past, defined not only by its forced contingency to the present's destructive practicalities but by the world of poetry which characterizes it. Ekphrasis gives place to narrative, but we can now understand more clearly the specialness of its design, depicting a pastoral scenario and therefore in this instance serving as a topos which participates in the rubrics of pastoral poetry itself.

The phrase *sera nocte* tugs us into still another generic world, this time that of the *Georgics.* It recurs in one of the more remarkable pauses in that poem when, in the fourth book, Virgil sequesters time from his apiary universe to spend some thirty lines telling us what he will not teach—the care of gardens, flowers, and vegetables.[32] The protagonist of the passage is a Corycian old man dwelling in Calabria. His life is rugged and at the mercy of seasonal vagaries, yet it has its distinct rewards. His small acreage is not fit for cattle or vines. Nevertheless, he is the first to pick roses in the spring and fruit in the autumn and the first to harvest honey from his bees. Whatever the poverty of his circumstances, in Virgil's words, "he equaled the resources of kings in his mind" (*regum aequabat opes animis*).[33] One aspect of his daily habits stands out: *seraque revertens/nocte domum dapibus mensas onerabat inemptis*[34] (and returning home late at night he burdened his tables with unbought meals). The last item, which Horace also echoes,[35] speaks to a gently idealized autonomy where human and nature are complementary, while the first looks to the labor necessary to maintain this balance. We are after all in a georgic world now, not a pastoral one.

The fact that Virgil uses the phrase *sera nocte* also of the stag, intuitively returning home to its beloved late at night, might seem fortuitous or, at best, tangential, were it not for one other detail which pointedly draws us from georgic 4 into the events which occur subsequently in the ekphrasis and its immediate aftermath. Virgil specifies, with a care underlined by the narrator's profession of autopsy, that the Corycian *senex* came from "under the towers of the Spartan citadel" (*sub Oebaliae . . . turribus arcis*), which is to say Tarentum *qua niger umectat flaventia culta Galaesus*[36] (where the black Galaesus waters its tawny croplands). A reader of the *Georgics* recognizes the poet's purpose when the word *Galaesus* recurs as appellation of an initial victim of the skirmish that follows on Allecto's instigation of Iulus and his hounds. Only two men are actually named. The first is Almo, one of the sons of Tyrrhus and therefore brother of Silvia. Then there are other casualties:

> corpora multa virum circa seniorque Galaesus
> dum paci medium se offert, iustissimus unus . . .[37]

Many bodies of men there were round about and the old man Galaesus while he offers himself for peace in their midst, the one most just.

Both Almo and Galaesus are names of rivers, the first a tributary of the Tiber, the second Tarentum's stream. By giving these names to the first fatalities, Virgil suggests the death of the landscape and of what nourishes it that comes through war. It is as if Silvia's world suffers another, now fatal, wounding and as if the Corycian *senex* and his setting where the Galaesus flows were epitomized in the figure of *senior* Galaesus who, peace-loving and just though he be, must also die.[38]

The case of Galaesus has a particular point. He brings with him as intellectual baggage not only the splendid interlude of georgic 4, where the farmer, caught up in nature's demanding rounds, at last and for a fleeting instant takes on the individuality of a name. He also brings the symbolism of Tarentum itself. Readers of Horace, for instance, will remember his mention of the Galaesus in the context of an ode which idealizes this southern city as one of earth's most beautiful spots, one whose citadel (*arces*) demands "Horace" and his addressee for their final resting place.[39] This perfect landscape, Virgil would seem to say in *Aeneid* 7, is what becomes immediately vulnerable at the onslaught of war. The point leads us back to the connection of the old man near the Galaesus and the stag, both of whom return home *sera nocte*. It is the loss not only of a pastoral *Weltanschauung* that the ekphrasis prefigures but of the georgic world as well. The narrator will soon bemoan the fact that men now attend to the making of arms: *vomeris huc et falcis honos, huc omnis aratri/cessit amor*[40] (hither honor of the plowshare and the sickle, hither all love of the plow has yielded). War affects the further metamorphosis of a countryside as it moves away from living with the demands of nature reasserting seasonal cyclicity. This mutation, and the losses it implies, also begin at the moment the ekphrasis and its model contents come to a stop. In subject matter we leave behind the bucolic and georgic worlds and replace them with history's martial narrative. We also are reminded that Virgil defines his ekphrasis not only by content and context but by allusion to the poetic genres of his past works. The ekphrastic pause here brilliantly recalls what the adoption of epic and the abandonment of pastoral and didactic poetry mean for the Virgilian career.

Hitherto Virgil himself has been our primary focus for explanation of the ekphrasis, whether we were looking specifically at its place in

Aeneid 7 or at what it brings to bear from echoes of earlier Virgilian poetry. I would like now, while continuing to make use of allusivity as a tool for investigation, to turn outside the Virgilian corpus and look to the relationship our ekphrasis bears to an extraordinary group of elegies by Propertius, the opening five poems of his third book. Though their exact date of publication is uncertain (internal evidence points most logically to 22 B.C.E.), there is no question that they were being written at the same time as Virgil was bringing his *Aeneid* to a close. My discussion will not pursue the impossible task of deciding priority of influence but will merely observe how imaginative interaction can shed light on both poets.

For their grandeur and the spiritual consistency they display as a group, Propertius' poems have something in common with another group of exactly contemporary poems, the six so-called "Roman" odes which open Horace's third book of lyrics, as well as with the sphragis to his masterpiece, *c.* 3.30. But, to generalize, whereas Horace's primary purpose is to examine certain ethical problems of deep concern to present-day Rome, Propertius takes the opportunity such an introductory grouping offers to study his poetics, which is to say his poetic goals, the magical power of his verse to subvert time, and, in place of prominence, the conflict of elegy with epic and the poet's continuing refusal to embrace epic themes.

The first poem in particular looks to the speaker's inheritance as bard in the tradition of Callimachus and Philetas and examines the emblems which confirm him in this priestlike vocation. It is striking that two of these insignia Propertius shares with the ekphrasis of Silvia's stag. The first appears in the third line when the speaking "I" announces

> primus ego ingredior puro de fonte sacerdos
> Itala per Graios orgia ferre choros.[41]

I myself first, as a priest, am setting out to bear from an untouched source Italian mystic rites through the choruses of Greece.

However complex the symbolism of the pentameter, the meanings of *puro fonte* in this context of self-revelation are clear enough. The phrase expands on *primus* to declare the uniqueness of the poet's vocation and sources of inspiration, but it also speaks to Callimachean purity of expression and to a refined poetics that stands in contrast to the heavy expansiveness of epic.[42]

The distinction between epic and elegy is also central to the couplet in which the second parallel with the ekphrasis appears. Propertius has gone on to curse those who "delay Phoebus in arms," which is to say, who hazard the inspiration of epic. The speaker's unwarlike triumph, he continues, will find his chariot drawn by tiny Cupids. Then, after offering assurance that many will praise Rome's imperial ambitions in the form of *Annales,* while his own work is to be read in surroundings of peace, he addresses the Muses directly:

> mollia, Pegasides, date vestro serta poetae:
> non faciet capiti dura corona meo.[43]

Nymphs [of the fountain] of Pegasus, grant soft garlands to your poet: a hard crown will not suit my head.

Epic hardness has no part in Propertius' genius, only the pliancy of elegy's gentle themes.

Given the symbolic weight of the phrases *puro fonte* and *mollia serta* in their Propertian setting, their appearance in adjacent lines in the ekphrasis is all the more astonishing. We are no doubt meant to imagine Silvia literally bathing her pet in an untouched source and interweaving its horns with soft garlands, but the other metapoetic aspects of the passage give us license to speculate here also on Virgil's deeper intent. Allusion to Propertian elegy and its emblems confirms what we have already sensed in the ekphrasis but expands another dimension only hinted at before. We appreciate yet again the understated eroticism of the description. We once more apprehend the passage as deliberately illustrating a world at peace soon to be disrupted by war. But from the symbolic aspects of the echoes we are also allowed a further glimpse of Virgilian self-consciousness. His ekphrasis, like Propertius' consecration into the mysteries of poetry, is equally a study in origination and originality, for its subject matter and for its co-optation of the emblems of elegy, as listed by its greatest Roman practitioner. At the moment when ekphrasis itself takes us within the world of elegy, the mastermind of the ekphrasis also appeals to a contemporary expert in an antiepic genre so as further to define and refine the meaning of each poetic type.

Propertius also helps us make the transition back into the epic narrative proper. Within the ekphrasis we have soft garlands, but the *dura corona* which Propertius awards to the writer of epic soon takes metonymic shape in the "hardened farmers" (*duros agrestis*) that Silvia calls to her aid and in the "hard cudgels" (*stipitibus duris*) which they use.[44] But there is one further detail of Propertian symbolism that the postekphrastic context takes up which again emphasizes the difference with the ekphrasis itself. Toward the end of the third of the elegies that introduce book 3, Propertius imagines the epiphany of the muse Calliope, who declares that the speaker, whom we come near to calling the poet himself, will not be lured to arms by the sound of a brave horse— that is, will not write epic:

> nil tibi sit rauco praeconia classica cornu
> flare, nec Aonium tingere Marte nemus; . . . [45]

Let not the martial summons blare for you on shrill horn, [nor be it yours] to imbue the Aonian mountain with Mars.

We are reminded of the sequence whereby the tamed horns of the tamed stag suffer transformation first into the horn of Iulus' hunting bow and then, as artistry further evolves, into the brass horn of war as the consul calls the people to arms: *aereaque adsensu conspirant cornua rauco*. Once more, that which stands as symbol in Propertius, this time for epic, not elegy, is used by Virgil literally as battling begins in earnest. Propertius can employ the horn as part of a *recusatio,* to show emblematically that he will renounce thoughts of epic to continue on his career as elegist. Virgil embraces the horn as the declarer of war, but his phrasing would lose something special in its force were it not seen as part of a continuum with the stag ekphrasis and were Propertius not allowed to play his part in forging a link between ekphrasis and narrative, between a sequestered intellectual world that shares important touches with Virgil's earlier work and with Propertius' contemporary accomplishment, which is to say between pastoral, didactic, and elegiac poetry, and the epic's expanding view of arms and men in history. The ekphrasis of Silvia's stag is in many ways a mirror of what is probably the longest *descriptio* of a person in the poem, namely, the ekphrasis telling us the past history of the warrior-virgin Camilla at 11.537–84. I would like to conclude by comparing the two passages to see what light their relation can shed on one striking detail in the stag ekphrasis—the fact that the animal must be torn from its mother in order to suffer the metamorphoses that I have been tracing.[46] Why the need for violence and for separation from its mother for the process of humanization to commence?

The story of Camilla is as original to Virgil as is the episode of the stag. We meet her first at the end of book 7, but she becomes a dominant figure in the narrative only in book 11, where her *aristeia* and death occupy a major portion of the book's last four hundred lines. For some fifty verses before she enters the action for a final time we learn something of her past, how her father was exiled from Privernum, carrying her as a baby with him. We discover how, in escaping from his pursuers he dedicates her as perpetual virgin to Diana, how she is reared on the milk of animals and lives the life of a huntress without thoughts of marriage. And, of course, her role as huntress prepares her, as it does Iulus, to make the easy transition to warrior.

The complementarity with the stag episode can be succinctly put. Whereas the animal becomes anthropomorphic, leaving the wild for domesticity and a form of marriage, the opposite happens to Camilla. Humans foster the stag (*nutribant*) to become one with them, whereas Camilla's father "nourishes her on the milk of wild creatures" (*lacte ferino/nutribat*), suitable enough accompaniment to his own *feritas*.[47] She is brought up to choose the country over the city, the feral over the human, virginity over a girl's normal course toward marriage, a man's pursuits over those of a woman, pursuits that soon lead her into the violence and bestialization of war. In the course of her adventures the poet appropriately compares her to the Amazon warrior Penthesilea.

Virgil uses allusions to pastoral and elegy to secure in our minds the stag's adoption of a peaceful world where a creature ordinarily preyed upon by man can become a surrogate lover. In the ekphrasis of Camilla it is allusion to Catullus which tells us what will not happen in her life: *multae illam frustra Tyrrhena per oppida matres/optavere nurum*[48] (Many mothers throughout the towns of Etruria desired her in vain as daughter-in-law). Virgil is referring to a moment in Catullus' second epithalamium where the female chorus compares virginity to a flower: *multi illum pueri, multae optavere puellae*[49] (Many boys, many girls desired it). Catullus' girls, whatever games they may be playing, are sharers in a wedding celebration. This world of marriage, and the lyric environment that gives it spiritual shape, must be eschewed by Camilla (and her inventor) in favor of the epic prowess that brings her glory and death.

The stag is torn from its mother as it enters an apparently motherless family to be reared by humans. Camilla has no mother, and her would-be nourishment is replaced by animal milk and a father's care. She stays with a double wildness that leads to war. For the stag, the implication is that the world of his mother is equivalent somehow to wildness from which civilization takes him, doing violence but at the same time bringing culture. He is an animate version of the scepter of Latinus, described in book 12, which "lacks its mother" (*matre caret*), cut in the forest from the bottom of a stump.[50] Only by being violently severed from woods and mother can it become symbol of political order imposed on their territory by the Latin fathers. Virgil makes a similar point twice over in georgic 2 when he tells of anthropomorphic plants which the farmer must tear from their mothers' bodies, or remove from their destructive shade, in order for them to become productive.

Virgil may be suggesting here that fatherhood (except in the twisted version of Camilla's story, where paternity is in fact a form of maternity bordering on animality), and maybe even the male world in general by definition, shares in the artistry of civilization-making. Viewed at large, the *Aeneid* would seem to bear out the point. There are few what we might call acculturating women in the epic. Dido, *dux femina facti*, woman in a man's role, has embarked on a civilizing mission, but circumstances cause her doom. The Sibyl helps Aeneas on his way but only after experiencing the taming controls of the male god Apollo. Venus has her helpful side. But when we survey the epic as a whole, the female spirit is largely conveyed as violent and disruptive. Juno's rage sparks the epic's initial storm, and her jealous vendetta arouses Allecto as its second half commences. Mothers themselves as a group largely exert a negative force. Provoked by Juno, they burn some of the ships in book 5, and book 7 finds Amata and her fellow "mothers set aflame by furies in their heart" (*furiisque accensas pectore matres*), driven into the woods as ready victims of goddess and Fury.[51] And through Virgil's genius they also have nearly the poem's last word. As he prepares to kill his suppliant foe at the epic's end, Aeneas is described as being "set aflame by furies and terrifying in his wrath" (*furiis accensus et ira/terribilis*).[52] As his epic concludes he is made to appear a source of madness, not order, as Juno did at the start (*accensa*)[53] and as do the mothers at the second beginning in book 7.

Silvia's stag must be torn from its mother to suffer taming, and the ekphrasis that describes it is an oasis of civility in a desert of wildness. As commentary on the largest context in which it is embedded (the epic as a whole), the ekphrasis still has something to tell us about the topos itself. It serves as vehicle which here forces generic conflicts to life and which demands, as do all the artistic ekphrases scattered through the poem, that we grapple yet again with the tone and meaning of the whole and especially with the violence of its ending. Aeneas shouts that his victim must not be torn from him. He is not, and Aeneas kills. Had Turnus been snatched away—that is, had Aeneas practiced the paternal, civilizing role, practiced the *clementia* his father suggests to him in the Underworld, and spared his humbled antagonist—we would have quite a different epic, with Silvia and all she stands for in triumph at the end. But this was not Virgil's intent.

5
The Shield of Aeneas

Book 8 of the epic concludes with the lengthiest and most complex ekphrasis in the poem, devoted to the shield of Aeneas.[1] In this chapter, I will analyze the description in detail, looking in particular at the means by which Virgil uses words to delineate the creation of a piece of fine art and to give it spatial quality. I will trace how the poet elicits our concern with problems of balance and shape. The last episode, for instance, is longer than all the preceding ones combined, and the totality, though its subject is linear history, finds its place on a rounded, circumscribed artifact.

I will then examine the multivalent relation of the ekphrasis to the poem as a whole and, more briefly, to Homer's description of the shield of Achilles in *Iliad* 18. In conclusion I will return to the first episode found on Aeneas' shield and to Virgil's use of allusivity to lend the initiation of the ekphrasis special force (630–34):

> fecerat et viridi fetam Mavortis in antro
> procubuisse lupam, geminos huic ubera circum
> ludere pendentis pueros et lambere matrem
> impavidos, illam tereti cervice reflexa
> mulcere alternos et corpora fingere lingua.

He had fashioned, too, the mother wolf, stretched out in the green cave of Mars; around her teats hung the twin boys, playing, and without fear licked their mother; bending back her smooth neck, she fondled them in turn and fashioned their bodies with her tongue.

The ekphrasis proper begins with *fecerat*, a word which, in conjunction with the subsequent *et*, reminds the reader of three facts. First, Vulcan had caused the shield and the scenes crafted upon it to be made. Second, though he had done so in the past and in a different locale, only now, together with Aeneas in the sacred grove of Caere, do we "read" what the hero sees and respond to it. Third, what we are about to peruse is part of a larger whole, excerpts from the total sweep of Roman destiny as defined by the descendants of Ascanius and their wars, chosen by the narrator (and assigned to him by his crafter!) and touched by the prejudices any such selectivity implies and entails.

The initiation of the ekphrasis dwells on crafter and crafting and therefore on the object before Aeneas and us. The remainder of the line—*viridi . . . Mavortis in antro*—both sets in motion the description of what is detailed on the shield and posits a counterpoint to it. It is possible to engrave or otherwise depict a cave in metal, and the event soon to be told would serve as strong enough signal that this cave had close associations with the Roman god of war. But to imagine a "green" cave is to pass beyond the metallurgist's art into the immediate reality of the scene itself, to vivify what stretches inertly before us on the shield. Virgil complements this extraordinary transition from static to mobile, from frozen artistry to palpable experience, by shifting the infinitives from past to present. This change gives texture to ekphrastic time by reflecting how the action of the shield, unlike Vulcan's spate of crafting, is to be perceived as continuous, which is to say unfinished or ongoing.

Had he so opted, Virgil's narrator (or Vulcan's hypnotic genius) could have portrayed the whole scene as done and over. The wolf could have been visualized as having lain there, suckled the young twins and shaped their bodies, with pastness of event reinforcing the past act of crafting and therefore the artificiality of the vignette. Instead, and in spite of the perfect tense of *procubuisse*, the greenness of the cave, with its implications of freshness and youth, and the potential implicit in the adjective *feta* (What does it mean for this wolf to be "pregnant"?) prepare the reader for the freshness and vigor of what follows. The wolf has not given birth but she is visibly about the act of suckling the twins just as they are before us, playing and licking their surrogate mother.[2]

We plunge into the scene through the demonstrative adjective *huic* applied to the she-wolf. This strange creature is made to appear very much present before us. But it is the four present infinitives—*ludere, lambere, mulcere,* and *fingere*—carefully balanced in the first and fifth feet of their respective lines, which emphasize the graphicness of what we see. We are meant to be beholding a work of art, but the brilliance of Virgil's description allows the scene itself to take on a life of its own. Much of this immediacy comes from the combination of variation and sameness that the four symmetrical infinitives project. Each deals with a different aspect of the event, but the quadruple repetition marks the continuity to immediate action. The force of this repetition is supplemented by the constancy of assonance and alliteration throughout the description. As we move from *ludere pendentis pueros* to *corpora fingere lingua* the figures of sound, with their own forms of repetition directed toward the reader's ear, recapitulate the force which the infinitives gain through iteration. Rhetoric thus doubly lures us into imagining an event happening directly before us. We may be watching Vulcan's shield but we are also in the hands of another master artisan who animates the still pastness of art through the activity of words.

I will come back to this scene from several other angles as my analysis proceeds. Here I would like to pause only on motifs of importance for the evolution of the shield itself. One concerns the ramifications that arise from a matter of topography. The scene of the twins suckled by the wolf was memorialized in the shrine of the Lupercal, located most probably at the base of the Palatine, below its southwest corner.[3] This sacred spot was restored by Augustus, whose own dwelling was located nearby, virtually adjacent to where tradition placed the house of Romulus. But the Palatine is also the site for the temple of Apollo, which serves as setting for the final scene on the shield, dedicated by Augustus on October 9, 28 B.C.E. Since this structure likewise neighbored the emperor's home, Virgil has used the Palatine, especially the Palatine as monumentalized by Augustus, as a unifying feature of his shield, to be visualized by his contemporary Roman reader in his mind's eye from what he would have known well in person.

The episodes on the shield may lead us chronologically over a period of seven hundred years, from the mythic founding of Rome to the battle of Actium and its aftermath. But, and this is a point we will examine later in detail, the historical linearity of the shield's contents finds its counterpoise in the circularity of its shape. This shape, in turn, is emphasized by the artifact's bounding scenes which take us, through parallel allusion to the emperor and his domestic environment, from the founding of Rome to its renewal, at the end of a century of civil war, under Augustus. The wholeness of the shield, from one crucial vantage point, mimics the pretension toward wholeness of Augustus and his Rome which his propaganda fostered.

Two other motifs which run through the ekphrasis are established in its opening vignette. The first is the idea of twins and the power that resides in such doubling.[4] We find it directly in the double flames that emanate from Caesar Augustus' forehead as he leads his forces into the crucial battle off Actium.[5] It appears again in the double snakes of death which Cleopatra fails to notice as the battle turns against her.[6] We find it in more subtle form in the way the figures of the emperor and his chief lieutenant, Agrippa, are described as they lead the initial onslaught. First we have Augustus, driving (*agens*) the Itali into battle, with the household divinities and the great gods (*penatibus et magnis dis*), his brow spouting its flames (*geminas cui tempora flammas/laeta vomunt*).[7] Then we have Agrippa, with his favorable gods (*dis . . . secundis*), loftily driving (*agens*) his own battle line, his brows gleaming with the naval crown (*cui . . . /tempora navali fulgent . . . corona*).[8]

This type of repetition in contiguous lines is unusual for Virgil. Its effect in this context is, verbally, to accent the equivalence of the *princeps* and his colleague as together they launch the conclusive battle of the civil war. Virgil initiates his ekphrastic vision of Roman history with twin brothers, one of whom would, over the course of time, kill the other. The tradition of fratricidal strife thus established would come to an end, as nearly does the shield itself, with the battle of 31 B.C.E. The similarity of the two Roman leaders is a clear exemplification of this redesigning of the Roman past, at once echoing unity and purging any ruinous attempt at dissolution.[9]

The further motif which the Lupercal scene inaugurates is the intimate connection between man and animals. Here the relationship would appear at once anomalous and mutually beneficial. The miracle of Rome's origins, and a primary source of the shield's initiating dynamism, is the suckling of human twins in a primitive, natural setting, by a creature of the wild. Elsewhere in the lines to come Virgil will follow out, in diverse versions and with different emphases, the ambiguous suggestiveness of this collocation.

As the second episode begins, Virgil keeps both the craftsman (*addiderat*) and the object crafted (*nec procul hinc*) as part of his narrative (635–41):

> nec procul hinc Romam et raptas sine more Sabinas
> consessu caveae, magnis Circensibus actis,
> addiderat, subitoque novum consurgere bellum
> Romulidis Tatioque seni Curibusque severis.
> post idem inter se posito certamine reges
> armati Iovis ante aram paterasque tenentes
> stabant et caesa iungebant foedera porca.

Not far from here he had added Rome and the Sabine women lawlessly carried off from the theater's seated crowd while the great Circus games were being held; and suddenly a new war arose between the sons of Romulus and the old man Tatius and stern Cures. Afterward, the same kings, their struggle set aside, were standing before the altar of Jupiter, armed and holding libation bowls, and were joining together in treaties over the sacrifice of a pig.

But as time presses on and as an unnamed twin now gains sufficient sway to share his name with a city (*Romam*) and with his own followers (*Romulidis*), our eye moves from the base of the Palatine further into the valley below its southern slope, to the Circus Maximus. The potential force, which the first vignette leaves implicit, was contained within a wolf's den. Energy is now made explicit and transferred to the public space of a theatrical "cave" (*cavea*) which holds the viewers looking at games named after the enclosed area in which they were performed (*Circensibus actis*).[10] From this double "enclosure" bursts a series of actions which Virgil helps define with a pun. The Sabine women had been spectators at an event presumably celebrated with yearly regularity. The rape of the seated women (*consessu*), an act unexampled elsewhere in Roman history for its several violations of customary procedure, is the cause for a new war to rise up (*consurgere*). At the dawn of Roman history, an individual act of force provokes battling that ends only in a truce, not in any intimations of final peace or reconciliation.

Vulcan is present for the first segment of the scene. When we turn to the second part, nothing stands between us, as viewer-readers, and the event itself, which shows the two leaders in the ongoing posture of standing (*stabant*) and joining in compact (*iungebant*). Continued action cannot, at least here, be captured in the craftsman's frozen art. This immediacy is enhanced by the multiple images we have before us, the men in their armor, Jupiter's altar, the accoutrements of ceremony. The most poignant detail comes last. A pig was a standard offering at the Roman ratification of a treaty, but we are also meant to assume its symbolic value here as replacement for the human victims of war. Animal sacrifice comes when confrontation is past, but Virgil leaves us with *reges armati*, with the uneasy spectacle of peacemakers still in their panoply of weapons.

One further detail stands out in these final lines. Nowhere else in the tradition is the Sabine king Tatius called *senex*.[11] That he appears as an old man making peace with the "sons of Romulus" not only emphasizes the age differential between the protagonists. It further suggests that the struggle which has just come to an end is meant to emblematize a type of civil war, with sons set in opposition to their older, future fathers-in-law. The wolf of Mars would breed twin boys, one of whom would murder the other. His "offspring," making peace by the altar of Jupiter, would in their own way carry on the tradition.

The subsequent episode, the warlike events surrounding which Livy calls "most like a civil war" (*civile simillimum bello*),[12] carries the pattern forward (642–45):

> haud procul inde citae Mettum in diversa quadrigae
> distulerant (at tu dictis, Albane, maneres!),
> raptabatque viri mendacis viscera Tullus
> per silvam, et sparsi rorabant sanguine vepres.

Not far from there four-horse chariots, driven in opposite directions, had torn Mettus apart (but you, Alban, should have held to your words!), and Tullus was dragging through the woods the innards of the liar, and the splattered briars dripped bloody dew.

As in the previous episode, we are directed on to the next scene (*haud procul inde*), just as Roman history progressed some hundred years to the reign of Tullus Hostilius and just as the mind's eye now moves from the valley between the Palatine and Aventine hills to the territory of Fidenae, north of Rome. Once again, as in the preceding episode, there are two distinct actions which Virgil distinguishes by using first a pluperfect, then imperfects, one over and done with, the other ongoing. The faithless Mettus Fufetius has been torn apart. His punisher still continues, in words that enliven art's rigid temporality, to have his guts torn through the woods whose brambles are even yet bedewed with blood.

No Vulcan is here present to remind us of artisan and artifact, but Virgil tricks his reader into expecting him by the sequence of pluperfects that lead from *fecerat* to *addiderat* to *distulerant*. But for the last we find not Vulcan at work but chariots about the act of rending apart a human body. No crafting figure mediates between "viewer" and the horror of the depicted event, which Livy pronounces "was the first and last punishment among the Romans of a kind that disregards the laws of humanity" (*Primum ultimumque illud supplicium apud Romanos exempli parum memoris legum humanarum fuit*).[13]

As we watch the Romans directly accomplishing a hideous moment in their destiny, we find Virgil exercising his own skill in bringing the event immediately before us. Only a brief space in Roman, or ekphrastic, time separates the killing of a pig from the dismemberment of Mettus Fufetius. We move briskly from a verbal world ironically dependent on words of unity (*consessu, consurgere*) to one intent on separation (*diversa, distulerant*). But it is the gesture of apostrophe—*at tu dictis, Albane, maneres*—that enlivens both the event and, for one ghastly final moment, the victim himself. Who makes the address is left unclear—Tullus Hostilius, perhaps, as he chastizes his faithless enemy, Vulcan as he confronts the implications of his figurations, or, most likely, Virgil, the creator of the whole, perhaps also anticipating the response of the reader-spectator to what he sees. But its paronomasia on *maneres* makes the address all the more pointed. Whoever speaks takes bitter note, through the verb, of the difference between remaining whole and laceration, which is to say between abiding by one's word and treacherous infidelity, between truth and falsehood. A parallel wordplay likewise centers on the name Albanus. Were he to have lived up to his name, Mettus would have been clear and bright, which is to say true, honest, direct. His moral career is the opposite of what his nomenclature implies.

But the basic meaning of the name sets up another parallel pattern of signification. He who should be white of character is in fact *mendax*, (etymologically) given to blemishes, of soul, not body. But the result of such an ethical stain is something highly visible. Lack of inner candor complemented by inner blotchiness leads, when retribution occurs, to brambles stained with the red dew of human blood. The invisible is made apparent in one of the most conspicuous images of the ekphrasis, incapable of being crafted (How could the miracle-worker Vulcan show the continuous dripping of blood?), yet intensely ocular. We have an unmediated vision of an infamous moment of revenge in early Roman history which is also put before us as highly anomalous. Dew becomes blood only at a moment when human perversity alters natural into unnatural.

In the preceding episode the sacrifice of a pig had replaced the further human victims that war might bring. Here animality is in the ascendant. In the third georgic Virgil alludes to an occasion where Venus maddens Glaucus' horses (*quadrigae*) so as to tear him apart with their jaws,[14] and the *Aeneid* itself often illustrates how horses, literally or metaphorically, emblematize violence. Here they are not only the means for Tullus to execute his vendetta but also his own self-extension, his penchant for brutal violence given animal form. Livy, at the end of his account, can proclaim that, aside from the example of Tullus against Mettus, "in other cases we may boast that with no other nation have milder punishments found favor" (*in aliis gloriari licet nulli gentium mitiores placuisse poenas*).[15] Virgil allows us no ameliorating apothegm.

In the fourth episode our movement on the shield's space takes us back to the city and, in Roman time, to the end of kingship and the beginning of the Republic (646–51):

> nec non Tarquinium eiectum Porsenna iubebat
> accipere ingentique urbem obsidione premebat;
> Aeneadae in ferrum pro libertate ruebant.
> illum indignanti similem similemque minanti
> aspiceres, pontem auderet quia vellere Cocles
> et fluvium vinclis innaret Cloelia ruptis.

There, too, Porsenna was commanding that they receive the exiled Tarquin and was pressing the city with a mighty siege; the sons of Aeneas were rushing to the sword for the sake of freedom. You might see him like someone indignant, like someone threatening, because Cocles dared to tear down the bridge and Cloelia was swimming the river after breaking her bonds.

We find Porsenna trying to reinstate Tarquinius Superbus while the Romans, among whom Cocles and Cloelia were notable for their bravery, resisting his pressure. Once again Virgil varies his mode of presentation. Vulcan remains absent, but in this instance there is no attempt at placement. Moreover all the verbs of the description are in the imperfect, illustrating one continuous event, Porsenna ordering and pressing his siege, the Romans fighting for their own cause. But, even though the artisan is unmentioned, the poet makes us here twice aware that our act of reading is tantamount to our (inner) viewing of the artifact itself.

The first instance is the phrase *indignanti similem similemque minanti*. Unlike the way he plunges us directly into Tullus' brutish doings, Virgil here makes us aware that we are watching an image of Porsenna which is twice over like, but nevertheless only like, a real person actually indignant or threatening. The second means by which the narrator calls attention to the ekphrasis itself is through the word *aspiceres*. If the apostrophe in the preceding episode drew us immediately into the event itself, or into a narrator's comment which reanimates the event's protagonist, here the use of the second person conspires to have us join with Aeneas for the first time in the ekphrasis, under the pretense of actually viewing, and pondering, this particular episode on the shield. The fact that "you," Aeneas as initial viewer, and "you," the privileged reader, first merge here in the ekphrasis gives special stress to the denomination of the Romans, in line 648, as *Aeneadae,* descendants now not of Romulus but of the hero of the *Aeneid* itself.

But if reminders that we are viewing/reading an artifact simulating reality lead to detachment, the very novelty of the poet's rhetoric also involves the reader in the act of seeing and therefore in the elicitation of meaning from what he sees. We marvel at the central figure, Porsenna, as he appears almost alive, aggrieved and menacing in response to what he beholds. We also watch, as we yield to the narrator's suggestive signals ("you might perceive, if you had imagination enough"), the sons of Aeneas championing their newfound liberty, with Cocles tearing up a bridge and Cloelia rending her bonds. We will later find these objects, the gestures they evoke, and the implicit presence of Aeneas in the background all to be important in judging the final moments of the ekphrasis itself.

As we move ahead in Roman history from the doublet of heroes, Cocles and Cloelia, at the dawn of the Republic, to the crisis of 390 and the invasion of the Gauls, our eye moves from the river Tiber, at the base of the city's hills, to the citadel perched on the lofty Capitolium (*Capitolia celsa*), the "head" of the City in both a literal and a figurative sense, and crucial for its survival (652–62):

> in summo custos Tarpeiae Manlius arcis
> stabat pro templo et Capitolia celsa tenebat,
> Romuleoque recens horrebat regia culmo.
> atque hic auratis volitans argenteus anser
> porticibus Gallos in limine adesse canebat;
> Galli per dumos aderant arcemque tenebant
> defensi tenebris et dono noctis opacae.
> aurea caesaries ollis atque aurea vestis,
> virgatis lucent sagulis, tum lactea colla
> auro innectuntur, duo quisque Alpina coruscant
> gaesa manu, scutis protecti corpora longis.

At the top Manlius, guardian of the Tarpeian citadel, was standing in front of the temple and was holding the lofty Capitol, and the royal dwelling was freshly bristling with the thatch of Romulus. And here the goose, in silver, fluttering through the gilded colonnades, was crying out that the Gauls were at the threshold. The Gauls were at hand, through the thickets, and were holding the citadel, defended by the gloaming and by the gift of dark night. Their hair was golden and golden their garb; they glimmer with striped cloaks, and their milky necks are entwined with gold; each one brandishes two Alpine javelins in his hand, his body protected by a long shield.

In this case top also implies source in a temporal sense, as we contemplate the *regia* of Romulus, the founder of Rome's royal power and begetter of her sons. Virgil-Vulcan complements the topographical location of the event by giving it a parallel placement on the shield, *in summo,* at the apex, where we find Manlius on guard in front of the temple of Jupiter Optimus Maximus, the city's sacred center.

As the scene and its events unfold, Virgil makes use of the figure of chiasmus both to expound and to delimit their extent over verbal space and time. At the outset of the episode we have an association between *arcis* and *tenebat,* each ending the vignette's initial lines. We then, through Vulcan's wizardry, hear from the singing of the goose that the Gauls were present (*Gallos . . . adesse*). The bird's warning is soon reified in what occurs, and in direct statement proclaiming what we see as fact (*Galli . . . aderant*). And to complete the verbal balance, which is to say, in the episode's plot-line, the transference of power, we find, at least in Virgil's version of the event, that the Gauls do replace Manlius and "grasp the citadel" (*arcemque tenebat*). Our eye has moved over the rhetorical space and time which ekphrasis allows and along the edge of the Capitolium, to watch first Manlius in charge, then a token that the Gauls were at hand, and, finally, the truth of their presence and of their mastery.[16]

Treachery is part of this world, and its presence helps confirm the outline that rhetoric suggests. We have an initial sense of it in Virgil's use of the adjective *Tarpeia* to describe the citadel. The epithet takes its name from the daughter of Spurius Tarpeius who, during Romulus' struggles with the Sabines, was bribed by their leader, Tatius (whom we saw depicted in the second episode of the ekphrasis), to admit armed men onto the *arx,* and was forthwith crushed to death by their shields. We feel its presence again as the "action" of the episode comes to a close and we watch the Gauls "defended by dusk and by the gift of dark night" (*defensi tenebris et dono noctis opacae*). Livy uses the word *deception* (*dolus*) to describe the endeavor of the Sabines, and Virgil draws on it at an analogous moment in *Aeneid* 2, where night embraces the perfidy of the Greeks in its shadow and the friendly silence of the moon abets their destructive plans.[17]

Virgil avoids further allusion to the *rupes Tarpeia,* the cliff neighboring the temple to Jupiter at the Capitoline's southeast corner from where traitors and other criminals were flung to their death. In particular, he makes no mention of a fact we learn from Livy that one sentinel, upon whom blame universally fell for the encroachment of the Gauls into the citadel, was thrown to his death "from the rock" (*de saxo*). He would thus have continued the line of victim-scapegoats, animal or human, from *porca* to dismembered Mettus, who succumb before the destiny of Rome. Instead, Virgil chooses to feature figures as they would be seen during and then at the actual moment of capture.

This immediacy is first conveyed in the adjective *recens.* It forms part of a brilliantly patterned (nearly) golden line: *Romuleoque recens horrebat regia culmo* (and the royal dwelling was freshly bristling with the thatch of Romulus). The chiasmus is underscored by the alliterative and assonantal relationship between *recens* and *regia, Romuleo* and *culmo,* and by the hypallage of *Romuleo,* which by rights should belong with *regia.* This complex verbal design, like the larger chiasmus of which it forms the first of two central lines, verbally complements Vulcan's own accomplishment which, remarkably, can both bristle and have the appearance of freshness. We attend more specifically to Vulcan through the words *auratis* and *argenteus,* the first words in the ekphrasis reminding us that we are in fact examining a work of art manufactured of various metals. As commentators point out, *auratis* may be meant anachronistically to remind us of the gilded world of Augustan Rome, and *argenteus,* according to Servius, would have recalled a statue of the goose in that metal set up on the Capitolium to commemorate the creature's distinguished behavior.

More strictly to the point, the reader, in focusing on the material makeup of the shield, not only is drawn into the scene itself and its suggestiveness but also in particular marvels at a bird that at once is made of silver and capable of the act of flying (*volitans*, with no hedging *similis*). This pair of words could serve as a minuscule definition of notional ekphrasis itself, delineating an object temporally frozen in an artistic medium yet full of the vivacity that words bring through the act of describing which we absorb over the compressed time and space of watching and reading the written text.

The goose is forever flying and forever caught in the interplay of the two metals which turn action to artifice (*auratis volitans argenteus anser*). This combination of immediacy and material brilliance dominates the final four lines of the scene. Vulcan's craft remains before us in the gilded hair and clothing of the Gauls, and in the gold with which their necks are entwined. The glimmer of their cloaks (*lucent*), together with the metal's shimmer, contrasts with the darkness of night (*noctis*) which abets the Gauls' subterfuge. We vividly see them, in all the nominal details of their corporeal makeup (hair, neck, hands, bodies), clothing (*vestis, sagulis*), and weaponry (*gaesa, scutis*), with their careful touches of the exotic further to enhance the description's pictorial elements.

The graphic quality of the account is complemented by the first use of verbs in the present tense in the ekphrasis (*lucent, innectuntur, coruscant*). And once more Virgil-Vulcan enacts the impossible. Verbs enhance nouns not only to sharpen what we see but to make it seem to happen before our eyes. But they do something more. *Lucent* refers to the soldiers' glimmer as art objects. *Innectuntur* is a bow both to Vulcan's craftsmanship—he has bound up their necks with gold—and to the gold collars they might in fact have worn.[18] *Coruscant* takes the hint one stage further. Though the verb seems to ally itself with *lucent* to intensify the glistening colors of the object described, and Virgil so uses it elsewhere, its primary meaning here is transitive.[19] We behold the Gauls actually brandishing their javelins. However much wrought of gold and the product of a craftsman's ingenuity, they are made to appear alive, physically before us as they go about their affairs as well as in someone else's metallic imagining of them. Only in this double setting is Virgil's genius apparent for choosing the word *lactea* to portray the necks of the Gauls. On the one hand the adjective reinforces the brightness characteristic of the Gallic presence. On the other hand, in this context it could apply only to the necks of living humans, as it does to Ascanius/Iulus in a parallel depiction in book 10. There we learn that *fusos cervix cui lactea crinis/accipit et molli subnectens circulus auro*[20] (his milk-white neck receives his flowing locks and a circlet clasping [it] with pliant gold). Here the anthropomorphism of *lactea* lends further force to the "presentness" of the verbs, particularly *coruscant*, to keep the immediate moment of the Gallic invasion, and the palpability of the fighters themselves, before our eyes. As voyeurs we share in the horror of the event, miraculously unfolding before our eyes. It is an event seemingly without an end, and we are in its midst.

Yet the final four lines, with their abundance of particulars, find their counterpart in the subsequent three and a half verses with which they are joined by the introductory *hic,* which also echoes the use of *hic* at 655 (663–66):

> hic exsultantis Salios nudosque Lupercos
> lanigerosque apices et lapsa ancilia caelo
> extuderat, castae ducebant sacra per urbem
> pilentis matres in mollibus.

> Here he had forged the leaping Salii and naked Luperci, and the woolen caps and the shields fallen from heaven; chaste matrons in cushioned carriages were leading the sacred objects through the city.

Even though the Romans are not shown winning the upper hand, or even meeting force with force, the ekphrasis gives them the opportunity to present their own form of confrontation to the Gauls. Against the literally physical and linguistic challenge of Gallic cloaks (*sagula*) and javelins (*gaesa*), the Romans present their own apotropaic spiritual arsenal in the shape of priests—Salii and Luperci—and presumably their wool-fringed miters.[21] They are pictured as going about their sacerdotal duties, the Salii leaping (*exsultantes,* in Virgil's etymological wordplay), the Wolf-men naked. The Salii had special charge of the sacred *ancilia,* figure-of-eight shields modeled after one sent from Jupiter in heaven during the reign of king Numa, and upon the preservation of which the city's safety depended. They are Rome's sacred response to the oblong *scuta* of the Gauls and find appropriate place in the decoration of the round *clipeus* whose "untellable text" contains them both as part of the larger design of Roman destiny.

It is fitting that, after a lapse of some twenty-five lines, Virgil here reasserts the importance of Vulcan not simply as maker of the whole or adder to his material but as actual craftsman (*extuderat*). The god of fire had hammered out something more talismanic even than Numa's *ancile*, a representation for Aeneas', and our, contemplation of the course of all of Roman civilization and, in particular here, of the continuity of ceremonies and the appurtenances of ceremony that both govern events and, like the shield's all-embracing history, surmount their temporality. And, once again, the challenge between *extuderat* and its setting, especially as reified in words like *exsultantes, ducebat,* and *mollibus,* point up the splendid, paradoxical tension between (poetic) life and (metallic) art, between action and stasis, with the past enlivened yet forming part of an imagined shape available for the perusal of its initial viewer and for later contemplation of its verbal virtuosity.

The final lines of the episode encapsulate a smaller instance of the retrieval of power which the poet co-opts more strictly for himself. The mothers, who carry the sacred objects through the city, gained their privilege because they offered their gold to the state at the time of the crisis provoked by the Gauls. The conveyances in which they are riding are called *pilenta,* apparently a Gallic loan word used here for the first time in Latin literature. The invading soldiers, as we have seen, had appropriately been given Gallic vocabulary for Gallic armor. Once the danger is past, and the mothers rewarded, they can now be associated with a Gallic word that has become part of Roman idiom just as a Gallic carriage can now be arrogated for Roman usage.

For the final small vignette dealing with pre-Augustan Roman history, we leap ahead more than three hundred years to the last century of the Republic (666–70):

> . . . hinc procul addit
> Tartareas etiam sedes, alta ostia Ditis,

et scelerum poenas, et te, Catilina, minaci
pendentem scopulo Furiarumque ora trementem,
secretosque pios, his dantem iura Catonem.

Far from here he adds also the dwellings of Tartarus, the lofty gates of Dis, and you, Catiline, hanging from a menacing crag and trembling at the faces of the Furies, and the good sequestered apart and Cato giving laws to them.

This temporal jump is complemented by the distance the eye must travel on the shield itself (*hinc procul*). We presume that, just as the placement of the Gallic episode *in summo* reflected the topography of the event itself, which occurred on the crest of the Capitoline, so the situation of Catiline and Cato in the Underworld is mimicked in the scene's disposition, we may hypothesize, at the shield's base, opposite that of Manlius, the Gauls and the representations of Roman religion.

Brief as the episode is, Virgil gives it an extraordinary tension. Of the six verbs which the poet allots to Vulcan the artisan throughout the ekphrasis, *addit* is the only one that is not in the pluperfect tense. This difference helps make the change to present time all the more astonishing. Suddenly we are beholding the god in the act of manufacture, even now attaching further material to what he had accomplished some time before. Such presentness is amplified by two other rhetorical means. The first is the apostrophe to Catiline. Like the earlier address to Mettus Fufetius, the device draws us directly into the scene itself, to the actuality of Catiline's punishment as it is simulated in Vulcan's ongoing craftsmanship. The other means is the list of three present participles in a row which demand that we watch Catiline as he hangs and trembles, Cato as he gives laws.

But the brilliant paradox of the episode is that, for all the immediacy of the event itself and in its making, we are contemplating the permanence not only of art but of artificial figures who have themselves lived out their mortal existences to become emblems in the afterlife of good and bad behavior. This paradox in turn lends emphasis to the duality which begins with careful similarity of name (Catiline, Cato) and extends to complementary differences of character—the lawbreaker balances the lawgiver—and to the perpetuity of punishment for crime or of reward for piety.

Virgil initiated his ekphrastic survey of the contents of Vulcan's shield with a vision of twin boys, hanging (*pendentis*) fearlessly from the teats of their bestial nurse. He ends his overview of Republican history with another set of "twins," one of whom is hanging and fearful (*pendentem . . . trementem*). Both are given rhetorical stress, Catiline by being the subject of apostrophe and of present participles that bracket line 669, Cato by having his name be the last word before the great final scene commences. Their reciprocity is the climax of dualities that begin with Romulus and Remus. Sometimes we are dealing simply, as in the case of Manlius and the Gauls, with a conflict of Rome with foreign enemies, on another occasion with an antagonism between the new Rome (Cocles and Cloelia) and its earlier tyrant and his patron (Tarquinius, Porsenna).[22] In two other instances—the sons of Romulus challenging Tatius' Sabines, and Tullus' act of dismemberment—civil war remains disturbingly in the background.

The establishment of Roman power over time, as Virgil would have us see it, is a tale of animality, unwonted violence, retributive vengeance, and victimization, but also of the heroic search for *libertas* and of the strength of religion's rituals against the onslaught of incivility. It is no accident that Virgil chooses to conclude his presentation of the Republic with the antithetical yet parallel figures of Catiline and Cato. The first, an enemy of the Roman order from within, fomented a revolution against the state. Unlike the similar Mettus, it is not so much Catiline's manner of death as his eternal torture after death that stands as warning of the abiding punishment awaiting those who stand in Rome's way. The second died in 46 B.C.E., a suicide after being defeated fighting against Caesar in north Africa.[23] He may be included here as an exemplum of Stoic virtue, but the Roman reader could see him also, while the civil war enters its final reaches, as a patriotic Roman fighting for Republican *libertas* against the inexorability of empire and of one-man rule. At the end of the Republic he inherits the mantle which Cocles and Cloelia had donned at its start, and it is a matter of some daring that Virgil grants him the final, prominent position on the shield, before Actium confirms the principate of Caesar's great-nephew and adopted son. And his permanence both in the constancy of the shield's art and as an ever-enduring paradigm in death lends his appearance a double aura of *auctoritas*.

Virgil now turns to his major episode, the battle of Actium and its aftermath. In length of description, which is also to say, metaphorically, in extent of space on the shield itself, it more than exceeds the combination of all preceding segments. The clear implication is that, as interpreted through both verbal and artistic dimensions, this moment in Roman history and what it anticipates surpass in importance all the past of Rome to which it grants assurance but which it also outshines.

To initiate the grandest of Vulcan's designs Virgil takes his cue from Homer, who bounds the shield of Achilles with mentions of water.[24] At the first we have the sea as part of the natural universe in which the subsequent activities of mankind are set (671–74):

> haec inter tumidi late maris ibat imago
> aurea, sed fluctu spumabant caerula cano,
> et circum argento clari delphines in orbem
> aequora verrebant caudis aestumque secabant.

> Amid these scenes a golden image of the swollen sea flowed widely, but the dark blue [water] was frothing with white waves, and all around dolphins in silver were sweeping the seas with their tails in a circle and were cutting through the swell.

At the very end of his ekphrasis the Greek poet tells us of "the great strength of the river of Ocean around the outermost edge of the solidly crafted shield." For Homer, the water which surrounds his human cosmos makes a logical border for a shield which emblematizes that cosmos. Virgil transfers such a border to the center of his shield. In so doing he pays Augustus, and the event that confirmed his power, an enormous compliment. Homer's Ocean fringed a microcosm of our world, offering exemplifications of peace and war, of seasonal labors, of artistry. Virgil's allusion, as he shifts the sea from edge to center, is a way of acknowledging that Actium alone, in its importance for the poet's new cosmos, deserves the preeminence that Homer accords to all human endeavors. Its forceful particularity, Virgil might seem to say, preserved mankind for what Homer's shield illustrates as its ordinary existence.

We can also draw on the poet himself for further understanding of the transition from Cato to Actium. Toward the end of book 5, Virgil uses two analogies for the equestrian display, known as the *Lusus Troiae,* which the boy Iulus and his colleagues perform. He likens their maneuvers to the complicated structure of the Labyrinth on Crete and their own skillfulness to dolphins cutting through the sea.[25] The moment is liminal in many respects. For the youths it signifies the change from childhood to adolescence, which in this case is to say from cavalry display as game to warfare. For Virgil's text, the moment and its similes anticipate aspects of the epic's near future—Aeneas' descent into the labyrinthine Underworld and the events at and after Actium. Both represent a coming of age of sorts as they anticipate the initiation of Aeneas into the responsibilities of Rome. Distant happenings, as presented in the parallel exhibitions of Anchises' parade of heroes in book 6 and of the scenes on Vulcan's shield in book 8, Aeneas can only dimly glimpse. But the similes equally introduce the actions of the epic's last six books, where Aeneas' behavior sets a pattern that his progeny in time to come might emulate. For the first time his actions are paradigmatic for the ways and means of establishing Roman power.

We are thus able to reconfirm from another angle the reason why Virgil sets the final vignette of Republican Rome not in our sublunar sphere but in the Underworld. We will later examine the manner in which the pattern of the *Aeneid* as a whole is echoed in that of the shield, and vice versa. Here we must look at one particular instance of that pattern and note again the importance of the placement for the Cato-Catiline episode. In the story line of the epic, Aeneas' journey through the realm of the dead takes him from the damned to the blessed, to his father's vision of the Roman future and, in the final sextet of books, to his own implementation of it. On the shield our parallel progress takes us from a depiction of two notable Romans, saved or damned in the Underworld, to a grand picture of one of the great moments of Roman history to come. It does not take too great a leap of imagination on the reader's part to make the requisite connection between Aeneas and

Augustus, Rome's initiator and its refounder. Virgil, as we will see, helps confirm the link.

This introductory setting, as is the case with all the preceding episodes, has its special ways of holding the viewer-reader's attention. The shield as crafted object is always before our eyes. We watch the sea's placement among these other scenes. We admire the image of the golden water (the enjambment of *imago* and *aurea* both moves our eye along and focuses it on the gilding) and the silver gathering of dolphins that presumably fringed the whole.[26] But the event is equally enlivened. For one thing, colors like sea-blue (*caerula,* a metonymy, where adjective also replaces noun) and white are not normally connected with metal but with the sea. For another there is the enormous energy of the action itself, with an "image" that moves, a frothing sea, dolphins that sweep and cut.

In this context the adjective *tumidus* is particularly suggestive. At two important earlier junctures in the poem Virgil associates swollen water with infuriate behavior stemming from emotionality, particularly anger. The first, at the start of the epic, is the "swollen seas" (*tumida aequora*) stemming from the storm wrathful Juno stirs up with the aid of Aeolus and which must be calmed by Neptune.[27] The second, which occurs at the beginning of book 8 itself, is the swelling of the Tiber, which the river-god himself associates with the anger of the gods and which now, as Aeneas makes his way to the site of Rome, will be calmed.[28] Here, as texture and character merge, *tumidus* likewise suggests water's emblematic role as an image for human passions and the struggles in which they embroil their victims.

For in the midst of this sea, at once golden and tumescent, part of a static artifact whose motion apprehends human intensity, we find the battle of Actium ready to begin (675–84):

> in medio classis aeratas, Actia bella,
> cernere erat, totumque instructo Marte videres
> fervere Leucaten auroque effulgere fluctus.
> hinc Augustus agens Italos in proelia Caesar
> cum patribus populoque, penatibus et magnis dis,
> stans celsa in puppi, geminas cui tempora flammas

> laeta vomunt patriumque aperitur vertice sidus.
> parte alia ventis et dis Agrippa secundis
> arduus agmen agens, cui, belli insigne superbum,
> tempora navali fulgent rostrata corona.

In the middle the brazen fleets, the battle at Actium, were on view; you might see all Leucate ablaze with the array of Mars, and the waves gleaming with gold. On this side Augustus Caesar, leading the Italians into battle, with the senate and people, with the gods of the household and the great gods, stands on the lofty stern; his joyous brow spews forth twin flames and the star of his father appears above his head. Elsewhere towering Agrippa, with winds and god favorable, leads his column; his brow gleams beaked with the naval crown, proud ornament of war.

Virgil helps the transition by repeating the word *fluctus* and by reminding us, with the phrase *auro effulgere,* that gold is still a part of Vulcan's crafting. Likewise, *fervere* carries forward the ambiguity of *tumidus,* referring literally to the swirling of the waters but figuratively as well to man's emotionality which, in this instance, is given vent on the sea itself.

But the particular moment has its own poetic specialness. The fleets are made of brass not only because this is the way Vulcan would have created them but because, as the actual battle commenced, real ships with their brazen beaks would have been involved. Mention of these armadas, made of brass as part for the whole, introduces two metonymies: *Actia bella,* the war which the fleets help consummate, and *instructo Marte,* the war-god himself whose "arrangement" is the disposition of the battle lines themselves. Above all, we, like Aeneas, are urged, for only the second time in the ekphrasis, to look and ponder for ourselves. At line 650, "you might perceive" (*aspiceres*) Porsenna enraged and threatening. Here the possibility of viewing is redoubled. The scene is there for us to contemplate, and the narrator presses us ("you") to imagine it (*videres*) in our mind's eye in a way that parallels, yet surpasses, Aeneas' own experience. But our direct involvement here may not be so distant from our engagement at line 650. In the earlier moment, liberty was at stake as Rome's regal government changed to Republic.[29] Here liberty, too, is at issue, but the focus of the argument, as we will see by the time we reach the end of the ekphrasis, is less clearly defined and the outcome less incontrovertible.

As the first and foremost image of the final scene, and at the center of the ekphrasis (it pivots around line 680), which is to say also most likely at the center of the shield, is Augustus Caesar. Elsewhere (*parte alia*), presumably not far, as the initial *hinc* suggests, is the representation of Marcus Agrippa. Virgil, as we have seen, is at pains, through detailed verbal repetition, to show them as nearly balancing, analogous figures and therefore as both physically and morally parallel. They are the imposing, modern counterparts of Cocles and Cloelia (it is not entirely fortuitous that the names of both sets of heroes begin with the same letters) and are as complementary, at the start of the new regime, as Catiline and Cato are differentiated as the old order comes to an end.

But Rome's founding twins are not absent from this opening scene, which leads us to take note of the differentiation as well as the similarities between the two heroes. What distinguishes Augustus, and catches the eye of the beholder in a series of bright images, are the twin flames spouting from his temples and the star of his father's divinity. The double flames remind us of other occasions in the epic where fire associated with the head is a fortunate omen.[30] As critics note, they also in this case recall the "twin crests" (*geminae cristae*) that Romulus sports on his head when Anchises introduces his ghost to Aeneas in the Underworld.[31] Once more, origins and renewals are mutually supportive. The brows of Agrippa, in his turn, gleam with a more recent honor, the naval crown that he was awarded five years before the battle of Actium for his defeat of Sextus Pompeius at Naulochus. Just as he was Augustus' subordinate, so he comes second in the description and receives three lines to his patron's four. Nevertheless, his final verse is "golden," turning on the word *fulgent* and complementing through the deployment of words the pattern of Vulcan's artistic fabric.

Suddenly, and fittingly, the description is all couched in the present tense (*agens, stans, vomunt, aperitur,* for Augustus alone). Through the miracle of the shield we are watching figures around whom immediate action revolves. But Virgil, by self-allusion, even as excitement develops, causes the reader to pause and ponder the meaning of the present moment in relation to the epic itself. Line 679, for instance, whose inspiration is partially Ennian, looks directly back to book 3: "*feror exsul in altum/cum sociis natoque penatibus et magnis dis*[32] (I am carried an exile into the deep with my allies, my son, the gods of the household and the great gods). The beginning of Aeneas' lonely wandering over the sea, as he transports the sacred objects of Troy to their new setting in Italy, finds its modern counterpart in another maritime adventure, as Augustus calls on the same divine apparatus to assist in confirming his power. *Patres* and *populus* replace allies and son, as all of Rome now joins in support, and the Itali, who were Aeneas' opposition, now form the mainstay of Augustus' forces.

The phrase *stans celsa in puppi* which opens the next line has a parallel effect. Virgil uses it twice elsewhere in the epic, first at 3.527, of Anchises calling on the gods, as lords of sea, land, and storm, when Italy has been sighted, to lend favorable winds to the Trojan endeavor. The second occurs at 10.261 as Aeneas comes downriver with his new Etruscan forces to rejoin the beleaguered Trojan camp. From the initial situation Virgil both transfers to Augustus the patriarchal posture of Anchises and confirms that the power over the Italy which the Aeneadae only can imagine in the distance has now become the emperor's own.[33]

This second situation has still more direct bearing on the posture of Augustus. Aeneas is standing on his ship's poop "when he then raised up the burning shield in his left hand" (*clipeum cum deinde sinistra/extulit ardentem*). This is the first time that we hear of the shield after the conclusion of the ekphrasis, and Virgil proceeds to compare the huge flames its boss pours forth to the gloomy ruddiness of bloodred comets at night or to the burning of the Dog Star that brings "thirst and diseases to sick mortals."[34] The simile may look specifically to the terror which Aeneas' arrival might spread among the Latins, but we must not disallow the more universal, more negative implications, to which we will soon turn, that the shield, its innate force, and the dynamism of its contents might have for Aeneas, as he ensures his power by victory over Turnus, or for his modern alter ego, Augustus, as the final events depicted on it secure his omnipotence.

Returning to the shield, we find another word of placement (*hinc*), which counterbalances *hinc* with which the Roman leaders were introduced and initiates a four-line description of their opponents (685–88):

> hinc ope barbarica variisque Antonius armis,
> victor ab Aurorae populis et litore rubro
> Aegyptum virisque Orientis et ultima secum
> Bactra vehit, sequiturque (nefas) Aegyptia coniunx.

> On this side Antony with barbarian resource and variegated arms,
> victor from the peoples of the Dawn and from the ruddy shore,
> draws with him Egypt and the strength of the Orient and farthest
> Bactra, and there follows—the shame!—his Egyptian wife.

Once again Virgil plays with the alliteration of nomenclature, pitting Augustus and Agrippa against Antonius and his *Aegyptia coniunx*, the unnamed Cleopatra replaced by an unglorious metonymy, a noble pair against one in disgrace. Virgil allots Antony, even as *victor*, no exalting emblems on which the eye might dwell, only "variegated arms," which, especially because of the juxtaposition with "barbarian wealth" (*ope barbarica*), reminds us of the Gauls' assorted weaponry and vesture as they attacked the Capitolium.[35] In the case of Antony, the implicit decadence comes from association with the east, not with the unique, civilized *populus* that assists Augustus and from which he is now rhetorically excluded, but with a plurality of *populi*. His resources depend on his foreign connections, not on his Romanness. Worst of all is the Egyptian wife (688) who is associated with the conquest of Egypt (687). It is for her that the greatest scorn is reserved in the expletive *nefas*, though Antony, by taking her as *coniunx*, initiates the offense. For once the narrator assists our interpretative work, interjecting into the description a moral judgment that might be Virgil's, Vulcan's, Aeneas' (were he capable of comprehension), or our own.

The explicit, sharp detail devoted to the two sets of leaders yields to a brief spate of unspecificity. All become one, with no mediating particularities. And for this moment, by means of the historic infinitives, we are placed in past time, as if change of tense altered pictorial plane and took our eye away from the vividness of the leaders to a more general instant of blurredness. But, whatever its transitional nature, in the "narrative" of art it remains extraordinarily graphic, with *totum* holding us in suspense until it receives its noun, *aequor*, a line and a half later at the end of the subsequent hexameter. In-between, as we view the space on which everything is hyperbolically merged together, the sea is both active and passive, frothing and torn up, as the warships go about their work of disturbing what by etymology would ordinarily be flat and calm.

But the past does not endure for long, and suddenly, with the phrase "they seek the deep" (*alta petunt*), we are back in the present which is to suggest, in terms of ekphrasis, that our eye moves along to another segment of the same picture (689–95):

> una omnes ruere ac totum spumare reductis
> convulsum remis rostrisque tridentibus aequor.
> alta petunt; pelago credas innare revulsas
> Cycladas aut montis concurrere montibus altos,
> tanta mole viri turritis puppibus instant.
> stuppea flamma manu telisque volatile ferrum
> spargitur, arva nova Neptunia caede rubescunt.

All rush together and the whole sea froths, torn up by the pulling of oars and the three-pronged beaks. They seek the deep. You might believe that the Cyclades, uprooted, were swimming on the sea or that lofty mountains were clashing with mountains, with such bulk do the men attack the turreted sterns. Flaming tow and shafts of flying steel are scattered from their hands; the fields of Neptune grow red with fresh slaughter.

The new immediacy is accented by a continuance of exaggeration. The ships (Vulcan-Virgil does not now differentiate between the battle lines) swim about like uprooted islands or clash like mountains against lofty mountains, so great is their mass, with stern sections looming like towers. A sea-fight itself is an unnatural occurrence from several points of view, but the quasi *adunata* further dramatize the moment. Islands do not swim and mountains do not engage in battle.[36] We soon meet iron that flies (*volatile ferrum*), and in the phrase "fields of Neptune" (*arva Neptunia,* 695) Virgil invents a metonymy to suit this powerful overstatement. Terrestrial fields and Neptune's waters are, at least metaphorically, compatible entities—unless, of course, they are associated with the enormities of a battle at sea, not to speak of one, as the phrase *caede nova* suggests, that continues a tradition of marine engagements associated with civil war.[37]

The verb *credas* makes an appropriate, focusing introduction to the episode. It is the ultimate of three occasions in the ekphrasis where "you," the contemplator of the shield, has a direct invitation from the narrator. The first two concern the act of viewing and emphasize crucial instances where sight must induce insight (*aspiceres*, 650; *videres*, 676). This last advocates not what one sees but what one believes, a more strictly inner, mental vision. So strange is the event that its credibility is strained in the eyes of the onlooker. So great is Vulcan's art that what would ordinarily be impossible seems actually to be happening. Nevertheless the subjunctive is tantamount to a command that conviction is necessary.

The last word of the scene, *rubescunt,* is also carefully chosen. Virgil uses it elsewhere of the sea's ruddy glow at dawn, of the reddening glow of dawn itself or of cornel berries as they grow ripe.[38] All these are natural events. However, for the sea to grow red with slaughter is as unnatural as the swimming of islands or the collision of high mountains. These "impossibilities" are what any warfare brings about but especially naval fighting which forms part of a civil conflict. *Rubescunt,* as a color word, reminds us that we are contemplating a shield whose metals bring variation from scene to scene. But to turn any metal bloodred, and especially to show the color in the process of deepening, can only be part of a god's magical art as it imitates, in his own idiosyncratic tour de force, circumstances of an equally unexampled nature.

Vulcan's narrator now turns attention again to the protagonists of the action (696–703):

> regina in mediis patrio vocat agmina sistro,
> necdum etiam geminos a tergo respicit anguis.
> omnigenumque deum monstra et latrator Anubis
> contra Neptunum et Venerem contraque Minervam
> tela tenent. saevit medio in certamine Mavors
> caelatus ferro, tristesque ex aethere Dirae,
> et scissa gaudens vadit Discordia palla,
> quam cum sanguineo sequitur Bellona flagello.

In the middle the queen calls her forces with her ancestral rattle, nor even yet does she behold the twin snakes at her back. Monstrous gods of every shape and barking Anubis hold weapons against Neptune and Venus, against Minerva. In the middle of the struggle Mars rages, engraved in iron, and the grim Dirae from the heavens, and Discord makes her way, rejoicing in her torn robe, whom Bellona follows with bloody whip.

We look first at Cleopatra, *in mediis*. Since Virgil generally alludes to the civil aspects of Actium by innuendo, Antony disappears from view and the queen changes from *coniunx*, who follows in the wake of her husband (*sequitur*), to the *regina* who stands alone and who, through Vulcan's conjuring, calls on her forces with the *sistrum*.[39] This is to say that, as we view her on the shield, she takes on the guise of Isis and joins with the monstrous gods of her country to face three of Rome's *magni di*. But her aggrandized role as queen and her patent pretensions toward divinity are virtually undercut by the appearance at her back of the twin snakes of death which we see but she does not. Likewise, the zoomorphic features of her fellow divinities, and the barbarism their animality implies, make them no match for the triple Roman deities who need only be named to evoke their power.

But as so often with Virgil, matters are not left so cut and dried. There are other, specifically Roman divinities whom we see participating in the events, but this time, "in the midst of the struggle" that is, presumably, common to both sides, universal in their loyalties even though surrounded in the text by their Roman peers. First is Mars, given his ancient disyllabic name Mavors to honor his antiquity. He rages while at the same time "chiseled from iron," a sentient artifact made from the metal most useful in war.[40] His companions are goddesses, and all have distinguishing characteristics. The Dirae, grim for the grimness they bring, are observed as being from the heavens above. The designation is curious, but it partially explains one notable absence from the list of Roman gods present at Actium. The Dirae are the servants of Jupiter, as we learn from a dramatic moment in book 12 where the king of the gods sends one of them down "from the peak of the sky" (*ab aethere summo*) to expel Juturna from the battle.[41] Their presence here *ex aethere* intimates that their function is to represent the *deum rex* in his role not only as arbiter of fate but as extender of death, disease, and war to humankind in general.[42]

The companions of the Dirae are Discordia, rejoicing in the dissension her torn mantle symbolizes, and Bellona, who here is given the whip which Virgil accords to the fury Tisiphone in book 6 as emblem of her power to extract vengeance from her victims.[43] It is more than coincidental that many of the same or parallel figures, among them Bellum, the Eumenides (another incorporation of the Furies) with their "iron chambers," and *Discordia demens* are among the hideous representations that lurk at Hell's entrance, ready to bring suffering to mankind and that greet Aeneas as he enters. Their appearance here further confirms the omnipresence of these personified abstractions in the activities, especially in the destructive bellicosity, of humankind.

The tense now changes to imperfect and our eye turns to Apollo, himself in the position of reacting to what he sees (704–706):

> Actius haec cernens arcum intendebat Apollo
> desuper; omnis eo terrore Aegyptus et Indi,
> omnis Arabs, omnes vertebant terga Sabaei.

Actian Apollo, watching these events, was bending his bow from above. At that terror all Egypt and India, all Arabians, all Sabaeans turned their backs [in flight].

The framing formulation which alliteration abets—*Actius . . . arcum . . . Apollo*—gives us a sense of linear space, but horizontality is soon broken by the enjambed *desuper*, which gives a vertical thrust to the dimensionality. Apollo Actius, lord of the bow and presiding divinity of the headland off of which the battle was fought, takes aim from above. And to this singular figure the whole opposition gives way in retreat. Whatever distinctions remain between the enemies of Rome which the scene catalogues are obliterated by the triple repetition of *omnis, omni, omnes*. Individual names are each time subsumed in a picture of general rout where one immortal dominates all human resistance.

But there is particularity after all, as we turn again to the *regina*, now no longer calling her forces into battle but in full retreat, with the Nile opposite, in readiness to receive the conquered (707–13):

> ipsa videbatur ventis regina vocatis
> vela dare et laxos iam iamque immittere funis.
> illam inter caedes pallentem morte futura
> fecerat ignipotens undis et Iapyge ferri,
> contra autem magno maerentem corpore Nilum
> pandentemque sinus et tota veste vocantem
> caeruleum in gremium latebrosaque flumina victos.

The queen herself, after she had called on the winds, was seen to spread sails and now, even now, to relax the slackened ropes. The god of fire had fashioned her amid the carnage, pale at her approaching death, carried by the waves and by Iapyx. But opposite her was the Nile, his great body in mourning, opening out his folds and with all his garments summoning the conquered into his sea-blue lap and hidden streams.

In this context *videbatur* does double duty. Cleopatra is seen by her followers as she herself gives sail and loosens the ropes. Yet she is also an object to be observed by the viewer of the shield (and the reader of the ekphrasis). The phrase *iam iamque* lends weight to both possibilities.[44] In the withdrawal after Actium, as we yield to Virgil's narrative mode, she is in the act of slackening the halyards. On the shield she appears now, even now, on the verge of action which is to say seeming, through Vulcan's brilliance, nearly capable of carrying out such a task.

Virgil calls attention to the significance of this dual scene by strongly reminding us, exactly halfway through the seven lines, of the presence of Vulcan for the first direct time since line 637. Everything that we see has really been accomplished by the god of fire who, at least in this instance, lords it over the other elements—the winds, sea, and streams of the Nile which are the result of his craft. But the centrality of Vulcan also helps galvanize our attention on the representation which he creates and the emotionality which pervades it. For, when considered in conjunction with her earlier appearance, the metamorphosis which

Virgil-Vulcan creates in the figure of Cleopatra and in how we respond to her is not dissimilar to a parallel change of tone in Horace's great ode *Nunc est bibendum*.[45] There, as the poem progresses, we turn from celebration that Rome has been spared the queen's drunken madness to sympathy for her (she is a soft dove to Octavian's hawk) to admiration for the singularity of her heroism which preferred suicide to humiliation at Rome. Here we watch her pallor before death and the mourning of the Nile, expansively depicted as the river-god himself, receiving into his ample lap the conquered who have the episode's final word.

Again, an act of self-allusion can help extend our understanding of Virgil's meaning. The phrase *pallentem morte futura* echoes words the poet had used of Dido "pale before her death to come" (*pallida morte futura*) as she readies herself for suicide.[46] The parallel is purposeful. Dido is a prefiguration of Cleopatra, a quasi-eastern potentate who nearly seduced the ancestor of Rome from his fated mission and whose heirs would battle the city in three wars for domination of the Mediterranean basin. As any corrupt and corrupting enemy of the Roman order, especially one who aspired to be the female *rex* of the Capitoline, she should be put away, or at least forced into self-slaughter. But neither Virgil, in dealing with Dido and Cleopatra, nor Horace, as he responds to the evolving tale of the Egyptian queen, leaves matters so unequivocal. As *c.* 1.37 reaches its conclusion and throughout most of the fourth book of the *Aeneid,* our sympathy lies with Dido, not with Aeneas and Rome, however much we know that fate and a sense of duty must prevail. The same could be said in reduced form of this moment on the shield. The bestial, depraved enemy has been conquered, but it is upon her, preparing for suicide, and upon the mourning Nile and its vanquished countrymen that our eye, and perhaps our compassion, finally rest.

Virgil-Vulcan allows an appropriate ambiguity to tone our final vision of the Nile, his clothing spread wide to receive the conquered "into his caerulean lap" (*caeruleum in gremium*). We have already seen the adjective used as a noun at line 672, to describe the sea at Actium. The color is equally apt for a river-god (not long earlier in book 8 the Tiber had been described as *caeruleus*).[47] But *caeruleus* is also the color of grief and death's somberness, suitable accompaniment for the river's sorrow (Virgil allots the adjective to the fillets that bedeck Polydorus' funereal altars as well as to Charon's dusky bark).[48] As an artificial item on a shield, the Nile greets the onlooker with its sea-blue tint. As a palpable, emotional figure, brought alive in all its grandeur by the charm of ekphrasis, it is clothed in darkness that befits its mourning not only for the defeated but for its queen preparing to accomplish her own demise.

Virgil now marks one of the extraordinary transitions of the ekphrasis with the monosyllable *at* (714–19):

> at Caesar, triplici invectus Romana triumpho
> moenia, dis Italis votum immortale sacrabat,
> maxima ter centum totam delubra per urbem.
> laetitia ludisque viae plausuque fremebant;
> omnibus in templis matrum chorus, omnibus arae;
> ante aras terram caesi stravere iuvenci.

> But Caesar, entering within the walls of Rome in triple triumph, was dedicating his undying votive gift to the gods of Italy, three hundred imposing shrines throughout the whole city. The streets were resounding with joy, with games and with applause. In every temple was a chorus of mothers, in every one altars, and before the altars slaughtered bullocks strewed the ground.

In terms of the facts of history, we move from allusion to the Egypt of 31 B.C.E. (and, implicitly, 30, the year of Cleopatra's death) to Rome and the triple triumph of August 29, from a victory at sea to honors awarded Octavian in his capital. But the adversative particle, though it forces our imagination from one episode to another and makes a leap of space and time, nevertheless asks us carefully to contrast what precedes with what follows, as if they were *comparanda*. (And Virgil keeps the imperfect tense in both segments, to help authorize the juxtaposition.) We turn from a scene of sadness to one of happiness, from sounds of the Nile's lamentation, and its calling the vanquished to the refuge it provides, to the roaring of applause in the streets of Rome. We move from an anticipation of death (*morte futura*) to the fulfillment of a deathless vow (*votum immortale*). As at the conclusion of Horace's powerful ode,

Octavian's triumph is in part visualized by means of Cleopatra, for Horace by her conspicuous absence from the procession, for Virgil, more subtly, by the contrast of her sorrowing river with the joy of Rome. Yet there is also death in this world of celebration. The slaughtered bullocks (*caesi iuvenci*) that strew the ground before the city's many altars are the contemporary Roman equivalent of the "slaughtered sow" (*caesa porca*) that sealed the compact between the Romulidae and the Sabines. At the end of a spate of war, it is suitable that animals be sacrificed both as thank-offering to the gods for the end of conflict and as replacement victims for the humans who have already fallen, or might still fall, if fighting were to continue. But the phrase *caesi iuvenci* has more disquieting sides. We will turn shortly to its importance in Virgil's conception of human development and its bearing on the meaning of the ekphrasis.[49] Here we must look at the participle *caesi* and specifically at its connection with the cynosure of the finale of the ekphrasis.

When we first meet the emperor on the shield, at line 678, he is called Augustus Caesar, addressed with the title he was to receive from senate and people in 27 B.C.E. and by the cognomen which betokened his membership in the Julian *gens*. Here, at his final naming, he is called only Caesar, a word whose ancient etymology has a special reverberation in this context. Pliny the Elder is the first of several ancient authorities to connect the word with *caedo* and with the birth of Julius Caesar, "so-called from the cutting open of his mother's abdomen" (*a caeso matris utero dictus*).[50] This derivation, along with the balance between lines 714 and 719 which open and close this segment of the episode, helps link Caesar with *caesi*. He who had been one of the prime participants in the bloodletting connected with the battle of Actium (the cognate noun *caedes* appears at lines 695 and 709) now participates in a ceremony requiring only the killing of animals. But the poet's wordplay allows Octavian's share in the human carnage associated with Actium to remain in our thoughts even as the type of sacrifice suffers appropriate modification and limitation.[51]

The final segment of this grand scene is devoted strictly to the emperor (720–28):

> ipse sedens niveo candentis limine Phoebi
> dona recognoscit populorum aptatque superbis
> postibus; incedunt victae longo ordine gentes,
> quam variae linguis, habitu tam vestis et armis.
> hic Nomadum genus et discinctos Mulciber Afros,
> hic Lelegas Carasque sagittiferosque Gelonos
> finxerat; Euphrates ibat iam mollior undis,
> extremique hominum Morini, Rhenusque bicornis,
> indomitique Dahae, et pontem indignatus Araxes.

He himself, sitting at the snowy threshold of shining Phoebus, reviews the gifts of nations and fits them to the proud doorposts. The conquered races pass in long array, as varied in languages as in their style of dress and weapons. Here Mulciber had fashioned the race of Nomads and ungirdled Africans, here the Leleges and Carians and quivered Gelonians. The Euphrates was moving past, its waves now gentler, and the Morini, most remote of mankind, and the twin-horned Nile, the unconquered Dahae, and the Araxes, indignant at its bridge.

Our eye journeys back to where the ekphrasis had begun, to the Palatine hill and to the temple of Apollo which Augustus was to dedicate in October 28 B.C.E. The difference from the preceding lines is marked by pinpointing Augustus himself, through the word *ipse*, the way our attention had been fixed on Cleopatra through the initial *ipsa* of line 707, and by return to the present tense, which Virgil had not used since the central stage of the Actian battle. We are participants at one of Rome's more splendid occasions, brought vividly before us.

First there is the shrine of the emperor's patron god, here given the title Phoebus, the Sun-god, whose monument, constructed of the white marble of Luna, is as brilliant as the deity is resplendent. Its doorposts are "proud" (*superbis*), as lofty as the temple itself, perched on the southern edge of the Palatine, and as sumptuous. Then there is the emperor, sitting, inspecting, affixing offerings and the variegated conquered peoples who march before him. For a moment we seem to be witnessing actual events as they unfold, as we did when watching the

Gauls glistening in their striped cloaks or Mars and his frenzied colleagues urging on Actium's strife. But in those instances the Gauls are made partially of gold and Mars of iron, reminders that it is art, not epic "reality," that we are contemplating. Or there is the unmediated vision of Mettus Fufetius being dismembered. But that occurred in past time. Only here in the ekphrasis does Virgil seem to allow us to share in the impossible—to see for ourselves a snow-white marble temple (on a metallic shield) past which continue to parade, for the emperor's review, a motley group of captives (all on a static artifact, capable of only a limited number of aesthetic variations).

But only for a moment, for as the ekphrasis draws to a conclusion Vulcan makes a forceful, final appearance. The anaphora of *hic* lures us at first into thinking, remarkably, that we are still "here," spectators at the pageant continuing to pass by the seated emperor. But suddenly, with the reemergence of the artisan-god we are no longer transported to the Palatine of 29 B.C.E. but find ourselves sharing in the initial viewing of the shield, where repeated uses of *hic* merely highlight positions on the artifact. Details continue to be vivid, as our eye scans the shield's figures—and Virgil's lines—which process from loose-garbed Afri and arrow-bearing Geloni to untamed Dahae, now conquered, and last to the Araxes objecting to its bridge. But we are now again in past time. The Euphrates was flowing, then, in a gentler course. Above all, this piece of artistry is something that Vulcan had accomplished a while ago. And, at his last appearance, we are twice reminded of the god's role as maker of the whole, not merely crafter of its individual parts. First the verb that Virgil allots him, *finxerat,* looks particularly to his role of sculptor in metal (only *extuderat,* at 665, applied in its immediate context to Vulcan's production of Numa's shields on his own, is parallel). It is the immortal Lord of Fire who fashions the unwieldy, inchoate mass of instances that add up to history into an ordered, cohesive artifact for our contemplation.

And the placement of Vulcan within the final lines eases the transition back to Aeneas at Caere who, after the conclusion of the ekphrasis, admires his mother's gift (729–31):

> Talia per clipeum Volcani, dona parentis,
> miratur rerumque ignarus imagine gaudet
> attollens umero famamque et fata nepotum.

Such [sights] he admires on the shield of Vulcan, the gift of his mother, and, ignorant of the deeds, rejoices in their depiction, raising on his shoulder the reputation and destiny of his offspring.

The lines circle back to those which introduced the ekphrasis, where Vulcan is the subject:

> haud vatum ignarus venturique inscius aevi
> fecerat ignipotens, illic genus omne futurae
> stirpis ab Ascanio pugnataque in ordine bella.

The god of fire, by no means unaware of prophecies and ignorant of time to come, had made [it], there every generation of future stock [sprung] from Ascanius and wars fought one by one.

From the first we learn that the shield encompassed the history of the Roman race and its wars waged in their order, from all of which the ekphrastic narrative makes a selection. As befits a people among whose founders could be numbered twins nurtured by a wolf of Mars, military conflicts are one of its primary concerns. It is war, as the concluding verses suggest, that is the Romans' fate, and it is how they handle their power that will give them their reputation.

But there is one difference between these sets of lines surrounding the ekphrasis that Virgil calls to our attention through the repetition of the adjective *ignarus*. Vulcan can shape the contents of his extraordinary icon because he knows before they occur (*haud . . . ignarus*) all the events that make up the tale of Rome. But what of Aeneas' response? The narrator only tells us that he rejoices in the image while in ignorance of the deeds. But Virgil allows us to interpret this response in two ways. Does he rejoice, though he is ignorant, because, were he to find out the meaning of the whole, it would give him pleasure to contemplate the future time when image would become reality? Or does he rejoice only because he remains uninitiated into any deeper meaning behind mere superficial brilliance, which is to say, because true understanding of the shield's significance would bring not elation but its opposite? Exploration of this ambiguity will lead us back again to the ekphrasis itself and to a further examination of how the narrator influences our thinking about the events which the ekphrasis describes and about the larger poem in which it is incorporated. The reader is given an opportunity denied to Aeneas, and perhaps even to Augustus and Virgil's contemporary Roman readers, to look into and ponder the richer connotations of what he sees.

The ekphrasis of the shield of Aeneas is, on first reading, an extremely time-committed narrative, touching on seven hundred years of Roman history, that leads climactically from Romulus and Remus in the Lupercal to Augustus in triumph on the gleaming threshold of radiant Apollo. And the rhetoric of this narrative is prejudicially imbalanced, with the final episode, from Actium to the Palatine, lasting some sixteen lines longer than the totality of the previous scenes. This linearity serves as verbal complement to a teleology of empire that culminates in an idealizing of the Augustan accomplishment, with the emperor in glory, his enemies conquered, and civil war, presumably, a thing of the past.

Yet for all this forward thrust, abetted by the necessity of narrative flow even in ekphrasis, we are looking at an object where the crucial scene is actually *in medio,* at the center, with the rest of Roman history, of which the ekphrasis gives us a selection, distributed around it. The circle, as well as the line, must be a part of how we see, and "read," the shield. In observing a group of temple paintings, say, or autobiographical sculpture on a temple's doors, we might expect a certain temporality to come naturally to the narrative, which must have its own version of time's flow. But Aeneas' shield is a visible icon of circularity, and this aspect of its shape should give a different impulse to the inner eye which, as it views an artifact defined by roundness, could find itself not only looking forward in anticipation but also being steadied by the atemporality toward which ekphrasis strives here as it seeks to delineate a static, crafted object. Centrality and circularity should tell of acts of enclosure, not release, of bounds and involutions. They might suggest a series of layerings and repetitions that force us, with some irony, to reconsider surface meanings and attend, even in the ekphrastic narrative, to exemplifications of the shield's "objectness." This is to say that we must examine what the shield tells us of aspects of life that are outside of time's march in the sense that they mirror changelessness in human nature.

To initiate a discussion of this aspect of the shield as an icon not only of Roman splendor but of history's repetitiveness, let us turn back to the figure of Vulcan. Before the commencement of the ekphrasis and once during it, Virgil favors him with the epithet *ignipotens*,[52] but as it draws to a close he offers him the rare honorific title Mulciber for the only time in the *Aeneid*. The ancient etymologists by and large linked this denomination with the ability of Vulcan or his fire to soften, and, as Paulus-Festus puts it, "to soften is to soothe" (*mulcere enim mollire . . . est*).[53] Virgil twice during the course of the ekphrasis plays on these associations. Two lines after the appearance of the word *Mulciber* we learn that, in the new Augustan dispensation, the Euphrates "was now going more gently in its waves" (*ibat iam mollior undis*).[54] The result of Rome's victorious might is that one of the most powerful rivers of the known world has become more subdued. Vulcan, paradoxically pitting fire against water, seems to reinforce the energies of Rome, taming the opposing forces of humanity and of nature to its political ends.

Mulciber and his potency had already entered the ekphrasis at its start. The verb that Virgil gives Vulcan at the end is *fingo* (one of only two words of sculpting, we recall, associated with the god during the ekphrasis), but he had already used the word of a character in the opening vignette, namely, the wolf of Mars. Vulcan had made *illam tereti cervice reflexa/mulcere alternos et corpora fingere lingua*[55] (her, bending back her smooth neck, fondle them in turn and fashion their bodies with her tongue). The wolf enigmatically takes on the role of sculptor, savage animal become creative artist through the power of metaphor, to design and mold her charges into the proper shape. And, as further irony, it is as if a beast had the capability of controlling, and fashioning, human twins for their proper role as begetters of Rome.

But Virgil has a purpose in suggesting a parallel between the wolf and Vulcan, the Soother, dominating Rome's opposition through the strength and imagination of art. The ring-composition which the references propose, and which the communality of setting on or near the Palatine also supports, in confirming the circular shape of the shield, also suggest certain continua in Roman, which is to say human, life even as history, at least on the surface, appears to change. At the initiation of the Roman world we need someone, in this case even a creature of the wild, to manage those who will manage Rome. At the end the Euphrates will take on human demeanor and appear softer in the face of the might of Augustus.

But behind both these situations there lie the presences of Mulciber and of Virgil, shaper of the shaper, and the implication of their roles is of some consequence. Like the wolf who, on the shield, is the product of his own imagination and the waves of the Euphrates calmed by Rome, Vulcan is equally a Softener but this time of all of Roman history. He has the capabilities of modeling the past to fit the stringencies of a circular enclosure. But recourse to this skill intimates that there is constant need for control not only in the re-creation by Vulcan of Rome but in the individual events that make up that vision. There is multiform energy in the twins that found the city and in the natural might that symbolizes those mollified by its refounder. But there is also need to manage those in control, lest the bestiality that lies barely beneath the surface itself become paramount, not only in the people who oppose it, but in Rome itself.

I will return to this point later when dealing with the relationship of the shield ekphrasis to the poem as a whole. For the moment let us return to repetitiveness within the ekphrasis as a means of complementing its circularity. We have taken notice of some of these recurrences earlier. The motif of twins and twinning, as we have seen, runs through the whole description, associated with both creativity and death. The killing of the pig, in episode 2, is echoed in the bullocks slaughtered at the celebration for Augustus, and both events take place before altars.[56] The variegated garments of the Gauls in episode 5 are reflected in the varied languages and garments worn by the conquered peoples who parade before the emperor.[57] Both episodes are associated with temples, and both allude to mothers as essential components of religious festivity.[58] In the same scene, the posture of Manlius, as he stood (*stabat*) and held the lofty Capitolium (*Capitolia celsa*), anticipates the posture of Octavian at Actium (*stans celsa in puppi*).[59] Both are defenders and saviors of the city.

Two of the early episodes in particular find reflection in the grand finale. The first traces how, after the rending of the body of Mettus Fufetius, "the splattered briars dripped bloody dew" (*sparsi rorabant sanguine vepres*).[60] Virgil utilizes similar imagery at the beginning of the description of the battle of Actium. After the water has been "torn up" (*convulsum*) by oars and the ships themselves compared to islands wrenched loose (*revulsas*) in the sea, we hear how flames of tow and flying weaponry were scattered and how Neptune's fields reddened with carnage.[61] Aspects of one of the bloodiest acts of revenge in Roman history are re-evoked as the battle of Actium unfolds in the Ionian Sea.

Closer still, and yet more challenging intellectually, is the connection between the scene of Porsenna, Cocles, and Cloelia, as kingship is rejected at the dawn of the Republic, with the sequence from Actium to Augustus' triumph. Once again imagery of plucking (*vellere*) is common to both scenes, and to this we must add the notions of rushing and swimming.[62]

But the heroism of the Romans fighting for freedom from tyranny looks not only to the battle of Actium—a battle where the forces of both sides rush together like swimming islands wrenched from their settings—but also to its aftermath and in particular to the concluding figure of the river Araxes "indignant at its bridge" (*pontem indignatus Araxes*), unaccepting of the regimentation imposed by Rome. Indignation, common to both opponents in defeat, is transferred from Porsenna, objecting to the Romans' energetic search for liberty, to the Araxes, troubled at Rome's imposition of its might.

This transference of resentment from the opposer of Rome's freedom to the sufferer of its domination is accompanied in each case by the symbol of the bridge. For Cocles and Cloelia, the bridge and the river Tiber, which it spans, stand in the way of Republican autonomy. They are, respectively, to be torn down or swum across as symbols of a type of ruling power which must be abolished and superseded. The bridge over the Araxes, by contrast, comes at the climactic moment of the shield and indicates Augustus' consolidation of power.

But, on a deeper level, in echoing the Tiber bridge which must be destroyed, Augustus' spanning of the Araxes can be seen also as mastery that encroaches on natural freedom. Liberty, in different ways, strives to obliterate bridges. Absolute supremacy replaces them as symbols of control. It may now seem less bizarre that Cato has, literally, the last word in the segment of the ekphrasis devoted to pre-Augustan Rome and that mention of the Araxes concludes our view of Augustus. Just as Cato recollects Cocles and Cloelia, so he anticipates the Araxes. The fighter for freedom at the end of the Republic, who kills himself rather than accept the rule of Caesar, now in death spends an everlasting existence giving laws to the pious. The Araxes, an instrument of nature in our sublunar world, is forced to accept the yoke of Augustan domination from which, at least in Virgil's text, there is no apparent escape. And we must not forget the fate of Cleopatra, who likewise decided on suicide rather than be enslaved to a later Caesar.

I have been examining some salient moments of repetition in the figuration of the shield and therefore in the history of Rome which it artistically encapsulates. Deployment of words mimics the patterning of art and fosters an impression not only of a teleology of grand destiny culminating in Augustan Rome but also of a circularity which encourages us to see the recurrence of certain constants in human life, among them the ubiquity of violence in human affairs or our craving for freedom counterbalanced by the regimentation that limits it. This aspect of the shield ekphrasis sustains its aim to bring eternal consistency to history's narrative or, in other words, through the static inclinations of art, to serve its larger symbolic role as atemporal, circular icon of certain universals that persist in our lives. Ekphrasis, like the art it describes, exerts its own forms of control.

The Shield of Aeneas and the *Aeneid*

I would like now to turn from aspects of the shield that underscore its (literal) self-centeredness to ways in which Virgil has his ekphrasis look out toward the larger text in which it is embedded. I would like to look first at some individual points in the Augustan narrative where the equivocations of literature, achieved often by irony or ambiguity and confirmed by allusivity, are passed on to the art it describes through the verbal potency of ekphrasis.

Take the phrase *terram stravere caesi iuvenci,* which we have looked at before from other angles.[63] The wording calls attention to itself. This is the first occasion in Latin letters where, in the language of the dictionary, "the thing strewn" is subject of the verb *sterno*.[64] At this paradoxical moment Virgil's inventiveness contrives slain animals with the strange capability of spreading themselves on the ground, as if on this festive occasion they were making a pavement with their bodies or laying their enemies low instead of being killed themselves.

Virgil's earlier uses of the phrase *caesi iuvenci* have particular bearing on this multivalent Augustan setting. One occurs early in georgic 3, where slaughtered cattle form part of a celebration for the victorious Caesar Octavian.[65] This festivity includes a poetic temple, constructed by the narrating "I," in whose decorations many critics find an allegory for an incipient Augustiad, later modified to form the epic which we now possess. But at the conclusion of the preceding book, Virgil had utilized the same phrase in a different context, as part of a concise but illuminating distinction between a golden, idealized moment in Rome's past, when Remus and his brother gave laws together, and a later time when men blew war trumpets and hammered out swords. The first was golden Saturn's time, in Virgil's accounting, before Jupiter held sway and before "an impious race dined on slaughtered cattle" (*impia . . . caesis gens est epulata iuvencis*).[66] In the case of early Rome, the sacred banquet was held by a race considered to lack *pietas,* presumably because Romulus killed Remus and established the paradigm for civil war.

That we are at another transitional moment, as Rome celebrates the victory of Augustus, is clear enough, but Virgil leaves unresolved the extent of the ambiguity he would have us ponder. A deliberate glance back to the crucial moment in the life of the founding brothers might lead us to believe that war, especially civil war, after the defeat of Antony and Cleopatra, will be a thing of the past in the history of Rome. As the city prepares for the celebratory meal, at which Virgil only hints, we may expect that sacrifice will purge it of the traces of *impietas.* But by allusion to georgic 2 the poet makes another suggestion. Perhaps impiety may be eliminated along with civil war, but Augustus Caesar, though publicly (and directly, in the poet's verse) is associated with his patron god, Phoebus Apollo, on another level becomes Jupiter, the follower of Saturn and repealer of the golden age. It is not civil war which we can expect in the Roman future but the preeminence for which Jupiter and his Dirae, whom we saw brooding over the Actian battle, stand.

It is not fortuitous that Aeneas, as he prepares to kill his humbled opponent at the end of the poem, takes on characteristics of the king of the gods. His spear is likened to a thunderbolt or to a whirlwind, to whom Jupiter's Fury had shortly before been compared.[67] By the time Ovid writes his *Metamorphoses* the comparison can be openly made. For Virgil it remains only an intimation that, by routing his enemies and forcing their leaders to suicide, Octavian puts an end to civil war. But by this very act, by symbolically killing a potential Remus very different from his "twin" Agrippa, he assures his position as the new Romulus. For all the earlier implications of shared authority, unique rule now returns to Rome, and with solitary power comes the immortal omnipotence of Jupiter as well. Once more, now as it reaches out to Virgil's earlier writing, the ekphrasis tells us of the repetitions and circularities of which history is made.

Much the same can be said for the phrase *superbis postibus,* the "proud doorposts" on which Caesar hangs up his gifts and to which the poet gives emphasis by enjambment. It reflects two earlier uses by Virgil of the words *foribus superbis* ("proud doorjambs"). The first occurs in the second georgic, not long before the passage I cited above, as part of an indictment of the corrupt morality of modern Rome where a house of the mighty is said to vomit forth a surge of morning greeters from its haughty doors.[68] And Virgil also uses these words earlier in *Aeneid* 8, in connection with the dwelling of Cacus, the bestial son of Vulcan who fastens the gore-dripping faces of his victims to his arrogant doorjambs.[69] Are we meant to find traces of the hauteur that typifies a decadent contemporary patrician, or of the presumption distinguishing the monster who lorded it over the site of early Rome, in the present conduct of Octavian during his great moment of acclaim? Is the power which has now accrued to him conducive to a positive or a negative self-esteem?

Irony is less indirect in a still more explicit parallel. This time we find ourselves in book 2, hearing Aeneas' description of the fall of Troy. He sees the death of Priam, bloodying his own altars, and how

> quinquaginta illi thalami, spes tanta nepotum,
> barbarico postes auro spoliisque superbi
> procubuere; . . . [70]

Those fifty marriage chambers, the great promise of progeny, the doors proud with the spoils of barbarian gold, have suffered ruin.

Barbarico here refers not, as most commentators take it, to Phrygian gold, but to the riches that Troy has amassed from foreign enemies.[71] It anticipates the *ope barbarica* by means of which the shield ekphrasis shows Antony supported and also, presumably, the spoils from the exotic peoples whose captives, as stand-ins for their nations, parade before Augustus. But such a parallel makes an analogy between the Troy of Priam and the Rome of Augustus in its magnificence the more disquieting. It says that empires, even in their loftiness, have a history of collapsing and that Rome, even Augustan Rome, can in its moment of pride draw little comfort from any resemblance to the pride of Priam's Troy. Once more the ekphrasis tells us, even while announcing the grandeur of the emperor's sublime achievement, that history repeats itself and that such moments of arrogance are as transient as the empires which gave them birth, however moving a poet's occasional, idealizing predictions of their immortality might be.

One further instance of the ekphrasis reaching out into the larger text also concerns the figure of Cacus. At lines 680–81, as we saw in another connection, the ekphrasis tells of Augustus, standing on his ship's high stern, *geminas cui tempora flammas/laeta vomunt* (whose joyous brow spews forth twin flames). This remarkable moment is complemented by the description, immediately preceding the start of the ekphrasis, of the helmet, also manufactured by Vulcan for Aeneas, terrifying with its crest and "spewing forth flames" (*flammasque vomentem*).[72] These two parallel phrases, from the introduction to and from within the ekphrasis, draw the reader's attention to the confrontation between Cacus and Hercules, which Evander described earlier in the book. There we find the monster first "spewing forth black fires from his mouth" (*atros/ore vomens ignis*), and then, as his demigod antagonist chokes him to death, he "spews forth vain fires in the darkness" (*in tenebris incendia vana vomentem*).[73] That Virgil would have us form a connection between the two scenes is confirmed by the fact that he uses the same phrase to describe the Arcadians gawking at the corpse of Cacus (*nequeunt expleri corda tuendo:* "men were unable to sate their hearts with gazing") as he does of Aeneas who "cannot be sated" (*expleri nequit*) with looking at the armor.[74]

It is received critical opinion that Hercules prefigures Aeneas-Augustus. The Greek hero rids the world of monsters, just as Aeneas does away with Turnus along with his Latin opponents and Augustus defeats Antony and his barbarous allies. Virgil's text both confirms the similarity and complicates it by drawing a series of verbal parallels between Hercules and Cacus.[75] The correspondence between Cacus and Aeneas' weaponry (his helmet and a figure on his shield) has the similar effect of further problematizing what might seem at first simple and straightforward. We have already observed some of the ambiguities raised by the ekphrasis itself and by connections it makes with the larger text of the poem, ambiguities which question a reading of the shield as an essentially honorific gesture to the accomplishments of Augustus. The connection between Cacus and Aeneas' armor deepens this complexity. It forces us to ask what might be the common ground between Vulcan's monster son and the god's artifact, what might be intellectually skewed about the iconic shield itself and about the tremendous vision it projects.

Let us continue our pursuit of such ambiguities, and of the idea of recurrence that circularity abets, by looking now in more detail at the relationship between the shield and the *Aeneid* itself. I will take my start here from an anecdote that the *vita* of Donatus attributes to Virgil, who said of the composition of the *Georgics* that "he produced his poem after the manner of a she-bear and fashioned it gradually into shape by licking" (*carmen se more ursae parare . . . et lambendo demum effingere*).[76] Aulus Gellius presents a more elaborate version of the same story, putting it into the mouth of the philosopher Favorinus musing on the recollections of Virgil by his friends. According to Favorinus, they had heard him say that "he produced verses after the manner and fashion of a she-bear [*more atque ritu ursino*]. For he said that as that beast brought forth her young formless and misshapen, and afterwards by licking [*lambendo*] the young cub gave it form and shape [*fingeret*], just so the fresh products of his mind were rude in form and imperfect, but afterwards by working over them and polishing them he gave them a definite form and expression."[77]

Virgil himself, in the process of creation, is like Vulcan-Mulciber, who fashions the features of Roman history (*finxerat*) and, as the etymological play on his name implies, composes them into shape. He is the godlike controller of time through art, rounding both out into something ultimately static, a shield artifact which symbolizes history's narrative conformed to the demands of an epic poem. This object in turn is contained in a scroll or in a codex of whatever shape, itself something out of time to be contemplated by the attentive reader. If Virgil is Mulciber, he is also, with a change of animal, the wolf of the shield's initial episode, artist-nurse, softening his newborn creations and licking them into shape with his imagination's tongue. One implication remains: that only through art, and in the mind's eye alone, can the wild actions that make up the story of Rome be tamed into submission.

We are not surprised, then, to find the same inventive talents that engender the shield as a whole and in its parts behind the entire poem and to discover confirmation of this omnipresence by means of specific parallels between the initial episodes of each. At the start of the ekphrasis we are beholding a scene which takes place in a cave (*antro*) where a nursing wolf (*fetam . . . lupam*) is fashioning the bodies of her charges and soothing them one by one (*mulcere alternos*). As we enter the action of the epic proper we also find ourselves in a huge cave (*vasto . . . antro*), a spot "pregnant with raging South Winds" (*feta furentibus Austris*).[78] Aeolus presides over this seething mass, and among his tasks are to temper their wrath and soothe their rancor (*mollit . . . animos*). We are reminded of this last duty again as the episode comes to an end. Juno charms Aeolus into forgetting his function as controller of his unruly charges. He releases them in pursuance of her hope that the storm they arouse would destroy the Trojan remnant who are so hateful to her. It is Neptune, lord of the sea and of Aeolus and his gales, who senses the deceitfulness and the anger of his sister as the cause of the uproar and restores calm to the natural universe.

In the epic's first simile, Virgil compares the winds to a mob to whom "fury lends arms" (*furor arma ministrat*) and their pacifier to someone "weighted with piety" (*pietate gravem*).[79] Neptune wields properly the power that Aeolus had abrogated, a connection which the last line of the simile makes clear: *ille regit dictis animos et pectora mulcet*[80] (He rules their tempers with his words and soothes their hearts). In dealing earlier with the etymology of Mulciber, we noted the link between the verbs *mollire* and *mulcere*. Here the reverberation of *mollit . . . animos* in *animos et pectora mulcet* underscores the intimacy. What Aeolus should have done, Neptune now accomplishes as he brings restraint and order to his world.

Looked at in larger symbolic ways, these two initiatory episodes complement and comment upon each other. The winds reify irrationality, in this particular instance, the madness of Juno, and their domination is as crucial for a civilized existence as their release is an augury of destructiveness. The cave of the winds is pregnant with negative potential. Should it be allowed to give birth, the results could verge on the catastrophic. Much the same can be said for the introductory scene on the shield, which appropriately represents the suckling of the newborn twins, which is also to say the birth of Rome. Virgil's narrator does not comment on what this beginning signifies for the city's future. It is enough to note that the infants are portrayed as fearless in the presence of their animal nurse and need to be soothed by her. Both characteristics are rich in paradox. We need only speculate on what it means for the potential of human twins, and for the political dynamism that springs from them, that they have no terror in the face of wildness and that the incorporation of that wildness must somehow bring calm and harmony to their inner beings.

The wolf quiets the twins' spirits just as Neptune pacifies the winds and Vulcan-Mulciber brings moderation to all the creatures of Roman history through the medium of art. And then there is Virgil, a higher Vulcan, who controls the whole through the medium of words, subordinating art's ekphrasis to his grander design and yet giving it special scope. But art, whether visual and apprehended through words or made of words alone, is as imagined as it is deceptive (and alluring). And what this art, be it of shield as described in the poem's longest ekphrasis or of the epic which enfolds it, seems to say of Rome is that the only way its energies, literal or symbolic, can be harnessed is through art. Kept to its own devices, and along with the brilliance of political accomplishment, it creates a world of war's constancy (and especially of civil strife), of dismemberment and forced suicide, of Jovian omnipotence and misplaced pride.

Much the same intellectual difficulties remain with us as we turn from beginnings to endings. The last figure on the shield, concluding the procession of conquered folk before Augustus, is that of the river Araxes "resenting its bridge" (*pontem indignatus*). The poem itself, in a powerful echo, ends on a similar note, heightened by repetition of the verb *indignor*. After Aeneas has buried his spear into his enemy's side, the narrative switches, for the epic's ultimate lines, away from victorious hero to victim: *ast illi solvuntur frigore membra/vitaque cum gemitu fugit indignata sub umbras*[81] (but his limbs are loosened with chill and his life with a groan flees resentful under the shades). Characters can be "indignant" in the *Aeneid* for a variety of reasons. We have seen Porsenna, on the shield, indignant that the Romans should oppose his plans.[82] The winds themselves in the first book are also *indignantes* because their animal energies are reined in by imprisonment in a mountain under the jurisdiction of Aeolus.[83] The same reaction could be attributed to the river Araxes, its vitality tamed by Roman might, by a bridging that bespeaks humans' control over nature. But the parallel with the life of Turnus, resenting its departure from the world above, complicates the correlation. We are not now dealing with animal energies or a natural force but with a human existence thrust toward an unwanted death. And Virgil's language gives small comfort from any such reading that might attempt to link winds, river, and the hero's life. The destructive intensity at the end of the poem is connected not with Turnus but with his killer, Aeneas, spurred on to his final sword thrust by a combination of ferocity, resentment, fury, and anger.

The meaning of the resentment of Turnus' vanishing life allows us to look again at its parallel at the end of the shield. The bridging of the Araxes, like the killing of Turnus, announces the final subjugation of anti-Roman or, in the case of Turnus, anti-Trojan opposition. War, especially civil war, is now over (Virgil is at pains to depict the strife in Latium as impious and therefore fraternal), and a river, standing for the might at empire's edge, is now dominated, just as are the negative forces in Latium at the loss of their leader. But the death of Turnus, killed in anger when the reader expects that Aeneas might act in clemency, suggests that we think of the indignation of the Araxes and of Turnus in a different light. On the one hand they serve as reminders of Rome's victorious agenda, whether under Aeneas or Augustus, both being examples of her goal-ridden teleology of accomplishment. On the other, both emblematize those who suffer the destiny of Rome and lose their individuality in the process.

It has long been pointed out how the language of Juno's emotionality at the beginning of the poem is ironically mirrored in the words by which Virgil describes Aeneas' wildness of mind before the killing of Turnus. This parallelism typifies what we have seen to be a reiterativeness in Virgil's view of Roman history that is echoed in the shield's curved disc which summarizes that history. It must come as no surprise that Virgil deliberately reflects this circularity in his own text and in the history of which it tells, extending from a cave, and the intensities it releases, to a river or a human life, both of which pay the toll for their contact with Rome. The course of the ekphrasis, when examined against the backdrop of the *Aeneid*, shows that the sweep of Roman events is mimicked by synecdoche in the contents of the epic itself. And yet, with brilliant complementarity, the smaller fragment, the self-contained emblem which is the subject of ekphrasis, tells of a grand sweep of history of which the poem at large, the expansive narrative of the *Aeneid*, encapsulates only a tiny portion.[84] Nevertheless both devices, ekphrasis and epic poem, incisive summary of all Roman time and extended survey of a short-lived instant in that history's mythic background, reinforce each other as exemplifications of life's occurrences and recurrences even over the passage of a thousand years.

These interconnections are important in our reading of what follows the ekphrasis in the poem. The description of the shield (and our understanding of Roman history) is positioned prominently at the end of the middle third of the poem. It and its contents have close similarities with Anchises' explanation, which ends book 6, of the presentation of future Roman heroes and their achievements. These two chronicles offer different ways for Aeneas and the reader to examine Roman time to come and help unify the epic's four central books. But the placement of the ekphrasis is particularly delicate. We find ourselves poised at a crucial intersection in the narrative. Art, and the presumably digressive ekphrasis which tells of it, is on the point of yielding to a resumption of narrative, to a detailing of the lived world of experience. The reader has been doubly prepared to ask how the events, of which the poem is soon to tell, jibe with what we have learned from the more distant happenings of which Anchises' display and the visionary ekphrasis have told.

The Shield, Homer, and Virgilian Originality

I have already suggested several ways in which ekphrasis and final narrative overlap and reinterpret each other. It is now time to turn back and analyze the creation of the shield, once more with the purpose of interpreting the ekphrasis and what it has to tell us of its larger context. To elucidate Virgil's artistry here we must look again at his extraordinary model, Homer's ekphrasis of the shield of Achilles in *Iliad* 18. We have already discussed the differences between the contents of each shield. Homer, as we saw, offers us vignettes that epitomize the regularity of human existence. His shield details a timeless realm of universals, strife and peace, the processes of law and life, seasonal activities, a dancing floor that celebrates art. We are shown its full contents, which would be readily comprehensible to the viewer in the narrative and to the hearer-reader outside. While the arrival of the armor makes Achilles grow angry and "glow with fire" and while the crafting of Hephaistos appears subordinate to the effect of power and enchantment which the object exudes, nevertheless we are told that the hero "takes delight gazing upon the art."[85]

Aeneas' shield, by contrast, deals not with Olympian universals but with the details of a particular history—events, places, unique individuals—as it evolves over many centuries. The ekphrasis outlines only excerpts from this general survey of Rome up to 29 B.C.E., but none of it, whether the whole or its parts, could have been comprehended by the shield's recipient, who rejoices in it but must nevertheless contemplate what he sees in ignorance of its meaning.[86]

But I have not hitherto touched on a major difference between the two presentations, which in turn affects the way that we interpret each ekphrasis and its context. In Homer's exposition we share in the making of the shield and—what Lessing in his famous critique found most praiseworthy vis-à-vis Virgil's imitation—we are direct participants in the immediacy of art and its creation. Virgil, on the contrary, makes the act of construction remote in both time and place. Though, as we have seen, the ekphrasis constantly reminds us of the artificial quality of the shield, by which I mean of the fact of its being fashioned by the god of fire, only once does Virgil use a verb in the present tense to describe Vulcan at work (*addit*, 666). Otherwise, the event is placed in past time, remote from the hero's present posture.

Though this temporal distance was not to Lessing's liking, Virgil's careful self-differentiation from Homer in this regard is for a purpose. By turning our attention away from the moment of manufacture to the moment of reception, Virgil removes the instantaneous gratification available to Homer's audience, who are to imagine themselves observant participants at the astonishing occasion when an artwork comes into being at the hands of an immortal artist and who can easily absorb a meaning for the shield's contents as accessible to them as it would be soon to Achilles himself. The Roman poet focuses attention instead on the receiver's act of contemplation.[87] In this case, pleasure comes to the reader not from enjoying the art-in-process but from sharing the role of Aeneas with the proviso that here this means being enlightened when he is uninformed. We are allowed the capability of deciphering a potent vision when the all-powerful hero lacks any clue to understanding.

But with this privileged position comes an implicit responsibility that Homer does not impose on his audience. The change of venue, so that instead of watching Hephaistos at work we "read" the shield along with its recipient, indicates that we must both become and surpass Aeneas himself, that we are asked to contemplate the shield both in ignorance and in knowledge, in anticipation and with hindsight, interpreting according to the signs that Virgil gives us and gaining a pleasure denied to the hero of gleaning connotations in a "text" very different from Homer's. We especially enjoy the act of seeing how ekphrasis and poem, static description and ongoing narrative, complement and support each other in a way foreign to Homer's immediate brilliance.[88]

The treatment of the shields by Homer and Virgil is different in another significant way, namely, in the story line that surrounds their production and delivery. In each case we are dealing with the same god, Hephaistos-Vulcan, and with a mother-son combination, in the first instance that of Thetis and Achilles, in the second Venus and Aeneas. But a major dissimilarity is immediately apparent. Thetis possesses leverage with Hephaistos because earlier she had saved him from his mother's wrath. Venus can make her plea on the basis that she is Vulcan's wife. In one case there is no question of sexuality. In the other, amatory response rules the scenario. And the fact that in the latter situation it is a notoriously unfaithful wife making a plea to her repeatedly cuckolded husband on behalf of her illegitimate child adds to the moral dilemma in which Virgil deliberately places his reader.

This dilemma is again not unlike a response to the shield that sees both glory and dread in its magnificence. Certainly Venus is using her relationship with Vulcan to help send her son along his fated way toward a resplendent future. The shield which he carries into battle allows him the majesty to become the extraordinary originator of Roman heroism, while in its essence it contains that very future of which he is to be the source and model. At the same time the scene itself, especially in its insistence on Venus' infidelity, was so troubling, even among ancient readers, that a character in Macrobius asserts that its immorality was the reason that Virgil expressed the wish on his deathbed that the *Aeneid* be burned.[89]

But whatever the reasons for our good fortune, Virgil himself did not see fit to excise the vexing lines, leaving it to his readers to sort out his several levels of intent. Certainly the grandeur of Vulcan's accomplishment must not be minimized, but already at the start of the episode it is the power of Venus that is the enlivening force behind the action. It is she, in the episode's initial burst of irony, who arrives (from where we are not told) at the "golden marriage-chamber of her husband" (*thalamo . . . coniugis aureo*) as the narrator asks us, through the word *aureo* that concludes the line, to fix our attention on a marriage-chamber from which she is regularly absent and on a husband who only sporadically fulfills his marital duties. It is she who from the start is in charge, "breathing immortal love into her words" (*dictis divinum aspirat amorem*)—a stunning line where alliteration and assonance combine with the first instance where *aspiro* has the meaning "instill" to epitomize Venus' power.[90] Irony continues in her address to Vulcan as *carissime coniunx*.[91] The apostrophe ends line 377, but Virgil is intent on following up the implication by emphatically repeating the word *coniunx* at the conclusion of lines 384 (referring to Aurora) and 393 (to Venus herself).

If air typifies the initiation of Venus' act of temptation (*aspirat*), fire is at its center. Though her arms are snowy, nevertheless she warms Vulcan in her embrace, he receives the wonted flame, and the heat enters his limbs like a lightning flash, as if the goddess had appropriated the power of Jupiter to her erotic undertaking. As critics have recognized, Virgil points up the moment by direct allusion to the opening lines of *De Rerum Natura*. He had prepared us for the reference by giving Venus the label *genetrix* at line 383, where the word appears at the same position in the line as it does in the opening apostrophe of Lucretius' poem, *Aeneadum genetrix* ("begetter of the sons of Aeneas"). But if, in the proem to the earlier poem, Venus was the symbolic beguiler of Mars, god of real warfare, "conquered by the eternal wound of love" (*aeterno devictus vulnere amoris*), here she is the literal seducer of the god of fire, now "bound by eternal love" (*aeterno . . . devinctus amore*).[92] In Lucretius, Venus' act of conquering befits her symbolic victory over Mars and the violence for which he stands. Binding, by contrast, suits an act of domination on Venus' part that captures the Protean artisan and puts his genius to work for her own purposes.

In another pertinent irony, she takes the role Vulcan once had adopted when he discovered his adulterous wife in bed with Ares-Mars and bound them together in their embrace, for the amusement of the gods.[93] It is à propos that Vulcan's final words of capitulation are an acknowledgment not only of her formidable power but of its masculinity: "cease by your praying to mistrust your strength" (*absiste precando/viribus indubitare tuis*).[94] In this patent reversal of roles, it is she who takes her husband's part, and, in the concluding lines of this part of the scene, lines which form the most explicitly erotic moment in the epic, though the narrator reminds us yet again that she is *coniunx*, he is the one who is poured into the lap of his wife, as if he were in part the passive object of her desire, to be molded to her wishes.[95] He is like the shield which he will soon make from the combination of air, fire, and molten metals, all of which now literally incorporate the metaphorical strength we have seen Venus exert upon her spouse.

The scene now shifts to the actual manufacture of the shield and to the Aetnaean caves of an island now called Volcano. This location is another among the hollow spaces of which Virgil was fond which serve as sources of energy, whether creative or destructive. He effects the transition through an astonishing simile which I will quote in full. The time is the waning of night:

> . . . cum femina primum
> cui tolerare colo vitam tenuique Minerva
> impositum, cinerem et sopitos suscitat ignis
> noctem addens operi, famulasque ad lumina longo
> exercet penso, castum ut servare cubile
> coniugis et possit parvos educere natos:
> haud secus ignipotens . . . [96]

when a woman, whose trial it is to make life endurable through her distaff and Minerva's humble work, first rouses the flame that slumbered in the ashes, adding nighttime to her effort, and sets her servants to some long task by lamplight so that she might keep chaste her husband's bed and bring up her small children: in such a way the god of fire . . .

The simile has antecedents both in the *Iliad* and in the *Argonautica* of Apollonius Rhodius. In *Iliad* 12 Homer compares the equipoise of the battle lines to a spinner holding weight and wool in a balance "to win a slim wage for her children."[97] Apollonius' two similes concern Medea. In the first he likens her, heart burning with love, to a spinner who kindles a blaze at night, and in the second, still closer to Virgil, we find her, love-sick and distraught, like a woman at her spindle who toils through the night "and round her moan her orphan children, for she is a widow."[98]

Virgil's brilliant allusions to Apollonius' Medea keep the note of eroticism before us, but whereas Medea in the second comparison is a widow with orphan children, Virgil leaves open the question of whether the matron's husband is dead or merely absent. I assume, however, that Virgil's vagueness about the wife's status, where Apollonius is explicit about her widowhood, implies the absence of the husband, not his demise. This in turn suggests that we consider yet again the relationship of Venus and Vulcan and its continuing irony. Inspiration for creativity is pervasively sexual, production itself is based on chastity, the virtue of a wool-working wife who is for the moment husbandless. Yet the implication still inheres that Vulcan is the faithful spouse, who cares for her and her husband's children while her mate is absent, unchaste, careless. But once again power lies with Venus, to seduce Vulcan only when and if she desires, to play the masculine role when he is the submissive female.[99] It is Vulcan who adheres to the Roman rules of marriage, remaining, as it were, *univira* while her consort is elsewhere, and it is Venus, *Aeneadum genetrix*, the immortal begetter of Aeneas and his sons, whose actions, as Virgil chooses to portray them, come under suspicion for their ethical dubiety according to Roman standards.

This highly charged eroticism continues on into the moment of the delivery of the shield. Venus finds her son in a sequestered valley of Caere and "offered herself of her own accord" (*se . . . obtulit ultro*).[100] A parallel phrase, lacking the word *ultro*, is used in book 2 of Venus' epiphany before her son in order to restrain his anger against Helen.[101] But the whole expression occurs first in Virgil in eclogue 3, where a shepherd boasts that his lover comes to him spontaneously,[102] and there is no reason to delimit the sexual element here. It is confirmed shortly later when "the goddess of Cythera sought the embraces of her son" (*amplexus nati Cytherea petivit*) and Virgil echoes language he had earlier used of the union of Vulcan with his love-goddess wife (*optatos dedit amplexus*).[103] In both the initiating stimulus for the creation of the shield and in its final presentation, Venus must bring her erotic powers to bear, first in the seduction of her husband, then in the gratuitous sensuality of her arrival with the shield, the only instance in the poem where she seeks rather than avoids her son's affection and where they actually embrace.

Like the shield itself and how we read it, sexuality in the *Aeneid* can be both inspiring in a positive sense and pernicious. (For examples of the latter we need only think of the events surrounding the figures of Juno, Helen, and Dido.) To see this ambiguity in relation to the ambiance of the shield, let us turn back for a final time to the seduction of Vulcan by Venus and to two further details in Virgil's narrative. The first is the characterization of Vulcan as "hesitating" (*cunctantem*) before he yields to Venus' embrace. Such pauses regularly occur throughout the *Aeneid* at moments of liminality where one of the epic's protagonists debates between two possible courses of action and the decision is crucial not only for its immediate results in the poem's action but also for the effect it has in helping form our judgments of the poem as a whole.

Dido hesitates before leaving her chamber to enter upon the fateful hunt with Aeneas.[104] The golden bough delays before it gives way to Aeneas' attempts at plucking, even though the Sibyl has told him that it will come easily, to the hero fated to break it off, or not at all.[105] Turnus and, shortly after, his antagonist, Aeneas, both hesitate as the poem comes to a close, Turnus before he faces his foe in the final duel, Aeneas at the moment before he kills. In the last lines of the epic the ethics of the Roman endeavor hang in the balance. Will Aeneas spare his now suppliant enemy, as his father had sententiously urged during their meeting in the Underworld, or will he allow his vengeful anger over the death of Pallas to gain the upper hand? An equally grand ambiguity centers on the golden bough. It is alive and dead, appropriate token for the hero himself, animate in the realm of the deceased, and it must be presented as a passport into and through Proserpina's kingdom. But it also grants entry to the Roman future, which Aeneas sees by means of the hero-ghosts of Rome to come whom Anchises marches before him. We end book 6 with Anchises' admonition to spare the downtrodden and, at the conclusion, with the funeral of Marcellus, as if to say that all this multivalent Roman might only brings some form of death in its wake.

We hear three times that the golden bough is a *munus*, a gift that in this case is accompanied by a duty or a task. The Sibyl calls the branch itself a *munus* before Aeneas plucks it, and, as he prepares to leave it as an offering and enter his father's Elysian fields, he is commanded by her to "accomplish the task you have undertaken" (*susceptum perfice munus*), an order he duly obeys (*perfecto munere*).[106] The shield is likewise part of a *munus*, as Venus' first words make clear when she delivers the armor: "*en perfecta mei promissa coniugis arte/munera*"[107] ("behold the gifts of my spouse, finished by his promised skill"). The golden bough is a *munus* that prepares Aeneas, and us, for the Roman future as illustrated in complementary fashion by Anchises. The *munus* of the shield likewise summarizes that future. Though there is little overlap in the personages or events described, the episodes balance each other, concluding parallel sectors of the central segment of the epic and rounding out a vision of Rome to come that serves as touchstone against which to measure the epic's final events. Twice over we are meant to sense the splendor of Roman heroism and its triumph in Augustus.

But the golden bough hesitates before submitting to Aeneas' touch, just as Vulcan delays before surrendering to Venus' embrace and allowing the warmth of love to metamorphose into the heat that makes a shield, and a future. The bough introduces a world, in Anchises' telling, where king Ancus "takes too great delight in the whimsies of the people," where Brutus, though he rids his city of the tyranny of Tarquin the Proud, still himself possesses a "proud spirit" (*animam superbam*) and axes of power that are savage (*saevas securis*), where Caesar and Pompey, though Anchises' apostrophe prays otherwise, will turn "their powerful strength against the guts of their fatherland" (*patriae validas in viscera . . . viris*).[108] And we have seen reasons enough in the ekphrasis of the shield to suggest why Vulcan might balk before succumbing to Venus' request. In each case, and even in dealing with the illustrious present-day savior of Rome from Cleopatra and her minions, Virgil takes the opportunity to explore the difficulties of the Roman rise to power and of the confirmation and continuity of that power. For to pluck the golden bough and to make the shield is to authorize Rome itself.

The second detail that I would like to examine more closely in the seduction of Vulcan is the attention Virgil calls to the wiles (*doli*) to which the love-goddess must resort: *sensit laeta dolis et formae conscia coniunx*[109] (His wife felt [her effect], happy in her machinations and aware of her beauty). We presume that Vulcan need not have hesitated or Venus have recourse to stratagems of cunning were the enterprise in hand totally innocuous. The results of these *doli* are the *dona* that Venus brings to her son and which we hear of three times in connection with the delivery of the arms. Virgil initially uses the word when Aeneas' mother arrives amid the clouds, "bearing the gifts" (*dona ferens*), and we soon thereafter find the hero himself "happy from the gifts of the goddess" (*deae donis . . . laetus*).[110] Finally, after the conclusion of the ekphrasis and as part of the ring-composition that makes shield and setting inseparable, the reader is once more reminded of the armor's origin. We hear for the last time that the contents which Aeneas so admires (*miratur*) are to be found "on the shield of Vulcan, the gift of his parent" (*per clipeum Volcani, dona parentis*).[111]

Even after the conclusion of the ekphrasis, Virgil thus allows himself a final irony regarding Aeneas' parentage. Because *dona* is a synecdoche in apposition to *clipeum,* the reader expects the parallelism to continue on in *Volcani* and *parentis,* that is, to have the two genitives refer to the same person. But they do not, with *parens* being a reminder that Venus begot Aeneas not with her lawful husband, the god of fire, but illegitimately with Anchises. However grand the creative efforts of Vulcan—he is, after all, siring the destiny of Rome—they still have an air of suspicion about them. This suspicion is fostered by the word *dona,* especially when the gifts in question are the results of the manipulation of *doli.*

Virgil has prepared the reader for this collocation in book 8, and for its deeper suggestiveness, through several earlier moments in the poem. The first occurs in book 1, and yet again Venus is a key figure in the action. Here the gifts in question are the offerings, salvaged from the wreckage of Troy, which Aeneas presents as tokens of hospitality to Dido. Even before Venus becomes involved the reader is made wary of their dark symbolism. They consist of a cloak, which Helen had worn when leaving Greece for Troy and "unlawful marriage" (*inconcessos . . . hymenaeos*), and a scepter and coronet belonging to Ilione, the eldest daughter of Priam who was forced to commit suicide.[112] The implication is that Aeneas, in what to all intents and purposes should be a positive gesture, unwittingly brings with him an illicit union that will lead the ruler of Carthage to self-slaughter.

Venus' *doli*, her sly intervention, merely expedite the effect of the *dona*. We first hear of her plot at 659–60 where she aims to "set aflame the maddened queen by the gifts" (*donis . . . furentem/ incendat reginam*). Soon thereafter the goddess addresses her son and we learn, first, of the *doli* with which she plans, up to this point at least metaphorically, to gird the queen with flames.[113] This will be accomplished by replacing Ascanius, who at this very moment is "bearing the gifts" (*dona ferens*) from the harbor to the city.[114] Ascanius, lest he learn of her wiles (*dolos*, 682), will be lulled to sleep and whisked away elsewhere, while for one crucial night Cupid can work his wiles for his mother (*dolo*, 684). And so it is that Amor, not Ascanius-Iulus, brings the gifts (*dona*, 695) to the royal dwelling, gifts which the Tyrians admire (*mirantur dona Aeneae*) as they do the features of Cupid (*mirantur Iulum*).[115] And both child and presents are linked together as they generate the effect which Venus desires specifically on the Carthaginian queen: "She is charmed alike by boy and gifts" (*pariter puero donisque movetur*).[116]

Like Aeneas in book 8, who contemplates Vulcan's shield in ignorance of what he sees (*rerum . . . ignarus*), Dido can be influenced by the gifts only while she is unaware (*inscia*) of the divine power that is manipulating her.[117] After she and Aeneas have become lovers, after she has learned of Aeneas' plan for departure and herself decided on suicide, she can be called "by no means ignorant of the future" (*haud ignara futuri*), just as the Vulcan who makes the shield is *haud vatum ignarus venturique inscius aevi*[118] (by no means unaware of prophecies and ignorant of future time). Enlightenment comes for Dido only after the combination of *doli* and *dona* have wreaked their damage. Unlike Dido, then, who came to late learning only when death is in the offing, and unlike the immortal Vulcan (and his equally omniscient creator, Virgil), who is endowed with foresight sufficient to imagine into art the whole future of Rome, Aeneas is not allowed to comprehend and act upon knowledge of either the distant mission of Rome or even his own nearer purposes. Only the reader shares the embracing wisdom of Vulcan, and therefore is aware not only of how crucial remains the god's hesitation—for in the case of the shield, to conceptualize in art is to institute as fact—but of how potentially lethal is the combination of gift and guile. It, too, as an important ingredient in the setting for the creation and delivery of the shield, supports what the ekphrasis suggests: that the march of events, which we call Roman history and which leads inexorably to the acclamation of Augustus, also has a duplicitous side of which we can appreciate only through wary scrutiny of the total epic, in which and for which it stands.

By the end of book 1 the reader is trained for the interaction of *donum* and *doli* and its consequences. This attention is rewarded by the most expansive instance in the epic of this juxtaposition in the epic which occurs in book 2, at the beginning of Aeneas' narrative to Dido of the fall of Troy. It, too, has parallels with the presentation of the shield which deserve tracing. The combination centers here on the wooden horse which is the essential object in the Greeks' stratagem for the taking of Troy, just as the gifts of Aeneas play a crucial role in the metaphoric besieging and capture of Dido, which only later mutates into the reality of her funeral pyre. We first hear tell of the "deadly gift" (*donum exitiale*) of Minerva and of Thymoetes' urging, perhaps by guile (*dolo*), that it be brought into the city.[119] Capys advocates that the suspect *dona* be thrown into the sea. Only Laocoön makes the connection directly in a rhetorical question remarkable for the assonance and alliteration that bind gift, guile, and Greeks together: "*aut ulla putatis/ dona carere dolis Danaum?*"[120] ("or do you think that any gifts of the Greeks lack treachery?") And he pursues his point with the equally memorable phrase—"I fear the Greeks even when bringing gifts" (*timeo Danaos et dona ferentis*)—of which the last two words link Greeks with Ascanius, soon to become Cupid, bearer of destructive gifts, and with Venus and her shield.[121]

The collocation persists throughout the first half of the book. We take note again, at line 189, of the *dona Minervae*, and, as the horse begins to disgorge its pernicious contents, we learn how nature sides with the Greeks to hide their deceits (*dolos*) and how Epeos, the "deviser of the fraud" (*doli fabricator*), was one of the first to leave the beast's belly.[122] But though the horse may incorporate the notions of both gift and cunning, it is the figure of Sinon who implements their potential. It is he who, in Aeneas' words, has made a decision either "to weave his web of deceit" (*versare dolos*) or to meet certain death, and it is by his *doli* and feigned tears, as the episode progresses, that the Trojans are mentally captured just as their city is about to be taken.[123] And there is one potent phrase that associates Sinon with the Venus who brings the shield. When his goddess-mother arrives with Vulcan's masterpiece, we remember, "she offered herself of her own accord" (*se . . . obtulit ultro*), and it is a version of the same expression that Virgil puts into Aeneas' mouth as he describes the sudden appearance of the treacherous Sinon before the Trojans:

> Ecce manus iuvenem interea post terga revinctum
> pastores magno ad regem clamore trahebant
> Dardanidae, qui se ignotum venientibus ultro
> hoc ipsum ut strueret Troiamque aperiret Achivis,
> obtulerat . . . [124]

Meanwhile behold Dardan shepherds, with loud shouts, were dragging toward the king a youth with his hands tied behind his back, who, though unknown, had offered himself of his own accord to them as they came up, so that he might accomplish this very goal and open Troy to the Greeks.

The beguilement of the Trojans by Sinon begins with the same action (*se . . . ultro . . . obtulerat*) as Venus' seduction of her son before the presentation of Vulcan's arms. Sinon, the Sneaky one, is the mouthpiece of the horse as well as the sly spokesman for the Greeks themselves. His cozening of the Trojan minds prepares the way for the breaching of the city's ramparts which anticipates by only a few hours the deadly birth from the horse itself. If there is a moment that parallels the hesitation of the golden bough or of Aeneas before killing Turnus or of Vulcan before creating the shield, it occurs when the horse, as it is being tugged joyously through the walls, "stopped four times on the threshold of the gate" (*quater ipso in limine portae substitit*).[125] But the Trojans, "blind with madness" (*caeci furore*),[126] place the horse on the citadel. They have their kinship to Aeneas, "set aflame by furies and terrible in his anger" (*furiis accensus et ira/ terribilis*), as he pitilessly slays his enemy, and Vulcan "bound by love" as he prepares to fulfill the behest of Venus.[127]

Horse, bough, and shield have their parallels. All serve as central symbols, prominent at transitional moments in the poem, and all therefore prepare for change, be it for the violent destruction of Troy or for Aeneas' initiation into the world of the dead and into Rome to come. Horse and shield, in particular, have further in common the fact that they are the most prominent examples of artwork in the poem: the first the product of the "immortal art" of Minerva and, as we saw, her deadly gift; the second, as Virgil emphasizes four times over, the result of Vulcan's magisterial *ars,* and also a gift of mother to son.[128] And there is guile connected with each, whether in the implementation of its potential or in the inspiration for its fabrication. In the one instance both deceit and artifact are part of a larger plot to raze the city of Troy. In the other they join to imagine the future of a still greater city. The extent to which Virgil means us to accept these similarities, when we ponder what the shield tells us of the violence attendant on the engendering of Augustan Rome, is left to his reader to adjudicate.

There exists yet another link between horse and shield which will return our attention one final time to the ekphrasis and, in particular, to its initial episode. As the horse climbs the walls, before entering the city, it is described by Aeneas as a "war-machine pregnant with arms" (*machina . . . /feta armis*).[129] The strange creature is as anomalous as the golden bough, both dead and alive, a siege-engine in the shape of a wooden horse that is teeming with weapons, where the word *armis,* standing for weapons alone or metonymically for the men who carry them, fosters the ambivalence. This gestation will soon result in the birth of the Greeks from the horse who, as they emerge from the creature's belly, are given the names that reenliven them and bring death to the city that is already symbolically "buried" through sleep and wine. We have seen the epithet *fetus* applied to the habitation of Aeolus and his wards, *feta furentibus Austris,* fertile with raging winds. The only other appearance of the adjective in the *Aeneid* is at 8.630, where it is applied to Mars' wolf suckling the twin progenitors of Rome. The commonality is appropriate. The horse gives birth to the destruction of Troy. The wolf fosters nurslings who in turn both establish a great city and set the pattern for fraternal strife which permeates that city's later annals.

All three moments are instinct with energy. In the first two instances, the cave of the winds and a cavernous horse, the force in question is powerful enough to wreak havoc over its opponents. In the third, the wolf in her den, as she nourishes her twins, is engendering Rome and its special dynamism. But the adjective *feta* and the scene in which it plays such a prominent part have a still further invigorating effect on the ekphrasis and therefore on the epic as a whole. Through allusion they take us back into the world of Virgil's literary past and to his co-optation of that past whose encapsulation lends the potency of tradition to his own individual achievement.

The Shield and the Virgilian Career

We have talked before about the Homeric tradition and in particular about how Virgil adapts Homer's description of the shield of Achilles to his own special purposes. The word *feta* expands this background by taking us into the Roman intellectual past of the ekphrasis and, appropriately, to the most influential of earlier Roman epics, the *Annales* of Quintus Ennius. In his gloss on line 831 of book 8, Servius observes that "nearly this whole section is Ennian" (*Sane totus hic locus Ennianus est*). Virgil's commentator is given to such generalities which are made suspect because, in the one grand instance where we can test him, namely, his assertion that the whole of the Dido story is borrowed from the *Argonautica*, he is found wanting. But in the case of the Lupercal vignette on the shield, he himself supplies evidence in support of his contention. In his annotation to *Aeneid* 2.355, on the point that in older writers the word *lupus* was common to both genders, Servius quotes, as a phrase of Ennius, *lupus femina feta repente* (suddenly a suckling she-wolf).[130] By the time of Virgil, *lupa* alone has taken the place of *lupus femina*, but there remains little doubt that Virgil's *fetam lupam* looks back to Ennius and therefore that, to whatever degree, the inspiration of the earlier epicist lay behind the scene as a whole.

I argue the point not to ponder the niceties of an allusion whose depth we will probably never be able further to plumb but simply to affirm the importance of origins and origination in the inaugural vignette of the ekphrasis. The episode in the Lupercal, as we have seen, echoes and therefore refigures the opening drama of the epic itself. But the allusion to Ennius also means that the beginnings of Virgil's ekphrasis recall the beginnings of Latin hexameter poetry, just as the contents of the ekphrasis, a selection from Vulcan's sweeping survey, form a miniature version of the *Annales* of the earlier poet (with the proviso, of course, that Ennius' exploration of Roman history extends only to events in the 170s B.C.E.). In any case, the initiation of the ekphrasis brings with it the initiating dynamic of Latin epic verse. It both incorporates that dynamism in an act of mastery that is itself originating and yet utilizes it as well to lend the authority of literary tradition, specifically in the genre of epic, to Virgil's own accomplishment. Once more the ekphrasis metonymically represents the poem.

A second poet that Virgil integrates into the opening episode of his ekphrasis is Lucretius. The wolf of Mars, who soothes her charges one by one, "her smooth neck bent back" (*tereti cervice reflexa*), is an immediate literary descendant of the war-god himself who, in the early lines of *De Rerum Natura, suspiciens tereti cervice reposta/pascit amore avidos inhians in te, dea, visus*[131] (looking up, his smooth neck laid back, as he gapes at you, goddess, he feeds his eager glances with love). And, given the similarity of contexts, the posture of the twins who hang (*pendentis*), playing around the wolf's udders, also recalls that of Mars: *eque tuo pendet resupini spiritus ore*[132] (and as he reclines his breath hangs upon your lips).

Once more we are dealing with the introductory lines of a masterpiece, this time from the generation directly preceding the Augustan age, and, though didactic in genre rather than epic, with the greatest Latin hexameter poem before Virgil. It was a poem enormously influential on the later poet, and Virgil, in absorbing the extraordinary impact of its proem, both acknowledges his own debt to *De Rerum Natura* and reprojects it as a signal part of the genesis of Roman intellectual history, which is of his own poetic genesis as well. Once again the history of Roman poetry and its effect on Virgil are important components of an ekphrasis bent on retelling the history of Rome itself. His literary heritage helps lend Virgil the authority and inspire his imagination to tell the tale of a different type of power and a different past from which it sprang.

But this interaction leads to two more specific reasons why Virgil here alludes to the opening scene of *De Rerum Natura*. For Lucretius, philosopher-poet of Epicurean quietude and inner calm, the "wild ways of war," emblematized in the martial god himself, must be gentled to inaction if his doctrines are to succeed and if his poetry, through the charm he prays Venus to lend it, will have the puissance to convince a Roman statesman to adopt its message of withdrawal from the practical world's confusion. Virgil's borrowing merely underscores the divergence from his predecessor. In the place of Mars lulled to sleep by Venus, we have his representative in the shape of a wild animal who molds her fearless fosterlings for a future, of which the remainder of the ekphrasis will tell, in which war is an essential ingredient. The Venus who brings arms (and a Martial paradigm) to her son is a very different creature from the incorporation of the Epicurean pleasure principle who, at the beginning of *De Rerum Natura*, must still the spirit of irrationality so that humankind may possess both external and internal peace.

The second specific reason for Virgil's bow to Lucretius follows readily from the first. It is to remind the reader, as we have seen, that the poet has already alluded to these very lines during the earlier occasion in which Venus seduces Vulcan into making the arms. There, we recall, the figure of Vulcan, "bound by eternal love" (*aeterno . . . devinctus amore*), serves as a remembrance of Lucretius' Mars, "conquered by the eternal wound of love" (*aeterno devictus vulnere amoris*). On one level Virgil's purpose, through allusion to the same passage of Lucretius at the engendering of the shield as at the commencement of the ekphrasis, is to point up the intimacy of the two. The emotionality that animates Vulcan as he prepares to create the artifact also charges the figures within that artifact. Through the double allusion to Lucretius the parallel between Vulcan, begetting his shield from his cavernous workshop under the erotic inspiration of Venus, and the wolf, licking her wards into shape, is strengthened.

Yet the metamorphosis in roles is worthy of note, as we compare the proem of *De Rerum Natura* with the two passages from *Aeneid* 8. Looked at simply by themselves, the figures of Mars, neck laid back, and wolf, her neck bent backward, are complements. The feral animal is appropriate nurse in Mars' cave for the twins of a god whom the ekphrasis will later show raging in the midst of the Actian battle lines. There is enough that is elemental in the god's character to make the conjunction readily comprehensible. But the parallel between Vulcan and Mars is, as we saw briefly before, both more complex and more ironic. Vulcan who, according to myth, captured the lovers Venus and Mars in a metal mesh, is himself now Mars, entangled in the toils of Venus who, in this context, takes on the powers of her husband. At the creation of the shield, the goddess of love, as we earlier observed, becomes masculine crafter and her consort the Mars figure, trammeled by her devices and at the same time, unlike Lucretius' Mars, releasing into being the martial magnetism of Rome.

The third and final author to whom Virgil refers in the opening segment of the ekphrasis is himself. The setting, "in a green cave" (*viridi in antro*) with the wolf lying down (*procubuisse*) while the twins hang (*pendentis*) from her teats, is analogous to the scenario in the first eclogue which the soon-to-be-exiled shepherd Meliboeus paints of his past in relation to his future: *non ego vos posthac viridi proiectus in antro/dumosa pendere procul de rupe videbo*[133] (after this, stretched out in a green cave, I will not see you [his sheep] afar, hanging from a rock thick with briars). In comparison to the opening of the ekphrasis, wolf, prone on the ground, has replaced reclining shepherd, and suckling twins have supplanted a flock suspended from its distant perch. But the setting in each case is closely parallel, and Virgil uses the phrase *viridi . . . in antro* only in these two instances.

Here, too, Virgil makes a point of echoing the opening of a grand poetic effort, this time of the first poem of his initial masterpiece, the *Eclogues*. And here also the ekphrasis assimilates and expresses in a new guise the intellectual nub of a poetic tour de force which now happens to be Virgil's own. In the first eclogue Virgil sets up a dichotomy between two shepherds, Tityrus and Meliboeus. The former, through the beneficence of a young god in Rome, is allowed to remain a leisured singer in an idealized pastoral setting. Meliboeus, by contrast, is caught up in the troubles of the real Roman world at the end of the 40s B.C.E. It is he who, with pointed irony, can call a Roman warrior someone who is *barbarus* and *impius*. The soldier is uncivilized in the sense that his behavior is worthy only of those outside Roman ethical influence and impious because it springs from the immoral horror of civil war. In Meliboeus' own concentrated words: *en quo discordia civis/producit miseros*[134] (behold whither dissension has carried our pitiable citizenry).

The reminiscence of this extraordinary moment at the start of Virgil's poetic career in the opening vignette has several purposes. The first is specific. Meliboeus' green cave, from which he is displaced by civil strife, becomes the green cave whence the twins bring *discordia* into the start of Roman history. Virgil chooses pastoral poetry, and a pastoral setting, for his initial meditation on the difference between ideal and real in Roman existence, a theme that would occupy the poet for his whole career. At the start of the ekphrasis the pastoral setting, with its particular recollection of eclogue 1, brings with it the same cluster of ideas, and the same problematics, as Virgil had outlined in his first extraordinary poem. The green cave might suggest pastoral quietude, unencumbered by life's importunities, as it once did for Meliboeus, or as the protection of the spreading beech still does for the blessed shepherd Tityrus in the poem's initial verses.

At the start of the ekphrasis, as he synopsizes the powerful beginning of his own poetic progress, Virgil suggests that Rome's pastoral infancy, like her later military career, could evolve in either of two directions: into the handsome generosity of a young god in Rome who gives assurance of stability in one shepherd's world and of continuity for song and for the life of the imagination for which it stands, or into the disruptive destructiveness of fraternal strife. Again it is up to the reader to decide which side of the spiritual balance Virgil weights more heavily in the lines that follow.

A second reason for the bow to eclogue 1 at the start of the ekphrasis is more general. We have seen how the ekphrasis reflects the *Aeneid* as a whole. Virgil, both in the epic and in the ekphrasis, takes us from a cave scene rife with energy to a figure, be it a tamed river or the life of a defeated hero, each indignant at the robbery of natural vitality. In the course of both ekphrasis and poem, Virgil has asked us to meditate on the intellectual value of line and circle, of history as idealized progress toward a transcendent moment or as a cycle of recurrences that ever turns in on itself and starts anew. Ekphrasis and poem, and the events of which each tells, could and no doubt should be interpreted as in some measure following each pattern. But the bow toward eclogue 1, like the analogy with the poem as a whole, suggests a prejudice on the part of the poet toward the notion of circularity.

This bias finds support in the fact that three times in the last book of the *Aeneid* Virgil calls our attention back to eclogue 1. The first comes at line 236 where Juturna, disguised as the respected Camers, urges the Latins not to let Turnus fight alone but to battle one and all against the foe:

> "nos patria amissa dominis parere superbis
> cogemur, cui nunc lenti consedimus arvis."

"We, our fatherland lost, will be compelled to obey proud overlords, we who now sit unresponsive in our fields."

Virgil would have us think back to the third and fourth lines of eclogue 1 where the departing Meliboeus compares himself and his fellow shepherds to Tityrus at ease in the shade: *nos patriae finis et dulcia linquimus arva. /nos patriam fugimus* (We are leaving the bounds of our fatherland and our sweet fields. We are in exile from our fatherland). For Meliboeus it is the advent of an impious and an uncouth soldier, spurred on by *discordia,* who uproots him from his paternal soil. For Juturna, urging on the susceptible Latins, it is the Trojans, whose arrival in fact sparks a form of civil war, who are in the process of becoming the haughty masters of Latium and therefore rulers of the fatherland their opponents are about to lose. The many levels of irony are not lost on the reader, for Troy, we know, is incipient Rome.

The other reminders of eclogue 1 in *Aeneid* 12 occur in one of the most astonishing episodes of the poem where Aeneas, on the urging of his "most beautiful mother," begins to capture and burn down the defenseless capital of Latinus. The first comes in words of Aeneas, threatening to level the city's "smoking rooftops" (*fumantia culmina*) unless its inhabitants accept his sway.[135] The second comes in the division (*discordia*) that affects its citizens (*civis*) as they debate whether to accept or deny his request.[136] The first returns our thoughts to the concluding lines of eclogue 1 where Tityrus paints a picture of nightfall for the departing Meliboeus:

> et iam summa procul villarum culmina fumant
> maioresque cadunt altis de montibus umbrae.[137]
>
> and now the tops of the villas smoke from afar and greater shadows fall from the lofty mountains.

In the eyes of the fortunate shepherd the smoking rooftops of the homes betoken the arrival of evening in a countryside at peace. For the reader with *Aeneid* 12 in mind and presumably, therefore, for the suffering Meliboeus, the smoke connotes something far less pleasant, namely, the havoc that results from civil war. Hence also the repetition of the phrase *discordia civis* in each setting (and in each case ending its hexameter).[138] Aeneas, in bringing his unnecessary attack, not only epitomizes the destructiveness such fighting can foster but foments discord among the citizens. For Meliboeus this discord in the abstract is what has physically effected his banishment from the dream existence of love and song into the harsh realities of the Roman world.

The bow to eclogue 1, at the opening of the shield ekphrasis, and therefore to the problematics which it so richly develops at the start of Virgil's writing, has a specific point, especially when taken in conjunction with its echoes in *Aeneid* 12. The ekphrasis as a whole may reflect the total poem, with the beginning and end of each paralleling one the other. But the acknowledgment of eclogue 1 illustrates another, still grander rounding off, this time of the Virgilian career as a whole. The Virgil who molds his poems the way a she-bear licks her cubs into shape (and the way the poet himself, Vulcan-like, shapes a she-wolf nourishing the future of Rome) tells us here something of the form in which his total oeuvre is formed.

It is a world built around Rome and its potential. The young god in the city who befriends Tityrus grows over the passage of time, and through Virgil's imagination, into Augustus in all his splendor, receiving the gifts of conquered peoples in front of his new shrine to Apollo. The forward thrust of Rome is the forward momentum of the shield—from Romulus to Augustus, from cave to shimmering temple—and of the poetry which defines them both. But the poetry, like the shield-poem, also has its roundings-off. For the shield-poem, the mountain cavern of Aeolus echoes the Martial cave of wolf and twins, just as Turnus' indignant life force echoes the Araxes, resentful of its bridge. For Virgil's total poetic accomplishment we have Tityran idealism pressing us ahead into the Augustan peace and, nearer to hand in the *Aeneid*'s circumstances, to the settlement in Latium that we assume follows on the killing of Turnus. But we also experience the tragedy of Meliboeus, the continuity of war's terrors and, at the end, the violence of heroes followed not by praises of victory but by the suffering of victims. This, too, typifies the shield but also the Virgilian career of which it is an exemplary part.

In the lines that introduce the ekphrasis the narrator describes the shield as a *non enarrabile textum*. The adjective is a Virgilian coinage and joins with *textum* to form a remarkable collocation which mixes a series of metaphors. The metallic shield, product of the sculptor's art, is also a type of fabric, a weaving together of strands and designs. It is a palpable object and therefore dependent for interpretation on seeing and on the proper exercise of any resultant inner vision. Yet unlike metal, it is also metaphorically supple, an intellectual form of cloth, say, or basket, or ship, made from meshing the pliable into a complete entity. It speaks at once of differentiations and wholeness, of details and integration, of yielding and strength.

This "text" also relies on descriptive words, whether voiced or written, in the attempt to deliver, or elucidate, its meaning. Like the ekphrasis itself, therefore, it is a magical fusion of the sculptor's and the poet's art, of metals and of words that convey their merger, of tangible and intangible. Again it is an object which we are made to see but only through a conception which the mind's eye makes available.

Yet this masterful display of art through art is *non enarrabile,* incapable of full recounting or explanation. One reason for this is superficial.[139] By some act of genius the images on the shield embrace all of Roman history. The ekphrasis is therefore only a form of synecdoche, a series of vignettes interwoven from a prodigious aggregate. To relate the whole history of Rome, especially a history conceived as ongoing, is as impossible an undertaking for a poet as we would expect it to be for a practitioner of the fine arts. But Virgil cannot allow himself, at least in this regard, the luxury of comparison with Vulcan. However similar their acts of craftsmanship, the mortal poet is merely capable of excerpts from the astonishing ensemble the god created.

But the phrase *non enarrabile* also looks beyond the superficial scheme of the shield. It is strange enough to expect, what ekphrasis posits as a given, that words can "narrate" a piece of visual art, that one medium of the imagination is capable of translation into another. In this case the impossibility of a complete narration suggests something about exposition as well. If the text cannot be fully recounted, neither can it be fully explained. And here what is à propos for the whole is also applicable for the part, for the ekphrasis of the particulars that Virgil does allow us to envision. Even the ekphrasis itself, not least because it bravely attempts the unrealizable mission of expounding an art object in words, is incapable of full exposition. And there is, of course, Virgil's own genius. The ekphrasis is no more open to an omnicompetent interpretation than is any aspect of the poet's brilliance. Readers are no more capable of eliciting a single correct explication of the ekphrasis than they can of the epic as a whole. And here again, and for the last time, poem and ekphrasis speak with one voice.

6

The Baldric of Pallas

We turn now from the longest to the briefest, and last, example of "notional" exphrasis in the *Aeneid*. It occurs in book 10 where the narrator, in a line and a half, depicts the contents of the sword belt of the dead Pallas which Turnus strips from his body and at some point assumes. We will once more examine the description, for its contents and context, for its poetic inheritance, and, finally, for the light it sheds on the poem as a whole and on a larger problem of Augustan intellectual history.[1]

First the content and context. Turnus has met and killed in single combat the young protégé of Aeneas. We pick up the narrative after the victor has stood over the corpse, announcing to the followers of Evander that the defeated got what he deserved and that he is sending the body back for burial (495–505):

> . . . et laevo pressit pede talia fatus
> exanimem rapiens immania pondera baltei
> impressumque nefas: una sub nocte iugali
> caesa manus iuvenum foede thalamique cruenti,
> quae Clonus Eurytides multo caelaverat auro;
> quo nunc Turnus ovat spolio gaudetque potitus.
> nescia mens hominum fati sortisque futurae
> et servare modum rebus sublata secundis!
> Turno tempus erit magno cum optaverit emptum
> intactum Pallanta, et cum spolia ista diemque
> oderit.

And after he had spoken such words he pressed the lifeless man with his left foot, snatching the huge weight of the baldric and the imprinted crime: on their single night of marriage the band of youths foully slaughtered and the bloodied wedding chambers, which Clonus son of Eurytus had incised with much gold. In these spoils Turnus now rejoices and takes delight in their possession. Mind of men, ignorant of fate and of future lot, and of holding a moderate course when buoyed by favorable circumstances! The time will come for Turnus when he will wish Pallas ransomed untouched for a great price and when he will hate these spoils and day.

The ekphrasis proper, which the narrator introduces with the phrase *impressumque nefas*—we are to learn of a crime given visible shape by engraving—lasts only one and a half lines but demands of the reader an unusual exercise of imagination. The belt tells of the slaughter of (presumably) forty-nine of the fifty sons of Aegyptus, all at once, by the daughters of Danaus on their wedding night. We witness one of the most graphic events in Greek myth whose feverish intensity is visualized as compressed, we are to imagine, in a series of vignettes equivalent to the number of murders, in the restricted space of a sword belt. The limited deployment of words metaphorically reflects the confined enclosure of the tangible object of which it tells.

The ekphrastic mode, as we have seen, aims for the impossible: to stop the passage of time (as narrative flows, and as we read) and to impart to and through words the apparent fixity of space. Virgil here comes close to accomplishing this goal. From absorbing the intent of a total of ten words stretched over an hexameter and a half we are made to imagine the repetition of forty-nine events happening contemporaneously. The simultaneity of action and the nearly instantaneous depiction of it in words complement each other. Brevity of time and brevity of space are captured in the concision of words which in a flash conjure up for us this exceptional object and its strange tale.

The words themselves are also a form of figuration for what they tell. As we begin an initial reading, with the phrase *una sub nocte iugali* which ends line 497, ignorant of what follows, we expect a happy vision of marriage based on the brisk suggestion of unity which both *una* and *iugali* suggest. Hence as we turn to the next, full line of the ekphrasis and its first word, *caesa*, the enjambment becomes particularly telling. From conjoining (and marriage) we turn abruptly to cutting (and murder), and the break between the lines, and the shock it arouses, signals both the violence of the deeds depicted and their sudden, unexpected quality. And because, verbally, cutting reflects the brutality of which it tells, the ekphrasis also subtly partakes in a form of iconicity which we see fully fledged in the figured poems we know most readily from the work of George Herbert but which are exampled from the Hellenistic period on. Once more poetry and the art and action of which art tells tend succinctly to merge.

Enjambment helps illustrate meaning, but the key word for understanding the moral thrust of the ekphrasis is *foede*.[2] We know that what we are going to see is a *nefas*, but *foede* gives the action of murder its ethical slant.[3] It is the pivotal element of line 498, caught appropriately between two caesurae, with seven syllables on either side. We must therefore attend to the poet's intentions here with particular care. Virgil puts his only other use of the adverb on the lips of Venus who, as part of her indictment of Juno to Neptune in book 5, speaks of Juno's continuing *ira, odium*, and *furor* against the Trojans and in particular of how the goddess had burned the Trojan ships, *foede*, after the mothers had been driven to criminal action (*per scelus*).[4] The implication is that such a course is both sly and dishonorable because it played on the infuriate emotions of women to perform a deed that would be unthinkable were they in their right mind.[5]

But both the adjective *foedus* and the verb *foedo* appear in contexts that also help us to comprehend the force of *foede* in book 10.[6] Most germane is the phrase *foeda ministeria* to describe the task of opening the twin Gates of War which Juno arrogates to herself when Latinus avoids it.[7] The passage takes us in a sweeping bit of etiology from Virgil's imagination of early Italian *mores* down to Augustan Rome. When Rome makes war now, says the narrator (speaking of Virgil's present time), it is against the Getae or to demand back the standards from the Parthi. The all too recent past had evinced a more ugly form of martial activity, when brother fights brother in civil conflict.[8] It is to avoid setting this gruesome precedent that Latinus now yields to Juno the "horrible functions" of releasing such antagonism into the world and into future Rome.[9] Jupiter in book 1 may dream of a time in which *impius Furor*, military madness based on impiety, is enchained behind War's iron doors. The inescapable reality of the *Aeneid*'s second half is of civil fury on the loose, and even Latinus, at the beginning of the last book, can exclaim that he took up *impia arma* when he allowed Turnus to make war against Aeneas.[10]

Virgil's use of *foede* at a center of the Danaid ekphrasis implies, then, that the action which the (unnamed) sons of Aegyptus suffered was treacherous and reprehensible (because the victims were unprepared), merciless, and ruthless (because they were defenseless) and has a particularly sinister, immoral slant, verging on an allegory of civil war, because potential wife killed potential husband and cousin killed cousin.[11] But before probing further the pertinence of the ekphrasis to the *Aeneid*'s final books I would like to turn back to Virgil's primary source, which is to say Homer, in both the *Iliad* and the *Odyssey*.

The scene of which the ekphrasis forms part is a condensed version of action spread over several hundred lines at the end of *Iliad* 16 and the beginning of the subsequent book. Before the actual clash between Pallas and Turnus, Virgil, through Jupiter's mention of Sarpedon, reminds us of the tears of blood which the king of the gods sheds for his son in anticipation of his slaying by Hector.[12] From there the parallels leap to the conclusion of the book where the lengthy dialogue between Hector and the dying Patroclus is replaced by Turnus' speech offering the body of Pallas to the Arcadians. Virgil has Turnus imitate Hector's gesture of putting his foot on the corpse.[13] We then jump to *Iliad* 17.125 where Hector strips the armor from the body (over which both sides fight in Homer) and thence to lines 186–94 where he dons the armor. This is immediately followed by a soliloquy of Zeus apostrophizing Hector, warning of his imminent death and remarking that he had seized the armor οὐ κατὰ κόσμον a phrase meaning something like "inappropriately."[14]

Zeus' words serve as spark for one of Virgil's rare moments of editorializing. Replacing the Olympian himself, the narrator speaks directly to his audience as if he were projecting the inner workings of the author's mind, his deeply felt beliefs voiced as general commentary on human action. Zeus remarks on the unseemly aspect of Hector's behavior, not because he despoiled his victim but because of the particular weaponry which he took, called by Zeus ἄμβροτα τεύχεα. In putting on the armor Patroclus had worn, Hector aims not only to become the greatest of heroes but to absorb his divine side as well. It will prove to be a fatal form of overreaching. By contrast with Homer, Virgil puts emphasis on the deed of despoliation itself and on the excess of pride such an action exhibits. And with this lack of moderation Turnus acquires not any symbolic parallelism with Pallas, such as Hector might have sought with Achilles, but rather the emblematic essence of the baldric itself. Homer tells of no decoration on the arms of Achilles which Hector wears. The details of Virgil's ekphrasis are therefore pointed when the episode is compared to its Homeric source. The narrator's words chiding Turnus, unlike Zeus' monologue, speak of arrogance followed by retribution. We are familiar with this ethical axis more from tragedy than from epic. It is therefore appropriate that Turnus be associated with a scene used in tragedy. Hector may foolishly strive to emulate the half-divine Achilles. Pallas' baldric brings to Turnus, as it had to its earlier wearer, a less obvious signification. He is now in the position of a Danaid (Virgil had given Pallas, too, before his death an *aristeia* with some ugly moments). He will soon take the more passive role of victim which is the description's primary subject.

Virgil gives Turnus a special relationship to the baldric and its art by repeating, within the space of two lines, the verb *pressit* through the participle of its compound, *impressum*. We must not leave unacknowledged the relation between Turnus' gesture of hauteur and the *nefas* inscribed on Pallas' shoulder-belt. To kill Pallas or, better, to tear his armor from him after death and presumably to put it on,[15] is parallel to the act of crafting itself, of preparing the visible insignia of a *nefas* which Turnus himself remakes. But before we probe further the meaning and effect of the ekphrasis we must turn back to Homer, this time to the *Odyssey* and to what would have been Virgil's model for the baldric itself—the only instance in classical literature before Virgil where a sword-belt is described ekphrastically. The occasion is Odysseus' meeting in the Underworld with the wraith of Hercules which comes upon him like black night, with bow stretched as if he were about to shoot (*Od.* 11.609–14):

σμερδαλέος δέ οἱ ἀμφὶ περὶ στήθεσσιν ἀορτὴρ
χρύσεος ἦν τελαμών, ἵνα θέσκελα ἔργα τέτυκτο,
ἄρκτοι τ' ἀγρότεροί τε σύες χαροποί τε λέοντες,
ὑσμῖναί τε μάχαι τε φόνοι τ' ἀνδροκτασίαι τε.
μὴ τεχνησάμενος μηδ' ἄλλο τι τεχνήσαιτο,
ὃς κεῖνον τελαμῶνα ἑῇ ἐγκάτθετο τέχνῃ.

and around his chest was a terrifying belt, a golden baldric, on which marvelous deeds were fashioned, bears and wild boars and lions with gleaming eyes, and fights and battles and killings and man-slayings. Now that he has crafted it may he never craft another, he who stored up in his craft that baldric!

The appropriateness of the baldric to Hercules is clear enough. It serves as metonymy for the hero himself, for, in Homer's punning, the belt is σμερδαλέος (609) like the λέοντες (611) which it contains. Hercules cinches himself with the battles (two types) and the killings (two forms) that typify the life of the warrior as well as with the wild animals whose characteristics a hero so often absorbs and displays as, in simile, he pursues his epic course.

In their way these two lines have as much energy as Virgil's line and a half, and we can be certain that the Latin poet, in creating them, is deliberately accepting the challenge that Homer puts into the mouth of his wandering hero. May he never create another such belt, says Odysseus at its sight, but this is exactly what Virgil, rivaling Homer, or his artist, confronting Homer's unnamed artisan, has accomplished. The changes are noteworthy. We move from an object that is dreadful and whose contents merely magnify the terror its wearer instills to something subjective, the ugliness of a crime whose allegorical association with its possessors only gradually becomes clear. We turn from a plurality of animals and generalized combats to one specific mythic moment which itself concentrates a specific number of ghastly events, a single tale of a singular night harboring a multitude of murders.

Unlike Homer, Virgil gives a name to his artisan, Clonus the son of Eurytus, and this exactitude is also a form of rivalry on Virgil's part because he takes the appellation from Homer and from the din of battle that resounds through the *Iliad*.[16] It is fitting that noise of battle be understood to engender its own emblem. But here also lies Virgil's greatest alteration to his model. What "Battle-din" creates in the *Aeneid* is not further Herculean conflicts, as obvious complement to the hero who wears the product of his artistry, but a moment from tragedy. In the person of Clonus and as one epicist rivaling another, Virgil offers here in metaphor a smaller version of one of his major accomplishments— the combination of epic with tragedy or, better, a metaphorical demonstration of the tragic dimension of all epic endeavors, especially those catalogued in the *Aeneid*. Virgil has remade Homer by means of a concentrated look at a particular tragic moment whose repetition within itself is constantly repeated as the epic's tragedy continues to unfold. Before watching this development more closely we must look at the tragedy itself.

The scene on the baldric comes from an event portrayed, or implied, in the trilogy which Aeschylus composed on the myth of the Danaids. We possess the first of the three plays, *Supplices*. Of the next two, plausibly entitled *Aegyptii* and *Danaides*, we have preserved only one assignable fragment where Aphrodite proclaims the universal power of *eros*, but their plot can be suggested in outline.[17] In the second play the women, at the instigation of their father, agreed to marriage only as a means for the treacherous murder of their grooms. Whether the second play showed the actual killings or only some preamble to them we can only conjecture. At some point, whether the incident was seen on stage or implied, Hypermestra spared her husband, Lynceus. The last play we can assume to have contained the trial of the Danaids and defense of Hypermestra. The fragment remaining of Aphrodite's speech suggests that Hypermestra's saving disobedience found acceptance and that her sisters, for all their initial repugnance, were ultimately reconciled to the idea of marriage.

In this tale of helpless victims become murderous victimizers, of hatred for and reconciliation to marriage, of the power of *eros* triumphant over *eris,* it is important to notice what Virgil has chosen to emphasize and what to suppress. The belt that the beautiful young Pallas, whose name implies both femininity and virginity, has worn into battle, that the handsome, prideful (and equally virginal) Turnus assumes after he has killed Pallas and the sight of which arouses Aeneas to kill Turnus in a furious rage at the epic's end, has depicted on it one of the most violent scenes in Greek tragedy, the treacherous mass murder of forty-nine (here) nameless husbands by their equally nameless wives inspired by a vendetta of their father against his brother or by their own hatred or by both emotions.[18] Much, even about the deed itself, is left to our imagination.

Equally vital to an understanding of the role of the ekphrasis for the denouement of the epic is what Virgil omits. The story of the Danaids is noteworthy not only for the ferocity at its center but for the two acts of supplication and sparing which frame this focal action. In the first, Pelasgus, king of Argos, receives the petitioning maidens into his custody; in the second, Hypermestra spares her husband, Lynceus (the descendants arising from the consummation of their marriage include among others Hercules himself).[19]

Thus whether the Danaids became resigned to marriage, as Aeschylus may have had it, or suffered among the damned in the Underworld the torture of carrying water in perpetually leaking vessels, as Plato and the Latin tradition generally maintained, Virgil forgoes mention of the two acts of supplication followed by what the Romans would have called manifestations of *clementia* which figure so prominently in their tale.[20]

There are two areas of exception to this regular picture of the Danaids undergoing eternal torture. The first centers on the figure of Hypermestra. We find her in *c*. 3.11 of Horace portrayed at the moment when she disobeys her father's command and saves Lynceus, anticipating in her thoughts the chains Danaus will load her down with "because in clemency I spared my poor husband" (*quod viro clemens misero peperci*).[21] She is also imagined, imprisoned and helpless, at some length by Ovid.

Before turning to the second exceptional aspect in the way the Danaids are treated in Latin poetry, we should note the anomaly in Virgil's handling of the myth in relation to his contemporaries. Among those tortured in Tartarus, as the Sibyl in the epic's sixth book describes to Aeneas this location of the most offending sinners, we find such regular denizens as Tityus and Ixion.[22] But, though the Danaids figure in such lists, as found in all his other coeval poets, they are absent from

Aeneid 6. Virgil, as we have been seeing, reserves them for a symbolic, ongoing role in the epic proper, for his development of a parallel between their lived experience and events in his epic story, not for relegation to a torture-house of the damned where they might serve as object lessons for the suitability of punishment to crime.

To have them listed in book 6, acting out the final, eternal segment of their notorious career, would detract from the immediate power of their presence behind the scene crafted on the baldric. Nor does Virgil make any mention of Hypermestra, Lynceus, and the possibilities of *clementia* which serve as moral compensating factors to the myth's central horror, though the fact that Horace explicitly and Ovid implicitly build poems around its force shows that this aspect of the myth was in the Augustan intellectual air, as an allegory for leniency toward the defeated or helpless.

Virgil leaves such construction of the myth to his fellow poets. Through the final underworld scene, where *pietas* finds fruition as son meets father, Anchises, of course, offers his own definition of *clementia* which, as we have seen, Virgil means to stay with the reader as ethical touchstone. Father addresses son as *Romane* and therefore grants him authority as standard for Roman behavior now and in the future. His son must remember to impose a custom for peace, which is to say to confirm the permanence of civil tranquillity by making its regularity a force in life. To this he adds his famous concluding demand: *parcere subiectis et debellare superbos* (to spare the subjected and war down the proud). The power of these words reverberates through the epic's second half and especially in the final battle books. Virgil may deliberately suppress any mention of the double manifestations of supplication and clemency that figure in the Danaid myth, just as Aeneas finally squelches any instinct to spare the suppliant Turnus as the epic reaches its violent conclusion. Aeneas does hesitate for a moment, but is moved to kill by sight of the belt of Pallas. As he acts, the hero assumes many roles as does his humbled antagonist, but the one most directly etched before us is of Turnus as a youth basely slaughtered and of Aeneas as a type of Danaid enforcing the vendetta of her father. Evander had, in book 11, stated to Aeneas in absentia that the hero's right hand "owed" (*debere*) Turnus to father and dead son.[23] It is the final role of the ekphrasis to make clear the archaic morality of this suggestion and its implementation. Meanwhile, the reader remembers the more reasoned, ethical demands of a different father, demands which the appearance of the baldric has helped expunge from his son's memory. Aeneas sees the baldric as metonymy for Pallas, but the reader has been made to concentrate on the meaning of its figurations as well.

The second area of exception to the general picture in the Augustan poets of the Danaids as watercarrying sinners is one which brings into play a unique aspect of this particular ekphrasis. It is the only one of the six Virgilian ekphrases that reflects an actual work of art, in this case one of the major monuments of the Augustan era. We know a great deal about the temple to Apollo that Octavian dedicated on October 9, 28 B.C.E., and archaeology is gradually clarifying more for us, especially about its intimate connection with the emperor's own *domus*. Prose sources tell us also that adjacent to the temple was a portico, but only the poets reveal in any detail what its decoration was.[24] Propertius, in a poem published within a few years of the dedication, speaks of the opening of the portico by Caesar and of its throng of women belonging to the old man Danaus set among Phoenician columns (*Poenis columnis*), which is to say made of *giallo antico*.[25] Ovid gives us a still closer look. In *Amores* 2.2 he mentions the *porticus* with its *Danai agmen*, where he saw a girl walking.[26] In *Ars Amatoria*, in one of his more blatant diminutions of Augustan aesthetic (and propagandistic) pretension, he visits the *porticus* of Livia

> quaque parare necem miseris patruelibus ausae
> Belides et stricto stat ferus ense pater.[27]

and the one where the Danaids dared to prepare death for their poor cousins and their father stands fierce with drawn sword.

This is a perfect place to go hunting for girls. Finally, in the *Tristia*, he combines Propertius' with his own characterization when he speaks of the place

> siqua peregrinis ubi sunt alterna columnis,
> Belides et stricto barbarus ense pater.[28]

where the statues alternate with columns of foreign (marble), the Danaids and their barbarous father with drawn sword.

Students of Roman art and architecture, as well as those interested in Augustan intellectual history and especially in the emperor's own ideology and its presentation in the tangible monuments of his reign, have long speculated on reasons for Augustus' choice of subject here.[29] Though there is general agreement that the portico, given its proximity to the Apollo temple, is connected with the battle of Actium and therefore with the warring it brought to an end, nevertheless two distinct schools of interpretation remain. One view, proposed by Paul Zanker, argues for the Danaids as exemplifications of sin and repentance.[30] It sees the murderous sisters as equivalent to Romans paying expiation for the guilt that nearly a century of war has brought upon them. The other interpretative approach explains the monument as suggestive of the final phase of the fighting that Actium and the deaths of Antony and Cleopatra at Alexandria a year later brought to an end.

Beyond this critics diverge. Some perceive the Danaids as emblematic of the Romans triumphing over the Egyptian queen, with Greeks standing in for Augustus and his colleagues repulsing an eastern moral and political threat.[31] This is also the core of the reading of David Quint in his fine chapter on the *Aeneid:* the Romans would have seen the portico and statuary as appropriate memorialization of revenge against foreign enemies.[32] Barbara Kellum, by contrast, sees the monument as emblematic of the evils of civil war, a constant reminder of the horrors that Romans had experienced and of what, by implication, the new regime had to put to rest in its final victory.[33]

This interpretation has much to commend it. The literary evidence, in particular that supplied by Ovid, leaves little doubt that the Danaids, led by their father, are meant to be visualized in a posture of killing, which is to say carrying out the revenge which he asks of them. But the poets are also unanimous in their condemnation of all concerned. For Ovid, Danaus is both *ferus* and *barbarus,* heady words to apply to a Roman leading his followers into action unless used in irony (something we should not disallow in Ovid).[34] As for the Danaids themselves, Horace styles them in one poem an *infame genus* and in the Hypermestra ode calls their deed a *scelus* and they themselves *impiae,* implying that their duty to marriage and to their husbands-to-be was greater than that to their father.[35] Ovid, in the *Ibis,* labels the group a *turba cruenta* while the passage from *Ars Amatoria* leaves little doubt that his sympathy lies with the victims (*miseris patruelibus*), not with the perpetrators of the crime. There is also no hint from any source of the saving presence of Hypermestra, which is to say of evidence for an emblem of *clementia* in the portico and its statuary.

The elegy of Propertius offers us two further details. The area contained a statue of Apollo playing the lyre, further reminder of the god's temple nearby and of how Apollo is leader of the Muses (and appropriate inspirer of those using the adjacent libraries) as well as god of war. Propertius also tells us of an altar around which were four statues of bulls by the sculptor Myron. The portico therefore suggested that Apollo also gains permanence, at least here, as a god of music and song, and that animal sacrifice, which is to say proper religious offerings, plays as important a role in the enclosure's total iconography as does the human victimization which is prominent in the Danaid myth. As for the Danaid statuary, whatever Augustus may have meant the viewer to experience as he or she entered the colonnade, the literary evidence sees this critical event in their myth represented by the statuary in unrelievedly bleak moral terms. The criminal vendetta they are carrying out, even at the command of a father, leaves them impious, while the father himself is behaving in a way more bestial than human, more uncivilized than enlightened.

Augustus may have meant the viewer to see the Danaids in positive terms: the Romans were defeating a foreign enemy, Augustus and his supporters pursuing a necessary civil war in order to achieve a moment of future revenge (whether it be against his father's murderers or against Antony and his consort or both) that from its horror would preclude further war and continued need for vengeance. If so, the ethical consensus of his poets is at odds with his intentions. If he means us to imagine what his poets saw, then he is indicting himself and his public image. We lack the visual evidence, which other aspects of the Danaid myth could have equally well exhibited, of the famous *clementia* of which he boasts in the *Res Gestae* and which, along with *virtus, iustitia,* and *pietas,* was engraved on his famous golden shield (*clupeus aureus*). This was awarded him by the senate and people and set up in the Curia Iulia probably in 27 B.C.E. and therefore nearly contemporaneous with the opening of the portico.[36]

Horace's ode was published four years later, in 23, and the *Aeneid* issued after Virgil's death in 19, so that their implicit criticism of what the Danaid monument said, and did not say, came soon after the opening of the portico. But there is one aspect which Virgil's ekphrasis and the Danaid statuary unquestionably share and which the poet's genius may want us deliberately to contemplate. The brevity of Virgil's line and a half, in which our mind's eye is allowed to contemplate forty-nine slaughtered youths and an equal number of bloodied marriage chambers, is parallel to what must have been the shocking briskness with which a viewer experienced the impact of the portico for the first time. This effect exemplifies what I suggested before was the goal of the ideal ekphrasis, namely to stop time. The direct linkage in this instance between verbal description and tangible artifact underscores the point and further cements the connection between poem and monument.

If the description itself nearly succeeds in achieving atemporality, the baldric and its message, as utilized by Virgil, take advantage of another means by which ekphrasis aims at suspending time, namely, repetition, which claims that any given moment in art or life, by reflecting another moment, prevents those acts of differentiation which time's progression causes. I would like to follow out this notion of repetition from two angles, one particular, the other more general. The first looks to moments where the words of the ekphrasis themselves look backward into the text. Several examples, such as certain details in Dido's preparations for the burning of her pyre[37] or our first look at the wounds of war in Latium, could be adduced where Virgil uses language similar to that which forms the ekphrasis. In the space of two lines, as the battle commences, we hear of those who have been slaughtered (*caesos*) and in particular of the "features of befouled Galaesus" (*foedati . . . ora Galaesi*) where the primary sense of *foedati,* disfigured by blood, is supplemented by the secondary meaning of "treat disgracefully." Galaesus, known for his sense of justice, had been killed while interposing himself between the initial warring factions in the search for peace.[38]

I would like to quote one instance of parallelism in somewhat greater detail. It occurs in Aeneas' presentation of Troy's fall to Dido. He advertises his presence as onlooker at the height of the horror in Priam's palace:

> ... vidi ipse furentem
> caede Neoptolemum geminosque in limine Atridas,
> vidi Hecubam centumque nurus Priamumque per aras
> sanguine foedantem quos ipse sacraverat ignis.
> quinquaginta illi thalami, spes tanta nepotum, ... [39]

I myself saw Neoptolemus raging in slaughter and the twin sons of Atreus on the threshold. I saw Hecuba and the hundred [daughters and] daughters-in-law and Priam amid the altars, befouling with blood the fires he had consecrated. Fifty were the wedding chambers, so great the hope of descendants.

We see through Aeneas' eye the murdering son of Achilles (*caede*) and his soon-to-be victim at the spot where he had been priest. (Once more *foedo* both denotes and connotes, with the stain of blood adumbrating a deeper defilement through perversion of sacrifice.) Then there are the marriage chambers (*thalami*) whose number gives an explicit reason to connect this passage with the tale of the slaughtered husbands of the Danaids. If *clementia* is an option in the Danaid myth, it does not figure in Virgil's ekphrasis any more than in his portrayal of the end of Priam, of his family, and of Troy.

The chief difference between the demise of Troy's royal house and the description on the baldric only serves to underscore their similarity. The one sets forth a series of simultaneous, instantaneous, undiscriminated events. The other leaves us to recollect a history of sadness as the children of Priam are either brutally killed or exiled while Troy comes to an end. But, of course, we do watch Priam closely, the second human sacrifice in the *Aeneid*'s chronological narrative, offering pitiful resistance as he is killed at his altars, slipping in the blood of his son Polites.[40] Before the death-blow the aged king shouts to his youthful killer, "You have befouled the features of a father with death" (*patrios foedasti funere vultus*).[41] Priam has been made to see the death of his son, but the reader thinks once again of the sons of Aegyptus, bloodied wedding-chambers, and treacherous, unsparing killings.

I quote this episode at length because it helps return our thoughts to the final books and to a different form of repetition toward which the ekphrasis points. The "history" of the *balteus* takes us from Pallas, Turnus, and Aeneas in book 10 to the same trio at the epic's end, with Pallas vicariously present in the dramatic reappearance of the baldric and in Aeneas' final words.[42] But Aeneas is playing many roles at the poem's conclusion as both the plotlines and Virgil's allusions make clear. As such he is repeating a series of past events that we know from within and without the epic. He is reincarnating Achilles killing Hector in the guise of Turnus, but Turnus is also an image of Priam before Achilles, save that the conquering hero now shows no mercy to his petitioner. More germane still, as we continue to draw out the Hector-Priam parallel, he is also Pyrrhus-Neoptolemus, killing now both father and son, first Polites, then Priam himself. Virgil's Priam, at the moment before his death, can remind Pyrrhus that (Homer's) Achilles "blushed before the rights and faith of a suppliant" (*iura fidemque/supplicis erubuit*).[43] During the epic's last scene Aeneas grants his *supplex* Turnus no quarter.[44]

The ending looks also to the reiteration of a nearer pattern of violence on Aeneas' part. Virgil, we recall, puts into Aeneas' mouth the verb *immolo* to describe how he, and Pallas vicariously, kill their victim.[45] Turnus is to be a form of human sacrifice, body for body, blood for blood. Both the verb, and the subsequent action it describes, are reiterated from book 10 where the narrator twice has recourse to *immolo* in describing the rampage Aeneas embarks upon after learning of Pallas' death. We find it first at 519 in connection with the eight human victims whose blood he will pour on Pallas' pyre. It recurs shortly thereafter in the account of the death of the duly-named priest Haemonides who is already dressed to suit his double role as sacrificer-sacrifice.[46]

These two killings, and the one which intervenes, have something in common which will help us further understand the poem's ending and the continued power of the Danaid ekphrasis throughout the last three books. Haemonides is entitled *Phoebi Triviaeque sacerdos* (priest of Apollo and Diana).[47] The only other figure in the epic so characterized is the Sibyl, likewise priest of Apollo and Diana.[48] Virgil has also carefully reminded us of Aeneas and the Sibyl as the hero prepares to kill Magus, his preceding victim, who is shown first escaping Aeneas' spear:

> et genua amplectens effatur talia supplex:
> "per patrios manis et spes surgentis Iuli
> te precor, hanc animam serves gnatoque patrique."[49]

and embracing his knees, a suppliant, he speaks thus: "Through the spirit of your father and the hope of growing Iulus I pray you, may you preserve this life for a father and a son."

The language is deliberately parallel to that which Virgil allots to Aeneas in book 6 as he turns to the Sibyl for aid. She has already specified his future posture as *supplex* as he goes searching for aid in Italy.[50] It then becomes his turn so to style himself:

> "quin, ut te supplex peterem et tua limina adirem,
> idem orans mandata dabat. gnatique patrisque,
> alma, precor, miserere . . ."[51]

"Indeed [Anchises] himself in prayer gave me orders that as a suppliant I seek you out and approach your threshold. Kindly one, I pray you, take pity on both father and son."

The reversals in fortune as well as in tone that have occurred between these two episodes, and which the parallels highlight, are astonishing. In his rage at Pallas' death Aeneas not only seizes eight human victims for gruesome sacrifice, he symbolically kills both the Sibyl, who receives and abets him as a suppliant, and himself in this very posture, praying for guidance to visit his father. He thus in book 10 twice over eliminates access to Anchises and his ennobling morality and brings to a violent, abrupt end a posture which had distinguished him until the arrival of his omnipotent weaponry in book 8. Before that he had been helpless in the face of Juno's storm and at the mercy of Dido. He had had to appeal to the Sibyl, to Latinus, and to Evander for aid. But with the advent of Vulcan's arms and especially with the killing of Pallas, everything is changed. From the first he gains power over his destiny. At the second, all thought of what it means to suffer the role of suppliant or to offer *clementia* in return seems to disappear and remain absent even to the epic's end.

We have seen how the language of the baldric connects books 2 and 12, as Aeneas' final conduct forces the reader to circle back to book 2 and to the earliest chronological events of the epic. Aeneas' Danaidic behavior at the end raises another topic which in turn serves to enforce further the notion of repetition and to complete a grander circle, namely, the human violence, associated so often by Virgil with women, which permeates the epic and its connection, finally, with Aeneas himself. For when Aeneas, after he has seen the baldric, has the memory of his *saevus dolor* rearoused and becomes "set aflame by furies and terrible in his wrath" (*furiis accensus et ira/terribilis*),[52] his conduct finds analogy not with model male figures such as his father with his ethical prescription combining force and leniency. Rather, someone *furiis accensus* is parallel to Amata and her mothers, made *furiis accensas* by Juno and her minion Fury, Allecto,[53] to Dido, in her own words *furiis incensa*,[54] and above all to Juno herself at the epic's opening, *accensa* by a very similar combination of *irae* and *saevi dolores* to that by which Aeneas is possessed at the poem's conclusion.[55]

Therefore, both in theory and in practice, in the topos of ekphrasis and in the tale it tells, the description of the baldric is in certain key senses a synecdoche for the poem as a whole. In the compressed simultaneity with which it feigns the stoppage of time, it echoes those larger poetic tools, repetition and circularity, which, as Murray Krieger has taught us, also help poetry mimic the stasis of art and which allow the poem itself, from one angle of vision, to assume the semblance of a large continuous ekphrasis. As for the tale itself, we can also see how it represents the poem as a whole.

The *Aeneid* has two distinct sides which it is Virgil's genius to have melded together. There is what we might call the historical narrative from Aeneas and Troy to Virgil's contemporary Rome. It couches in idealizing, almost impersonal terms a teleology which leads with apparent inevitability to a golden age of glorious *imperium* under Augustus, with *impius Furor* at last suppressed. And in the story line of the poem there implicitly lies ahead the marriage of Aeneas and Lavinia with all its potential for wide-ranging reconciliations. In counterpoint to this goal-directed orientation is what we might call the poem's lyric or tragic dimension. By contrast to the perfectibility which linearity suggests, it postulates a wholeness based on negative intensity. Art freezes time at a moment when victims become victimizers who do not spare. It monumentalizes vengeance and suggests that, when its narrative fully turns to the business of war and pious heroes suffer the empowerment of force, epic, at least in Virgil's hands, takes on the semblance of concentrated tragic action where *eros* and *eris* merge to tell a tale of nonmarriage and lack of *clementia*, with virgins killing virgins allegorizing a continuous circling back to uncreative fury in human destiny.

In freezing, art also frees, creating in the ending a series of ironies, and here the larger notions of the *Aeneid*'s lyric side triumph. The lyric voice enters the epic on many levels and in many ways, from the emotional rhetoric of Dido, and her past in Catullus' Ariadne, to the similes where Virgil, to describe the deaths of the androgynous young like Euryalus and Pallas, draws on flower analogies in Catullus and Sappho to imply that war devirginates by murder, not marriage. Viewing the baldric also frees Aeneas' inner, passional self, but in this liberation there are likewise a series of paradoxes. The hero who suffers Juno's violence at the epic's opening and who must regularly make prayer for aid until he receives arms and allies, is at the end in full control of his actions. But at the moment when victim becomes victimizer—and Virgil's language tells us that Aeneas in his anger is about to claim another human sacrifice—the reader must, at least for a moment, become Aeneas and debate whether the hero should or should not act. To choose the latter alternative would be to make at last the gesture of sparing, postulated by Anchises and craved by his suppliant, and bring about reconciliation and in fact a harmonious ending. He does not bring this about because he, too, is a passive victim as well, *furiis accensus,* set aflame by inner demons. This lyric voice, especially during the course of the epic's final books, strongly complements the power of ekphrasis, for it, too, aims to stop, or at least to moderate, the compelling force of temporality.

This Junonian, spiritual passivity, in the killing it engenders, takes us back into the center of the world of tragedy and of repeated, vengeful action of which the baldric, and the poem, forcefully tell. And it is with the *Aeneid* and tragedy that I would like to end. We have been schooled from the beginning of the epic to watch its events unfolding against a backdrop of dramatic presentation. As we have seen, one of the extraordinary similes of the poem finds Dido, pursued in her dreams by wild Aeneas, compared to two tragic figures:

> Eumenidum veluti demens videt agmina Pentheus
> et solem geminum et duplices se ostendere Thebas,
> aut Agamemnonius scaenis agitatus Orestes
> armatam facibus matrem et serpentibus atris
> cum fugit ultricesque sedent in limine Dirae.[56]

> as if maddened Pentheus sees the ranks of Furies and a twinned sun and a double Thebes display themselves or [as if] Orestes, Agamemnon's son, driven about the stage, when he flees his mother armed with torches and black snakes, and avenging Furies sit on the threshold.

Dido, *dux femina facti,* a woman once powerful in a man's role, is now equated with male figures we see representing heroes driven mad on the tragic stage.[57] Her fury is paradigmatic for repeated exemplifications, indeed reenactments, of victimizations by the Furies, who hold the simile in their embrace. Virgil would see no escaping from them. Orestes goes mad at the end of the *Choephori,* pursued by Furies who would avenge his mother. At the beginning of the *Eumenides* he is a suppliant, while the play itself, we recall, shows the Furies themselves evolve from vengeful to benign spirits.[58] No such progression happens in the life of Dido, *furiis incensa,* and preparing for suicide.

The same holds true at the conclusion of the epic. No third drama brings resolution or any larger sense of concord. No calming Eumenides arrive to take control of Aeneas and the poem. There is no epiphany of Aphrodite, preaching the power of *eros,* applauding the *clementia* of Hypermestra and turning her sisters toward appreciation of marriage.[59] (Turnus does cede Lavinia to Aeneas as wife in virtually the last words he speaks, but his offer has no final effect.) The only appearance—*apparuit* is Virgil's graphic word—is that of the baldric, which brings with it another uncompleted, uncompletable tragic plot, stopped yet again, like the poem itself, at a moment of violent, unforgiving action. In this respect, too, poem and ekphrasis share common ground. Ekphrasis breaks the forward thrust of epic and reminds us that, in Virgil's brilliant hands, the plot of Rome has a repetitively tragic dimension. It warns that, even as we advance idealistically toward Augustus' putative golden age, human nature doesn't change.[60]

Conclusion

This has been in no sense a theoretical book either about the phenomenon of ekphrasis or about the history of description, whether of real or imagined art. Rather, it consists of six separate but congruent acts of practical criticism based on the close reading of individual texts. In all instances we have been probing the words of poetry, their intention and deployment. But since the subject has been ekphrasis, that is, words used (in five of my *exempla*) to portray visual art, by the very nature of the undertaking we have been examining two types of narration in studied intersection, namely, the verbal depiction of artifacts and the epic mode in which such depictions are incorporated. But my analyses may prove useful at a moment in criticism where ekphrasis, as a discursive genre, has become a major subject of scholarly discussion. In recent years critics of literature have turned with renewed interest to the problematical relation of text and art or, specifically in the case of the present volume, of the interplay of images and literature where the descriptions of visual signs are a forceful part of the larger verbal enterprise in which they are included.

Nevertheless, though theoretical explanation of ekphrasis has not been my goal, we can draw some more general conclusions from analysis of Virgil's ekphrases. Ekphrasis is an encapsulation of visualized art wherein a verbal medium strives both to delineate a spatial object and, even while beholden to narrative's temporality, miraculously to capture the instantaneity of a viewer's perception. The focus of scrutiny may be one object in and of itself or a series of scenes which together compose a work of art. All Virgil's examples of notional ekphrasis, exemplifying written art that is itself thoroughly artful, help us contemplate, which is to say also to comprehend, the larger poem for which they stand as synecdoches. We pause as we become visionaries before art's stillness, but that pause, to exercise mentally our capacity for imagined viewing, is critical for the insight it offers us as we prepare to immerse ourselves once again in the yet more time-ridden events of epic.

Ekphrasis, in Virgil's hands, has much in common with simile. Both topoi on the surface appear as mere embellishments to adorn a text and entertain the reader, apparent diversions from the onrush of epic action. But both, in fact, as critics have come more and more to appreciate, are types of metaphor, offering us opportunities to reinterpret the text in which they are embedded, to gain a new angle for the apprehension of its meaning. Both devices are products of rhetorical artifice. But there is a multidimensional aspect to Virgilian ekphrasis which simile lacks. Simile helps us explicate an immediate moment by discovering a resemblance elsewhere. The very physicality of an object or objects delineated through ekphrasis suggests that it not only elucidates the particular circumstances for which it serves as intellectual enhancement but that it reflects the matter of the poem itself. The "materiality" of ekphrasis reclarifies, in a variety of ways, the substantiality of the poem that harbors it. The artistry that expresses itself in the writing of ekphrasis is also the artistry of its parent text, a virtuosity which finds a further, final parallel in its presentation through the palpability of a crafted book itself.

Ekphrasis of works of art, in Virgil's hands, also more often than not implies a multiplicity of interpretive perspectives. We find ourselves taking note, regularly in combinations of two or more which may also overlap, of the reactions of the creator of the artifact in question and of its commissioner, of its donor, receiver(s), and other viewers who form its "audience" within the text, an audience which, in one instance, is also a character in the ekphrastic tale. And at both ends of this spectrum there are the poet, maker of the descriptive text as well as its context, and we appraisers of ekphrasis, among whom we must in turn imagine the range of critical viewer-readers from the moment of the poem's appearance in the dozen years that followed upon the victory at Actium to the end of the twentieth century. The very variety of such responders, and therefore responses, to Virgil's ekphrases suggests an important consideration for his interpreters. Just as there is no possibility of a fixed, exclusive, all-comprehensive exposition of a work of art through ekphrasis, so we must not expect to retrieve any incontrovertible, secure interpretation of the host poem. Such symbolic richness, of which ekphrasis is capable, is especially relevant for a poem as dynamic as the *Aeneid.* Its ekphrases are as delimited, prejudiced, unstable, provocative, brilliant, and open to a varied spread of interpretation as the master poem itself. Just as a poet's mimetic language is never fully qualified to "narrate" a work of art, so no single critical perspective could, or should, be capable of evaluating the prismatic coruscations of meaning which a poem like the *Aeneid* as a whole projects. The very complexity of its ekphrases and their reverberations argues strongly against any reductive or tendentious reading of the epic itself.

Virgilian ekphrases, by and large, mimic the total poem in another paradoxical manner. Like the *Aeneid* itself, its ekphrases are both static and in motion. We read them for their circular structure and for the wholeness of their designs, yet we also sense their open-endedness. The mere linear act of reading ekphrasis urges us to accept the poem itself in a similar fashion. At the end of Virgilian ekphrasis we are regularly left hanging, in anticipation of a resolving finale which never comes— Ganymede in heaven, a father finally "crafting" his son, Io turned back to human shape, Hypermestra forgiven and betrothed. So at the end of the poem our expectations of artistic and narrative unity find few satisfactions. There are no acts of forgiveness, no renunciations of violence. In reactivating Juno's language from the opening of the epic to characterize Aeneas' deeds at the poem's end, Virgil both leaves us hanging, in respect to what might but does not happen, and brings us full circle back to where he and we started. For this procedure the best analogy lies in the poem's most extensive ekphrasis, the description of the round shield of Aeneas that contains all of Roman history of which we are shown a series of vignettes.

The shield, as we have seen, ends with the indignation of the river Araxes just as the poem concludes with the indignation of Turnus' soul. In comparing the two, the mind of the thoughtful reader posits not future reconciliations but continued acts of revenge and reprisal. Yet the poem itself does come to an end as does the ekphrasis, and as the final

CONCLUSION

verses bring a halt to linearity so they also retroject us back where we started. Just as history and poetry both change and repeat themselves, so history and ekphrasis likewise partake both in the linear and the circular, the time-driven and the time-controlled. The *Aeneid*, in this view, is itself one grand ekphrasis, one grand monumental artifact simulating the smaller verbal artifacts which it contains. I will return to this point in a moment.

We might note also the relationship of Virgilian ekphrases to the contemporary world of Augustan Rome. A compatriot of Virgil would no doubt have asked what connections should be made between Daedalus' sculptures on his temple of Apollo, detailed in Virgil's ekphrasis, and the sculptured doors on Augustus' Apollo temple on the Palatine, dedicated in 28 B.C.E. He would have also sought for plausible linkage with, and distinction between, the *clupeus aureus*, given to Augustus in 27 B.C.E. by the senate and people of Rome, and Virgil's shield of Aeneas. But the last ekphrasis of the poem, depicting the sword-belt of Pallas which contains the Danaid murders, deliberately parallels an Augustan monument that Virgil's coeval readers could easily have seen: the statues of the daughters of Danaus interspersed throughout the portico adjacent to the Palatine temple. The sight of some forty-nine women in the process of slaughtering their husbands must have been overwhelming and, in particular, must have urged its onlookers to contemplate visually the conflict between vengeance and clemency with which Virgil concludes his epic, as Aeneas kills after catching sight of the baldric.

We, too, in each case ponder the power of images, whether verbal or visual or visual engineered by verbal, to shape the imaginations of reader-viewers. Ekphrasis in this instance forces us to examine the differences and similarities between the viewing of an image or images in a public, highly politicized setting that is both culturally and religiously charged and surveying the same images through the mind's eye in Virgil's own complex intellectual setting. The meaning of the Danaid statuary as part of Augustan visual propaganda will be a continuing subject of debate, as will Virgil's representation of the same "artistry" and, equally, the affiliation between the two. Nevertheless, Virgil's readers, here especially in the *Aeneid*, are left to ponder in what ways the description, however brief, of a work of art resonates both within and without the poem, as he deliberately demands of us the contemplation of significant intellectual aspects of the social world in which both the *Aeneid* and the tangible monuments of the emperor's choice were produced. Virgil's context studiously complements, and challenges, that of Augustus.

In the present climate of criticism, studies of ekphrasis find a particularly appropriate place. Not only is it a powerful figure in and of itself but it also is especially worthy of attention at a time when the destabilization of meaning in literature and art is a subject of scholarly debate. Ekphrasis should find itself easily at the center of such discussion, first, because it pits together two modes of narrativity that bring with them a concomitant, still broader diversity of focalization, and second, because its presence posits the challenging interplay of art and text, of art in texts and of texts about art that are themselves artful. It asks us to ponder how verbal signs create visual ones and how poets both complicate and reveal the meanings of their texts by their incorporations of art.

It is apt, too, that a mode of discourse that helps open out a given text to a variety of interpretations should be a particular focus of study for the *Aeneid* at this time. For the earlier part of the twentieth century, the interpretation of the epic put forward by Richard Heinze in *Virgils epische Technik* held sway, namely, that the poem's essential purpose was the glorification of Augustan Rome. His view was sustained and modified in the equally influential work of Viktor Pöschl, *Die Dichtkunst Virgils*. Though he acknowledges the presence of evil in Virgil's world, Pöschl's interpretation finds in Aeneas the prefiguration of "the Christian hero, whose heart remains gentle through struggle and sorrow and beats in secret sympathy with all suffering creatures."[1] This interpretation is in essence echoed in the important volume by Brooks Otis, who stresses the poem's *humanitas* and "the quite clear-cut victory of the 'good' over the 'bad' cause."[2]

By contrast, the last chapter of my *Poetry of the Aeneid* examined the moral complexities of the poem's ending. In particular I looked at how they are fomented by actions of Aeneas himself who, as he prepares to perform his final deed, is "set aflame by furies and terrifying in his anger" (*furiis accensus et ira/terribilis*), thereby apparently embodying the very characteristics that his immortal enemy Juno had exerted against him from the initial episode of the epic. The bleak tonality adumbrated in my essay was powerfully plumbed a decade later by W. R. Johnson in *Darkness Visible*.

The present volume follows in this pattern. My appraisal of Virgil's ekphrases finds much in them that, in varying degrees whether we are dealing with manner or content, echoes both the epic's unfulfillments and the constancy of violence and resentment as a pervasive element of Virgil's poetic scheme—all in a poem that is, in fact, brilliantly cohesive and conclusive. The paradox is at the core of the poem and, finally, of criticism about it. Like the ekphrases that it contains, the *Aeneid* is a capacious masterpiece, open to a variety of interpretations, a combination of which seems to do it most justice. It is a poem whose idealistic visions of a golden future for Rome under Augustus, and therefore for humankind under any fostering dispensation, are constantly tempered by the reality of a narrative which charts its titular hero's progress from passive to active, from sufferer of his destiny to its emotional implementer.

The very human anger that Aeneas exhibits at the poem's conclusion contrasts crucially with the *clementia* urged on him by his father. But it is the friction between the two, an interaction that could not exist without the complementary presence of both vantages, that at the present moment in Virgilian criticism seems to give the *Aeneid* its special power. Virgil asks us to measure carefully both perspectives and, if my own reading of the epic inclines toward giving primacy to Virgil's view of the emotionality that pervades his universe and to its intellectual complement in the incompletions of his art that smack more of tragedy than of epic, I can espouse this interpretative stance only because the poet's richness of mind gives his readers the chance to study it in a context that also sees the possibility for humanity, and the potential for poetry, to bring order and redemption in the political sphere which could then likewise become the fit subjects for art's wholeness.

In this regard the ekphrasis describing the shield of Aeneas has perhaps the most to tell us about the poem as a whole. This is true not so much for its size as for its "narrative" history, or histories, of Rome. The *Aeneid* in its plot may offer an expansive view of a single major moment in the legendary prehistory of Rome's foundation, while the shield ekphrasis casts into sharp, brisk relief singular events or personages in that history itself. Each in certain important aspects serves to analogize the other. We see Aeneas in terms of Actian and post-Actian Augustus, which means that we see both the glory that accrues to each, as Philip Hardie has eloquently shown,[3] but also the violence that goes into shaping that accomplishment and the sadness and finally the resentment that, at the end, seems to permeate the reaction of her subjects to Rome.

The multiple perspectives that we bring to the ekphrasis complement the complex reactions which the poem itself arouses. We, the receivers of Virgil's *non enarrabile textum,* have something in common with Vulcan and Aeneas, seduced into our own idiosyncratic acts of contemplation and re-creation. We may have parallels to the maker of the shield, who knows all, to its recipient, who is "ignorant of its matter," to the "you" within the ekphrasis, perusing now a work of art, now a scene within that art that comes magically alive before our eyes so that we are "there." We may attempt to apprehend both ekphrasis and poem with the eyes and ears of a Roman of the first century B.C.E. or with the perspectives and prejudices allotted to us at the end of the second millennium C.E. Whatever our angle of vision, just as, for Virgil at least, ekphrasis is a crucial figure in aiding us to interpret his art, so the poet's brilliant descriptions of art may serve as guides for readers of other texts where, as for the Roman master, ekphrasis stands as multifaceted metaphor for the work it challenges us to understand.

Notes

In addition to standard abbreviations for classical works, the following abbreviations are used in the notes.

LIMC	*Lexicon Iconographicum Mythologiae Classicae* (Zurich, 1981–)
OLD	*Oxford Latin Dictionary* (Oxford, 1968–82).
Platner-Ashby	Ashby, T., and J. Platner, *A Topographical Dictionary of Ancient Rome* (Rome, 1965).
RE	*Real-Encyclopädie der classichen Altertumswissenschaft*, ed. A. Pauly, G. Wissowa, and W. Kroll (Stuttgart, 1893–).
RG	*Res Gestae Divi Augusti*, ed. P. Brunt and J. Moore (Oxford, 1967).
Richardson	Richardson, L., Jr., *A New Topographical Dictionary of Ancient Rome* (Baltimore, 1992).

Introduction

1. I adopt the term *ekphrasis* more out of convenience, and because it is standard in commentaries, than out of any certainty that Virgil would have approved, or perhaps even known, of its use, which only became fully established as a rhetorical designation during the Second Sophistic. Though it occurs twice in the works of Virgil's contemporary Dionysius of Halicarnassus (*De Imitatione* fr. 6.3.2 and *Ars Rhetorica* 10.17), it is not in common usage until the second century C.E. The late Republican writers on rhetoric would have used the words *descriptio*, *evidentia*, or the borrowed *enargeia* to describe the phenomenon of bringing before the mind's eye a variety of objects, the most common of which are people, places, animals, and, most usually, artifacts.

The authoritative analysis of ekphrasis is by Friedländer (1912), 1–103. The most recent general discussions of its meaning and usage are by Krieger, Heffernan (1993), and Hollander (1995). I am indebted to each. D. Fowler (1991) offers an extensive listing of treatments of the topos in ancient (25, n. 1) and modern (25, n. 2) literature, which the bibliography of the present volume supplements (I would call attention in

particular to the discussions by Alpers, Baxandall, Becker, Cage and Rosenfeld, Hollander [1988], and Onians). Besides Fowler's, I have found especially useful the treatments of Bartsch (7–13, with notes), Lausberg (399–407), Vasaly (20, 90–91), and G. Zanker ([1981], 297–311).
  2. Hollander (1988), 209–19, and (1995), 4.
  3. Krieger, especially 1–28.
  4. Heffernan (1993), 46–47, 108–12, on ekphrasis and gender. He deals primarily with Virgil's use of ekphrasis at 23–36.
  5. Heffernan (1993), 69.
  6. *Aen.* 8.611; *ecl.* 3.66.
  7. 4.471–73.
  8. 10.272–75.
  9. 12.946–47.
  10. Cat. 64.115; *Aen.* 6.27.
  11. Cat. 64.113; *Aen.* 6.30. *Caeca vestigia* also intimate the "blind steps" that Theseus must take as he embarks on his adventure.
  12. On this point see Laird (1993), 18–30.
  13. Ancient citations to both temple and portico are collected in Platner-Ashby s.v. "Apollo Palatinus."
  14. *C.* 3.11.
  15. Cf. Augustus' *RG* 34.2. On the Curia Julia see Platner-Ashby and Richardson s.v. The importance of the golden *clupeus* for Augustan iconography is discussed by P. Zanker (1987), 97–102 and 341, trans. (1988), 92–97 and 350.
  16. 7.789–92.
  17. 9.730–33.
  18. 7.371–72, and cf. 409–10.
  19. 7.286–87.
  20. 7.291.
  21. The genealogy is as follows: Io, Epaphus, Libya, Belus, Danaus.
  22. Moschus 2.43–62.

Chapter 1. Dido's Murals

  1. Out of the lengthy bibliography on the ekphrasis I have found the following particularly helpful: Williams (1960); Johnson, 99–105; Dubois, 32–35; Clay (1988); Leach (1988), especially 311–19; Fowler (1991); Lowenstam, 37–49; Barchiesi (1994).
  2. On this point see Barchiesi (1994), 116. The very anonymity of the effort is striking, especially by contrast to the prominence of Daedalus and Vulcan as creators in the poem's other two ekphrases of some length, as is the plurality of artisans mutually involved (*inter se*). Both notions may underscore the roles of Dido as guiding spirit behind the artistic re-creation of Troy and of Aeneas as empathetic respondent to this endeavor.

3. On aspects of the difference between how Aeneas reads and how we read, see Leach, 311, and the critiques of Fowler (especially 23 on the problematics of focalization) and Barchiesi (115, 119 and 120, n. 21). We take note of Aeneas seeing, but we as readers are manipulated by words to perceive very different things, to "read" quite dissimilarly. This in no way invalidates Aeneas' response or our appreciation of the *dolor* which the scenes bring to him. We are meant to study Aeneas' reaction to what he sees and use it as a touchstone for any further interpretation of the representations. But readers have the luxury of time and knowledge of the epic's plot, a situation impossible for an actor in the text, which allows us the opportunity to probe still further levels of meaning.

4. Cf. Barchiesi, 120–22, for the ominous presence of Juno and its implications for future Roman involvement with Carthage. Horsfall (1973–74) speaks of the "greed and brutality" (138) which the Carthaginians might find congenial in the story of the conquering Greeks.

5. To trace the ambiguities in this setting in the light of its Homeric background is a major purpose of Clay's important essay.

6. On the meaning of the phrase *pictura inani*, see Arkins, 42. The irony of *inani* must be directed at both Dido and Aeneas. For the Trojan hero, the murals could be styled empty because they elicit only an immediate emotional response and remain devoid of deeper implications. It could be taken as a warning of Virgil's greater expectations of the reader that, for Aeneas, art reproduces the past without any emblematic, ongoing experiential value.

7. Barchiesi (118) observes that the miniaturizing effect of the scenes is Virgil's way of controlling Homer and the Greek poetic past. The poet could also be said, through the dynamism of ekphrasis, to intensify the past, giving it the force of a brilliant series of nuclei that exert their power over present and future as well.

The very fact that the episodes are nonchronological and that the reader must search for "nonhistorical" connecting strands among the episodes abets the atemporal ambition of ekphrasis. Though we are presented with a chain of discrete events, the reader is constantly expected to think backward as well as forward in order fully to appreciate Virgil's intellectual design. The act of reading itself encourages the rhetorical stasis to which ekphrasis aspires.

8. Selden, 486 (with notes).

9. On this point see Williams, 151, and Heffernan, 1993, 27–28 and 199, n. 40.

The parallelism and balance between *agnoscit lacrimans* and *avertit* encourages the reader for a moment to see Aeneas, as well as Diomedes, as the subject of the latter verb, as if he had a part in turning the horses aside, i.e. in causing the demise of Troy. Because the verb anticipates the posture of Athena, eyes turned aside (*aversa*, 482) from Trojan supplication, we may be briefly meant to sense Aeneas' failure to see the causes of tragedy or his part in the initiation of his city's collapse. (The connection is furthered by the link between *animum . . . pascit* [464], of Aeneas, and *pabula gustassent* [473], of the horses of Rhesus, between the fostering of the mind that comes from aesthetic attention and the literal eating that nearly occurs for figures within the object of that attention.)

10. See the eloquent pages of Heffernan (27–28) on the dragging of Troilus' spear as a metaphor for a type of writing symptomatic of the near-eradication of the line separating image and word.

11. On the effective appearance of the word *peplos*, art within art, as the ekphrasis begins its second half, see R. Thomas, 181. The "infelicità" of the *peplos* as a gift is discussed by Barchiesi, 123.

As in the case of Aeneas and *avertit* (see above, n. 9), Athena's averting her eyes from a work of plastic art is preparation for the enactment of tragedy.

12. The point is made by Williams (1960), 151.

13. Penthesilea *furens* also anticipates the varieties of *furor* which will soon overtake the Carthaginian queen (cf., e.g., at 4.65, 69, 101, 283, 376, 433, 465, 474, 501, 548, 697). For further parallels between Dido and Penthesilea see Segal (1990), 3–7.

14. The connection is made by Lowenstam, 43–44, who also remarks on the linkage with Camilla and of the latter's death with that of Turnus.

15. For Achilles' domination of the ekphrasis see Clay, 204–5. Anderson (in particular 24–30) was the first to draw out the analogy between Aeneas and Achilles at any length. See also Boyle, 96–101. On the figure of Achilles in the epic as a whole see King, 31–57.

16. Pl. *Bac.* 953–55. The Palladium and the wooden horse are linked together in Turnus' speech at *Aen.* 9.150–52.

17. On the interconnection of Troilus, Rhesus, and Troy's fate, see Austin (1971), on 1.474.

18. Williams (1960), 149, n. 2, allows for the possibility "that a mental association can here be made with the loss of the *Palladium.*"

19. In fact, Virgil constructs the first half of book 2 around the figure of the horse. We reach the book's midpoint at the moment when the Greeks (briefly) seek shelter back within its belly (400–401).

20. 1.673, 717, 719.

21. 4.77–79. The clear echo in line 79 (*pendet . . . iterum narrantis ab ore*) of *De Rerum Natura* 1.37 (*eque tuo pendet resupini spiritus ore*) urges the parallelism of love-sick Dido with Mars, lulled by the repeated words of Aeneas-Venus. The symbolism, with Dido's loss of masculine heroism occurring at the hands of an Aeneas who is at the mercy of the machinations of Venus and Cupid, forms part of Virgil's strategy, as he links the mural ekphrasis with what follows. Virgil pointedly repeats the verb *pendeo* at 4.88 (*pendent opera interrupta*). Dido's "hanging" on Aeneas' words causes the building of her city to come to a standstill. The metamorphosis of heroic queen into elegiac lover means the halt of Carthaginian civilization. Such a moment characterizes Virgil's great conjuring trick in the *Aeneid:* to write a poem allegorizing a teleology of Roman greatness climaxing with Augustus that is also about the triumph of

nature over culture, of paradigm over syntagm (whether we are dealing with rhetoric or with human behavior).

22. Note also the echo of *audire laborem* (2.11) in *audire labores* (4.78). Repetition of narration means repetition of the content of narration. The future is absent in Dido's world. The doom of Troy portends her own demise. In the case of the murals, Dido in her artistry and Aeneas in his response cannot grasp what the poet's ekphrasis proposes to the reader. The same holds true for the effect of Aeneas' storytelling, the tragic consequences of which neither teller nor hearer—only reader—can comprehend.

23. 4.669–71.

24. On the gendering of ekphrasis, and in particular on the word-image antagonism, see the trenchant discussions by Heffernan, 6–7, 46–47 (on Ovid's Philomela), 108–112 (on the Grecian urn of Keats).

25. The point is elaborated by Barchiesi, 122–24.

26. On this echo see Putnam (1995), 223–24.

27. 6.469–71.

28. 4.366–67.

29. 4.143–49. The simile balances Dido's comparison to Diana (1.498–502) and is modeled in part on *Il.* 1.43–45 where Apollo arrives as the god of disease and death for the Greeks.

30. *Demisit lacrimas,* 455; *lacrimas ciebat,* 468; *prosequitur lacrimis,* 476.

31. On the relation of the scenes on the murals with events in the last books of the epic, see Knauer, 103–4; Clay, 203–5; Lowenstam, 37–49. On the possibility of such recollection, Barchiesi, 115, n. 11, comments: "Mi sembra però riduttivo legere il testo come un enigma che viene gradatamente risolto dallo sviluppo della sua trama." But if we find the ekphrasis effectually operative in its own surrounding context, then its echoes in more distant books will not seem so incongruous. The Trojan war repeats itself again, with the difference that in the final books the Trojans in part become Greeks and the analogy of Hector-Aeneas with Achilles is strengthened. The relation of the ekphrasis to the conclusion of the epic suggests that recapitulation and reperformance are essential to Virgil's view of human nature, on the deepest psychological level.

32. 12.930–31, 936–37.

33. 7.321 (Paris), 363 (*Phrygius praedo*). The passage in book 11 is, of course, based in part on *Il.* 6.297–311, where the Iliades pray for help against the Greeks led by Diomedes.

34. Virgil may also be thinking of Phemius (*Od.* 1.326–27), as he sings to the wooers of the "sad return of the Achaeans" and Penelope weeps, but the general framework of *Odyssey* 8–9 is much closer to *Aeneid* 1 and what follows.

35. On the dispute in question see Nagy, 21–25.

36. On Odysseus' responses to the songs of Demodocus, see Pucci (1987), 221, and Segal (1994), 24–26, 32, 99, and especially 118–20.

37. On the phrase *sunt lacrimae rerum* with bibliography on the history of interpretation, see Lyne (1987), 209–10.
38. Macr. *Sat.* 7.1.14, Servius *ad* 1.742, both quoted by Austin (1971) on 1.742.
39. Tib. 2.4.17–18.
40. Prop. 3.5.25. Lines 26–38 list various topics for the speaker's future study in the natural sciences.
41. On the notion of cosmic order and the "ironic tension" which develops between the song and its setting, as well as for an insightful interpretation of the song as a whole, see Segal (1971), 344. The notion that Iopas' song marks the point at which Dido changes from hospitable queen to erotic lover is perceptively developed by Brown.
42. Virgil's other major source for Iopas' song is the cosmogony that Orpheus chants to calm the strife among the Argonauts, at A. R. *Arg.* 1.496–511.
43. 1.755–56.
44. 1.460, 597 (Trojan *labores*), 1.628 (Dido and the Carthaginians). On the possible connection between Iopas and the realities of recent Trojan and Carthaginian history, see Segal (1971), 337 (referring to Pöschl [1962], 151–54, and Quinn, 108 and 345).
45. 2.11; 4.78.
46. The transition from the material of Iopas' song to the narrative of Aeneas in books 2 and 3 is echoed in Pallas' request to Aeneas at 10.161–62: *quaerit sidera, opacae/noctis iter, iam quae passus terraque marique*" (he asks of the stars, of the path of the dark night, now of what he had endured on land and on sea).
47. It is no accident that the mixing of gifts (*dona*) and guile (*doli*) that figures in the main narrative of book 1, as the duping of Dido proceeds apace, is absorbed by Aeneas as he takes up the tale of the deceit surrounding the story of Sinon and the offering of the wooden horse. His tale fosters his own continuing deception of the Carthaginian queen.

Segal (1994), 118, shows how the second song of Demodocus is related to the *Odyssey* as a whole, both being tales of revenge by the wily underdog for real or potential adultery. This insight is applicable to the relation between Iopas' song in the *Aeneid* and its larger context, where it forms an essential part of the seduction of the queen away from loyalty to her dead husband (and to her newly founded city) into more treacherous hands.

48. For discussion of the ancient criticism of this simile see Austin (1971), on 1.498.
49. *Od.* 11.375. Among the gifts that Aeneas offers Dido are a dress and veil that Helen wore when she sought *inconcessos hymenaeos* in Troy (1.651). In accepting the gift Dido becomes Helen, with all the potential for tragedy that such a gesture implies. But the giver, Aeneas, is also a type of Helen, male for a moment changed to female seductress, luring Dido to become unfaithful to the memory of Sychaeus, just as Helen had abandoned Menelaus.

NOTES TO PAGES 54–61

50. The ending of the poem, where ekphrasis is also involved vicariously, tells a carefully reversed tale, as we will see. Aeneas hesitates as he observes the suppliant Turnus and withholds action. On seeing the baldric of Pallas, which the reader knows from the brief ekphrasis at 10.497–98 has engraved on it the murder of the sons of Aegyptus by the Danaids on their wedding night, he kills.

Chapter 2. The Cloak of Cloanthus

1. The standard discussions of the figure of Ganymede are by Drexler, Friedländer (1910; 737–42 deal with Ganymede in literature), and Sichtermann, who also has a detailed discussion of depictions of Ganymede in art in *LIMC* 4.1.154–69. Two recent treatments of particular *exempla* are by Gazda and Clarke.

For Ganymede in the pederastic contexts of Martial see Richlin 40, 136, and 159. Discussions of later developments in the treatment of Ganymede in western literature may be found in Boswell (ch. 9), Saslow, and Barkan (1991).

2. It is, of course, possible that the ekphrasis proper ends with the phrase *anhelanti similis* and that the subsequent three and a half verses are a resumption of the story line proper, where the narrator offers continuing details and commentary on the weaving. If this is the case, it further tightens the connection of Virgil himself with both the content of the ekphrasis and its contexts, both limited and expansive.

3. Cf. the similes at 9.563–64, where Turnus, tearing Lycus from the Trojan ramparts, is compared to an eagle snatching up a hare or swan (the words *pedibus Iovis armiger armis* are common to 5.255 and 9.564) and 11.751–56 where Tarchon, grabbing Venulus from his horse, is likened to an eagle bearing a serpent aloft.

4. On the importance of circularity to ekphrasis see Krieger, ch. 7 and in particular 220–28. I need not emphasize further how the wholeness which this circular construction intimates contrasts with the fragmentation, alienation, and desolation which defines the contents it encloses.

5. *Il.* 20.232–35. Cf. also *Il.* 5.265–69 for mention of the horses which Zeus gave to Tros in recompense for the boy's loss.

6. Pliny gives the following description of a statue by Leochares: "Leochares [fecit] aquilam sentientem, quid rapiat in Ganymede et cui ferat, parcentemque unguibus etiam per vestem puero" (*H.N.* 34.79).

7. *Arg.* 3.114–27. For the deliberateness of Apollonius' alterations to Homer see Feeney, 66.

8. *M.* 10.155–61.

9. Ida is mentioned at 30 as well as 52 and 70.

10. Likewise, the richly interwoven word order of line 251, the end of the frame, is echoed in the equally complex enmeshings of line 252, which initiates the ekphrasis proper. In the first the initial four words are noun, noun, adjective, adjective (AABB), though the grammar is built on chiasmus (with the order noun A, noun B, adjective B, adjective A) and the sound patterns on alternation (ABAB). In the

second, adjacent line the last four words are noun, adjective, adjective, noun (ABBA), though their grammar conjoins them as ABAB.
11. I quote from H. A. Shapiro, 271–72.
12. *Il.* 3.125–28.
13. *Il.* 22.440–41.
14. The chlamys is associated with six figures in the course of the epic, because it is either worn or received as a gift. The only woman is Dido (4.137), preparing for the hunt (as a man would?). The others are Iulus (3.484, a gift from Andromache), Evander (8.167, a gift from Anchises), Pallas (8.588), the unnamed son of Arcens (9.582), and the priest Chloreus (11.775). We thus have a woman about to depart on an adventure that will lead to her death, three pubescent youths (the father of one of whom will soon lose his son in battle while one other is the son himself), and two warriors (connected verbally: with 9.582 cf. 11.772), one of whom is about to die, the other to become the cynosure of Camilla but who in fact proves her undoing. The garb as associated with the latter two seems to imply effeminacy. Camilla, who also appears to be wearing a purple cloak as she prepares for battle (7.814–15), is drawn to Chloreus' garb *femineo praedae et spoliorum . . . amore* (11.782). Remulus' rebuke to the Trojans about their clothing at 9.614, following closely on the description of the *filius Arcentis—vobis picta croco et fulgenti murice vestis* (you have clothing embroidered with yellow and gleaming crimson)—further suggests something unmanly about a chlamys. Iulus, though he is not killed, is stopped from killing by Apollo and therefore from making the full transition from adolescence to manhood. The evidence therefore points to the appropriateness of the rape of Ganymede to a chlamys, of scene to setting, context to *puer intextus*, craft to meaning. All figures are (or were, in the case of the young Anchises) observed as they, or those associated closely with them, undergo a crucial moment of change which is always ominous and in three instances betokens death.

The only other preserved mention of a *chlamys aurata* in classical literature is at Tac. *Ann.* 12.56 where Agrippina wears one at a naumachia presented by Claudius (cf. also Pliny *N.H.* 32.63).
15. Cf. Putnam (1965), 93, and Hardie (1993), 32–33.
16. I owe this connection between Attis and Atys to Raymond Marks.
17. The fact that Iulus-Ascanius is called *regius puer* at 1.677–78, the same designation that Ganymede receives at 5.252, is not accidental.
18. *Geo.* 4.498.
19. Cf. also 2.153, 688; 5.686; 6.685; 9.16; 10.845.
20. 12.930–31, 936–37.
21. 12.919, 922–23.
22. *Geo.* 4.499–500.
23. 2.791. Cf. 4.278, 9.658, 5.740, 12.592.
24. 12.948–49.
25. Lyne (1987), one of our finest Virgilians, defends Aeneas' action on the

grounds that the hero must "avenge dishonour" because Turnus has been "the slayer and dishonoror of Pallas" (220). But in the editorial comment following on the death of Pallas (10.501–502), the narrator, speaking in his own voice, takes Turnus to task not for what he did to Pallas but for lack of *moderatio* in the doing. Mezentius says shortly later that "there is no crime in killing" (*nullum in caede nefas,* 10.901), and we have no reason to disbelieve him, given the abundant slaughter perpetrated by both sides in the final three books of the poem. We contemplate Turnus' *superbia* more than once as book 10 progresses (he is called *superbe* directly by the narrator at 514, soon after the editorial intervention), but at the end we are made to see Aeneas thinking, impassionately, of his reactions to Pallas' death—not dispassionately, of the failings and now supplicatory posture of Turnus—as he angrily kills.

26. 1.191.
27. 4.71.
28. The first is at 2.355–58 where Aeneas and his fellow Trojans are compared to *lupi* driven by rage against the Greeks. The balance between epic's start and conclusion is clear enough. The second is at 12.715–22 where Aeneas and Turnus are equated with bulls.
29. 1.92; 12.951.
30. *Sat.* 5.16.10–11.
31. 7.55; 8.589–91.
32. Nor need we seek far to find reasons why the muse Erato (7.37) and the various forms of *eros* which she brings with her serve as instigators of the poet's memory in the epic's second half.

Chapter 3. Daedalus' Sculptures

1. The most recent discussions of the Daedalus episode are by Pöschl (1975), who sees it as exemplifying the failure of art when the artist confronts the truth of his suffering, Weber, for whom the sequence serves as model for a miniature epyllion, and Fitzgerald. Fitzgerald's important essay views the two major segments of the tale as illustrating the change from "a finished work of art" to "the narrative of Daedalus, unfrozen and released into history" (54). In his earlier discussion (1950, 244–46 translated as 1962, 149–50), Pöschl draws analogies between Aeneas and Daedalus. Both are exiles, both offer pity at crucial moments (Daedalus for Ariadne, Aeneas for Dido), and both exemplify *pietas* (Daedalus' love for Icarus is parallel, according to Pöschl, to Aeneas' yearning for Anchises with whom he is soon to be reunited). See also Weber, 40, n. 33.

Such analogies are further developed by Segal (1965, especially 642–45) in his sympathetic analysis of these lines. For Segal, Daedalus "foreshadows the sufferings of the individual in the *mythical,* not the historical world, sufferings which lead to no lasting fruition in history, hence no transcendence of death."

The legend of Daedalus has been treated in depth by Frontisi-Ducroux and by

Koerner, who draws analogies between Daedalus and the modern mind dealing with its labyrinthine past while being drawn toward self-sufficient flights into the ahistorical and the novel. Cf. also the remarks on Daedalus as typifying "the artist as magician" by Kris and Kurz, 66–71.

2. 6.851–53.

3. The authoritative discussion of the phrase *ut fama est* is by Norden ad loc. The variations on tradition which it implies are numerous. Foremost is the connection of Daedalus with Italy. Writers of the generation before Virgil return Daedalus to earth in either Sicily (Dio. Sic. 4.78) or Sardinia (Sall. *Hist.* fr. 2.7 [Maurenbrecher] from, among others, Servius on 1.14). By having him aim directly for Cumae, Virgil emphasizes the parallel with Aeneas which will gradually grow clearer as the ekphrasis evolves.

By feigning to repeat tradition unemotionally and then significantly varying it, the narrator claims control over the history of his subject. The poet does the same generically. Virgil's model for Aeneas' arrival at Cumae as prelude to his visit to the Underworld is the opening of book 11 of the *Odyssey*, where Odysseus reaches the land of the Cimmerians and immediately conjures up the spirits of the dead. No ekphrasis intervenes (cf. Knauer, 130, n. 1). Therefore, even where Daedalus seems as yet indifferent to, or even unaware of, his loss, the narrator-poet is very involved with the tale so as to mold Daedalus, to make the sculptor his own artifact, to impress his stamp of originality on his artisan-hero. If Daedalus deepens his emotional involvement in his subjects over time, as he sets about the crafting of his psychic biography, the narrator has a deep imaginative commitment from the start.

4. According to Austin (1977), on 18, following Norden, on 18f., the dedication to Apollo "marks his gratitude for a safe landing and also his retirement from air-travel, in the manner of many Greek dedicatory epigrams." But these strange oar-wings are also an offering for passing safely through the god's province on which men do not ordinarily trespass. (Virgil's only other use of the phrase *remigium/remigio alarum* is to describe the means of Mercury's descent from heaven at *Aen.* 1.301. The repetition here suggests a momentary equivalence between god and mortal who ascribes to the supernatural.) The overreacher might be expected to pay a penalty for challenging Apollo in his territory. The passive *redditus* implies that throughout this stage of his adventures Daedalus has in fact been the god's subject. Virgil may portray him as flying *praepetibus pinnis,* but Horace, in an ode of which Servius twice reminds us (on 15 and 18), sees the means of his journey as *pinnis non homini datis* (*c.* 1.3. 35). Perhaps the implication is that Phoebus Apollo does claim recompense, in the form of Icarus, for earthbound man's sally into the skies, for momentary human arrogation of divinity. As god-man, the ultimate in spiritual hybridization, the Orphic artist, fulfilling for an instant his imagination's divine claims, suffers a profound human loss.

By forcing us even here to meditate on the negative demands of progress, Virgil reminds us that, in the unfolding epic story, it has not been long since Neptune exacted *unum caput* (5.815), one life for the safe completion of Aeneas' journey to Italy through the god's watery element.

5. *OLD* (s.v. 1b) would translate *enavit* here as "to fly forth," but it is more enriching within the context to take the meaning as a metaphorical example of the dictionary's first definition: "to swim out or forth; (esp.) to escape by swimming; swim to safety." But, since Daedalus escaped the danger and the (pointedly) unnamed Icarus did not, the reader should rightly sense ambiguities in *praepetibus* and *levis*. The first is an augural word, discussed in detail in relation to these lines by Aulus Gellius (*N.A.* 7.6). It appears four times in Ennius (Gellius mentions two instances) and lends a tone of majesty to the description of the artisan's epic accomplishment. As a term in augury it means "propitious," the opposite (according to Gellius' source, Figulus' *Augurii Privati*) of *infera*, which he defines as a low-flying, less auspicious appearance. Its etymology is from *prae-peto*, "forward-seeking." As Gellius (followed closely by Servius on 6.15) expounds the meaning, the word becomes closely complementary to *enavit: idcirco Daedali pennas "praepetes" dixit, quoniam ex locis in quibus periculum metuebat in loca tutiora pervenerat* (on this account he labeled the wings of Daedalus "propitious" because from a place in which he feared danger he had reached a safer place.) The reader, wondering why the narrator does not have Daedalus here include Icarus in his daring, sees *praepes* as "well-omened" (at least for Daedalus), as "flying directly ahead" (without a concern for the tragic events occurring behind?), and as "lofty" (unlike Icarus who, after rising too high, fell into the sea?). *Levis*, then, while primarily defining Daedalus' nimbleness, hints at a certain fickleness as well. Physical dexterity (or artistic talent, for that matter) does not necessarily ally itself with stability of mind.

6. Even here Virgil may be alluding to Aeneas' tale. The seven bodies (*septena corpora*) of sons sent to Crete each year by the Athenians are reviewed shortly thereafter in the *septem iuvencos* (38), the seven bullocks and the same number of heifers which Aeneas must now present to Apollo and Trivia. As the two myths follow their parallel progress, human offering is replaced by animal, but in each case sacrifice is essential.

7. The most inclusive article on Daedalus' Labyrinth and its resonances for Virgil is by Enk.

8. The language is close to *Aen.* 7.282–83 where the horses given by Latinus to Aeneas are described as coming *illorum de gente patris quos daedala Circe/supposita de matre nothos furata creavit* (from the stock of those [steeds] which cunning Circe, stealing them from her sire, bred bastard from the mare she had mated). *Aen.* 6.24 and 7.283 document Virgil's only uses of the perfect participle of *suppono* in a sexual sense, and *furata* (7.283) echoes *furto* (6.24). The connection is further secured by Circe's epithet *daedala*. Circe is prone to the same erotic supposititiousness and "thievery" as the Athenian artificer. This supposititiousness is both literal and figurative. To "put under" sexually is fraudulently to replace the usual with the unexpected. The resulting miscegenation is, in book 7, between mortal and immortal (in the animal kingdom), and, in book 6, between human and animal. In each case generic

mixing, as performed by Circe and Daedalus and re-created by the latter in sculpture, is typically Daedalian. Circe's hybrid horses anticipate the figures on the armor of Turnus: A chimaera on his helmet (7.783–84) which, like Circe's horses (*spirantis naribus ignem*, 281), spouts fire (*efflantem faucibus ignis*), and Io in the process of metamorphosis from human into animal, *iam saetis obsita, iam bos*. Hybridization and metamorphosis complement each other in both instances. The latter, especially metamorphosis down from a higher to a lower sensibility, typifies book 7 as a whole (lines 660–61, e.g., offer an example of the furtive "mixing" of god and mortal). I have elsewhere (1970) traced the book's patterns of metamorphosis in further detail. On the association of Turnus and the Minotaur see Dubois, 39–40, part of a thoughtful discussion of Daedalus' sculptures.

9. It remains deliberately ambiguous whether *caeca vestigia* refers to the unseeing steps of Theseus or to the Labyrinth's dark path. Support for the former proposition comes from Catullus' reference to Theseus' *errabunda vestigia* (64.113) and from later imitations (cf. Austin [1977], on 30), for the latter from Virgil's earlier description of the Labyrinth with its dark walls (*caecis parietibus, Aen.* 5.589) and from the sentence structure whose logic suggests a sequence from *ambages* to *caeca vestigia*. In either case the artisan is directly involved, though his duplex activity lends different shades of meaning to *regens*. He becomes Ariadne and empathetically "leads" her lover to safety, or "straightens" the windings of his Labyrinth, unraveling the unravelable out of pity. *Inextricabilis* (27), Varro's coinage to describe Porsenna's Etruscan labyrinth (Pliny *H.N.* 36.91), helps define the Labyrinth's puzzlement and toils and adds a further dimension to Catullus' parallel, *inobservabilis* (64.115, itself a coinage), whose point is absorbed into Virgil's *caeca*. Virgil's Daedalus first creates, and then solves, the problems of his "text."

The influence of Catullus 64 on the Daedalus episode as a whole, most recently treated by Weber (47, 50–51), deserves still further study. It begins with similarities between the Argonauts and Daedalus through the primacy of their daring (there is a common emphasis on nimbleness, rowing, and swimming in both initial episodes), develops in close parallels between the poets' treatments of Androgeos (64.77–83; *Aen.* 6.20–22) and the Labyrinth (64.113–15; *Aen.* 6.28–30), and concludes with loss. In Catullus the loss is double. Ariadne loses Theseus, and Theseus, Aegeus. In Virgil, Daedalus misses Icarus alone.

10. Perhaps the artist unravels his artistry, out of manifest pity, to abet the love of others for fear that it might bring doom on himself. At the least his uniting of two other lovers anticipates the loss of love in his own life. (For the relation of pity and fear, see Pucci [1980], especially 169–74.)

11. This point is valid for the ekphrasis as a whole. We are earlier made aware of the placement of the sculptures (*in foribus*), of the dynamic interrelationship between episodes (*respondet*), and of the specifics of location within a scene (*hic . . . hic*). The absence of a word for crafting in the Ariadne vignette is particularly telling. Because the Icarus scene could not be started we assume that Ariadne's story, which precedes

it, was brought to completion, but nothing in the narrative attends to this. Instead, while Daedalus implements the penultimate and second most emotional episode in his artistic biography, the narrator of his tale shows him in the emotional act of unraveling his past art, not in the dispassionate formation of it. Even here, though we are led to presume one act of artistic fulfillment, emotion directly undoes the mind's creation.

12. Though Virgil on three other occasions repeats *bis* in a line or between adjacent lines (*Aen.* 2.218; 6.134; 9.799–800), only once elsewhere does he employ it in anaphora at the opening of contiguous verses, 11.629–30, which is also the only instance where the two uses of *bis* contrast with rather than reinforce each other. The context is the ebb and flow of war which in turn, if we look at the last four books as a whole, analogizes its futility.

The parallel with 6.134–35, where the Sibyl remarks on Aeneas' *cupido—bis Stygios innare lacus, bis nigra videre/Tartara* (twice to swim the Stygian lakes, twice to see black Tartarus)—strengthens the bond between Daedalus and Aeneas. Though Aeneas does in fact complete his underworld journey, whereas Daedalus fails to finish his sculpture, the verbal interconnections may be one of Virgil's several subtle ways in book 6 of questioning the success of Aeneas', or Rome's, enterprise. There is, however, a later moment in book 6 with an even richer correlation to lines 32–33. When Aeneas finally reaches Anchises, son tries to embrace father (6.700–701): *ter conatus ibi collo dare bracchia circum;/ter frustra comprensa manus effugit imago* (three times there he attempted to throw his arms about his neck; three times the vision, embraced in vain, fled his hands). The lines are repeated from book 2 (792–93) where Aeneas fails in his attempt to clasp the ghost of Creusa. Both events document the hero's inability throughout the epic to achieve emotional fulfillment (he does embrace his mother at 8.615 but at her insistence, not his). As critics note, Daedalus' inability to sculpt Icarus after two attempts may be modeled on Odysseus' triple attempt and triple failure (*Od.* 11.206–208) to embrace the spirit of his mother (cf. Pöschl [1975], 121; Fitzgerald, 63 n. 18). This, of course, was Virgil's model in the episodes of book 2 and 6 (the imitation, in the case of the latter, has most recently been noted by Austin [1977]). But further potential meanings of this last anticipation in the Daedalus story of the later narrative of book 6 must not be overlooked. If Daedalus cannot perfect the loss of his son in art, can Aeneas finally fulfill the *pietas* owed to Anchises, especially given the strong need for *clementia* with which his father overlays his future loyalty?

It is noteworthy that the fall of Icarus is alluded to only by paronomasia in the word *casus*. The fall of Daedalus' hands, however, suggests that now, finally, the artisan experiences a version of his son's misfortune. Father becomes son. The son's physical fall is reiterated in the father's emotional collapse. Empathetically, literal death is the death of art.

13. I examine the reasoning behind Aeneas' actions at this crucial moment in Putnam (1995), 152–71.

14. *Geo.* 2.45–46.
15. *Geo.* 1.41–42.
16. *Geo.* 1.44.
17. See especially Duckworth (1957) and (1962), 11–13.
18. The parallels between the wooden horse and Daedalus' cow and Labyrinth are noteworthy. In each case they include *doli* (2.44), accompanied by the supportive wiles of Thymoetes, Sinon, Epeos—the Daedalian *doli fabricator* (264)—and the Greeks (34, 62, 152, 196, 252), trickery (18, 258), and *error* (48). In both instances a hybrid animal produces a monstrous birth. Both the cow and the horse are mounted on wheels as they implement their subterfuge (Dio. Sic. 4.77, Apollodorus 3.1.4, for the cow; *Aen.* 2.235–36, for the horse). Daedalus' gift to Pasiphaë therefore resembles the Greek's gift to Minerva, the *innuptae donum exitiale Minervae* (2.31), which the art of the goddess has helped produce (*divina Palladis arte*, 15). At this stage of his career and in this particular instance, Daedalus anticipates both duplicitous Greeks and crafty Minerva as they bring into being the *machina . . . feta armis* (2.237–38), and the horse and its destructive brood.
19. Allusions to deceit begin, in book 1, at 130 where Neptune becomes aware of the *doli* and *irae* of his sister Juno. Out of eighteen uses of *dolus* in the *Aeneid,* ten are in books 1–4.
20. Dido, in this matter as in others, is an accomplice in her own downfall, asking, at the end of book 1 (750–52), for Aeneas to retell the known as well as the novel in Troy's demise, and reiterating the request as her tragic love deepens (4.77–79).
Yet, whereas the sculptures of book 1 lead diachronically toward Aeneas' narrative, as he "sculpts" Troy's fall and manages Dido's death, and the shield of book 8 details Rome's future in linear progression, Daedalus' artistry analogizes the whole of the epic on several levels, offering a series of synchronic paradigms. The two longer ekphrases, by dwelling in the first instance on Aeneas' response, and in the second on Vulcan's craftsmanship, retain a strong specific point of focus that the Daedalian sculptures, with their lack of concern with the crafter at work or the viewer reacting, carefully forgo.
Aeneas' perception of the sculptures on Juno's temple is discussed with great sensitivity by Johnson (99–105). By contrast with the earlier episode, the narrator does not allow us to learn how far in his examination of Daedalus' sculptures Aeneas had proceeded (*quin protinus omnia perlegerent oculis, ni . . .* , 33–34), though we presume that his "reading" was near completion. In any case, only narrator and reader, not the poem's protagonists, know of Daedalus' final suffering. But perhaps a similar event will occur in Aeneas' life. At the moment in book 8 when Aeneas is about to set out from Pallanteum, taking himself and Pallas to war, we find him "pondering many hardships in his sad heart" (*multa . . . dura suo tristi cum corde putabant,* 8.522). To break his spell of contemplation Venus sends as sign a lightning bolt and resounding thunder (*iterum atque iterum fragor increpat ingens,* 527). Aeneas will not explain what *casus* (533) this betokens, only that he must go into battle. But he may already

sense the loss of Pallas with its many ramifications of incompletion in his life. It is a *fragor* (493), three times heard in Avernus, which, in the fourth georgic, signals Eurydice's death caused by the *furor* (495) of Orpheus. The reader schooled in Virgil's symbolic modes is prepared to await a parallel misfortune as the *Aeneid* draws to a close and Aeneas, potential artist of Rome, undoes his work by his own version of madness.

21. 4.305–306.

22. Looked at within the bounds of books 1–4, the story of Dido shares common ground with that of Daedalus and, partially, of Aeneas. It begins with double artistic accomplishment—an extraordinary city being built with a magnificent temple at its heart, and a disciplined civilization arising to bring order to the territory around it—and ends with a series of *dolores* (419, 474, 547, 679, and the death agony at 695; cf. the uses of *doleo* at 393 and 434). These destroy, literally, the queen and, symbolically, the city she had founded. Pöschl ([1950], 246 and note, trans. [1962], 150 and 207, n. 17) recognizes the parallel between Ariadne and Dido *regina*. See n. 1 above.

23. 6.473–74.

24. 4.693–95.

25. The complex *resolveret* is simplified shortly later in *solvo* (703). For Dido here, as for Pasiphaë, passion creates the need for subterfuge, for *doli* (663), which only augment and finalize the *doli* of Venus and Juno which initiate her tragedy (95, 128) and of Aeneas who furthers it (296, the narrator's word). In Daedalus' artistic, which is to say psychic, life, *doli* precede *dolor*. For Dido *dolor* both anticipates and is precipitated by her resort to *doli* (see n. 22 above). The release of Dido from her entrapment, cares and body unmeshed at once (*me . . . his exsolvite curis*, she cries to Aeneas' *dulces exuviae*, at 652) is the reader's release into the middle third of the epic. Aeneas is the major Daedalian figure in Dido's life, but it is Virgil who frees her from his text.

26. Fitzgerald (63, n. 13) sees a probable connection between Labyrinth and Underworld. The link is strengthened by appeal to the Sibyl's definition of Aeneas' *labor* (128): *sed revocare gradum superasque evadere ad auras* (but to recall one's step and make one's way out to the breezes above). Though Aeneas' "mad enterprise" (*insano . . . labori*, 135) works on the vertical plan while the Labyrinth presents a horizontal complexity, the parallels between the two adventures, where the hero must enter treacherous territory, engage in an arduous challenge or challenges, and return out alive, are suggestive. They are supported by the narrator's striking, ironic designation—and presumably Daedalus' depiction—of the Labyrinth as a *domus*. It will not be long before Aeneas will cross the *atri ianua Ditis* (127) and enter the *vestibulum* (273) in order to make his way *per . . . domos Ditis* (269).

Among the monsters Aeneas must soon thereafter pass by are *Scyllae biformes* (286). (Virgil's only two uses of the word are at 25 and here.) It will not be long before he crosses the *inremeabilis unda* of the Styx (425), an adjective used of the *error* of the Labyrinth at 5.591 and akin to the rare *inextricabilis* at 6.27. These difficulties past, Aeneas, as we shall see, continues his Daedalian enterprise with his pity for Dido and with his manifold inability to embrace his father.

27. Cf. also Dido's plea to Aeneas at 4.318—*miserere domus labentis*—and her later command to Anna, *miserere sororis* (435).

28. 6.476.

29. 5.350–54.

30. 9.66.

31. 9.136–39.

32. See n. 13 above.

33. If we pursue the analogy between Daedalus and Aeneas as we reach the poem's conclusion, we could say that in terms of life's terminations the two are successful. Each has reached a goal. Daedalus gains Cumae and constructs a notable artifact (*immania templa*), an awesome temple to Apollo. Aeneas, too, has come to Italy and defeated the enemy who, presumably, has stood in the way of his founding the Roman race. But to turn biographical completions into art, to make them appear as art, is for each a different, highly inconclusive matter.

34. By the end of his epic Aeneas could also be seen as an Icarus figure, the most palpable sign of his father's artistry, realistic proof of how idealizing are Anchises' notions of *clementia*. (We remember that it is Anchises, not Aeneas, who initiates the sparing of Achaemenides in the epic's third book.) Daedalus' *dolor*, yearning for his lost son which may well include resentment and self-hatred also, results only in artistic incompletion. Aeneas' *dolor*, where loss is directly linked to the Furies' fires, to *saevitia* and *ira*, leads to a resentful, passionate killing with far more complex intimations of failure.

Forgetful Aeneas is made to mimic careless Icarus with the forceful difference, of course, that Aeneas lives on. For him, in Virgil's richly ironic narrative, survival is the equivalent of overreaching Icarus' plummeting into the sea, and this survival means the end of his father's art.

The "celestial" plot of the *Aeneid* concludes with Jupiter yielding to Juno's demand that all things Trojan submerge their identity in the Latin present and future. What follows, therefore, up to the epic's last lines, is in fact the intellectual birth of Rome, as Aeneas becomes, according to his father's definition, *Romanus* (6.851). Two actions are paramount. First, Jupiter co-opts the Dirae to warn Juturna and her brother of the latter's impending death. Second, Aeneas kills Turnus. In the first deed, heaven summons hell to motivate earthly doings for the last time in the epic but for the first time, one could surmise, in Virgil's Roman history, as history's cycle starts anew. The second, Aeneas' concluding deed, becomes the initial Roman action. Motivated by inner furies, it betokens a continuum of passion and anger, portending the impossibility of any new aesthetic or ethical wholeness.

35. The case for the authenticity of the *Odyssey* from 23.297 to the end is argued persuasively by Moulton (1974).

36. 12.816–19.

37. 12.805–809. His beloved Virgil is here on Statius' mind, but the Virgil not of the *Aeneid* but of georgic 4 (525–27).

38. The abrupt conclusion of *De Rerum Natura* offers the closest parallel in earlier literature to the end of the *Aeneid*. I strongly support the view of Clay (1983), 251, that Virgil's "grim and unresolved" finale deliberately echoes both the style and tone of his great predecessor.

39. The reversals of the *Iliad* in the *Aeneid* deserve separate study. The *Aeneid* ends in one respect where the *Iliad* begins. Achilles' anger at the start of the *Iliad* turns to forgiveness at the end. The story of Aeneas, on the other hand, begins with the hero's suppression of *dolor* (1.209), for hardships experienced in the past, and ends with his outburst of *dolor* over the loss of Pallas. In at least one episode of the *Aeneid* the reversal directly concerns Achilles. In Pyrrhus' vengeful killing of Priam, Achilles' anger lives on. It too, of course, is an emotion that spurs on Aeneas to his final deed (*ira terribilis* is the narrator's characterization of Aeneas immediately before his final speech, 12.946–47). Is it mere coincidence that Helenus bestows the *arma Neoptolemi* (3.469) on Aeneas as his parting gift?

40. The parallel is developed with sensitivity by Segal (1966), 50–52. Cf. also Rutledge, 311, and Pöschl (1975), 120.

41. Fitzgerald (54) rightly notes that Daedalus' tale delivers him "from the past [that his artwork first encapsulated] into the painful and unfinished world of history." He pursues his insight by concluding that Aeneas, as Daedalus, is forced into a tragic history "that forfeits the comfort of closure."

42. The truth of Aeneas' emotions at the end of book 12, as in the Helen episode in book 2, leads to artistic inconclusions, in the first instance because the text (2.567–88) would be expunged by, and nearly lost because of, Varius and Tucca, in the second because it leads not to potential elimination but to aspects of incompletion. The first episode suggests, too early and too strongly, it might have been said, the truth of the hero's emotionality. The second cannot be argued away, though its author sought to destroy it as part of his whole epic. It forms a special complement to the first. Virgil stops at a moment of the greatest honesty which demonstrates Anchises' model to be one based on wishful thinking while Aeneas' violent response to Turnus and the emotional thrust behind it speak the truth. This truth brings about, literally and splendidly, the end of art.

Chapter 4. Silvia's Stag

1. For non-"notional" ekphrases, that is, for examples of such *descriptiones* not dealing with works of art, the usual introduction involves some form of the verb "to be" (*cervus erat, est locus*, etc.). This reminds us that, in whatever way the description may be extended and whatever the diverse manifestations of temporality it may contain, as far as its context is concerned it is essentially a static, rhetorical phenomenon. The motion of narrative proper for all intents and purposes comes to a halt, and,

though the future story line may be enhanced by such a pause, the reader must stop to absorb a compressed, intense vision, however animate aspects of that vision might be, before the activity of narrative per se can be resumed.

2. Macrobius (*Sat.* 5.17.1-2) offers evidence for ancient disapproval of the passage. A pejorative word on occasion applied to it is *sentimental* (see, e.g., Williams [1973], on 7.475f). For a summary of the responses of ancient and modern critics to the passage and for a sensitive reading based on comparison with the simile at *Aen.* 4.68-73, see Griffin, 170-72. The connection is also made by Boyle (93) in the course of a discussion of deer imagery running throughout the epic. Horsfall (1993, 110 and notes) finds Virgil's source in an epigram of Meleager on the death of Phanion's pet hare (*A.P.* 7.207 in Gow-Page 4320-27). Examples of ekphrasis in the Greek novel dealing with animals are listed by Bartsch (11-13, and n. 12) as part of a valuable discussion of the development of the topos.

3. 7.203-204. The main difference between Latinus' characterization and Evander's later depiction of the evolution of humankind on the site of future Rome is that Latinus sees no need for laws, whereas Evander tells of Saturn as giving laws (*leges*, 8.322). The dynamic of energies already inherent in Italy at the time of Aeneas' arrival has been well discussed by Moorton.

4. See above, n. 2.
5. 4.553.
6. 4.551.
7. Cf. the uses of *ilia* at Catullus 11.20, 63.5, and 80.8.
8. It is possible that the animal serves as a sacrificial victim, symbolizing perhaps the loss of Italian integrity before the onslaught of (civil) war or before a different, merged world. This may well be part of Virgil's purpose. But *serta*, through their association with *convivia* and poetic creativity, are distinct from the *vittae* that bedeck a victim. We think of Sinon as potential human offering (2.133) or of the priest Haemonides at 10.538, sacrificed (*immolet*, 541) by Aeneas. Moreover, the stag is only wounded. We never hear of his death (cf., e.g., 8.641, 11.197-98, and 12.213-15, where animal sacrifice does occur).

How close the language of hunting is to that of war may be seen by comparing line 478—*insidiis cursuque feras agitabat Iulus* (Iulus was harrying wild beasts with snares and horses)—with 2.421—*fudimus insidiis totaque agitavimus urbe* (we routed them through ambushes and were harrying [them] throughout the city).

9. 5.254; 8.649.
10. Several words in the passage abet the undercurrent of eroticism. *Erilis* (490), e.g., may refer to the mistress of an animal or the *domina* of an elegiac lover (Cat. 68.136; Ovid *H.* 9.78. *Erus* is equivalent to husband at Cat. 61.109). Both *aestus* and *levare* can refer not only to external heat and its assuaging but to love's "swirlings" as well (*aestus:* Cat. 68.108, Prop. 2.33.43; *levare:* Cat. 2.10, Prop. 1.9.34).
11. Cf. Nänny, passim.
12. 479, 493-94.

13. 496.
14. 492, 496.
15. 491, 498.
16. 483, 488.
17. 497.
18. Virgil also uses *intendere* of stretching the strings of a lyre (*Aen.* 9.776). There is thus a further musical aspect to the metaphor and a further hint that war corrupts the artistry of peace to its own malicious ends. On the musical as well as martial aspects of the metaphor cf. Landels.
19. The phrase *novas artis* is used of Venus' trickery in exchanging Cupid for Ascanius and thus precipitating the downfall of Dido. On the connection between Venus and Allecto see Lyne (1987), 18–20.
20. See *OLD* s.v. *manus* 13b and 20.
21. 7.248.
22. 338.
23. For the senses of *labor* in erotic contexts see Pichon, 180–81.
24. *Ecl.* 10.44–45.
25. *Ecl.* 2.49–50.
26. *Ecl.* 5.31.
27. For *intexo* and artistic weavings, cf. *geo.* 3.25 (*intexti Britanni* on a stage curtain) and *Aen.* 5.252 (Ganymede on a cloak). For use with other "woven" objects, see *Aen.* 2.16 (the wooden horse) and 10.785 (a shield). At *geo.* 2.221 we are told how a particularly creative soil "will interweave for you elms with productive vines" (*tibi laetis intexet vitibus ulmos*).
28. 21–22.
29. Cf., e.g., Prop. 1.3.10, where fidelity or its absence is crucial for an understanding of the poem.
30. 6.68, 7.25; 6.16–19.
31. 8–9.
32. For an incisive reading of the passage and its idealizing aspects, see Perkell, 130–37, with notes.
33. *Geo.* 4.132.
34. 132–33.
35. *Epode* 2.48.
36. *Geo.* 4.125–26.
37. *Aen.* 7.535–36.
38. The death scene of Galaesus also caught the attention of Macrobius (*Sat.* 4.4.3).
39. C. 2.6.10, 22. For further details on the attractions of Tarentum, see Nisbet and Hubbard, 94–95. It is a curious fact of literary history that Propertius places Virgil singing of Thyrsis and Daphnis, that is, composing his *Eclogues*, *umbrosi subter pineta Galaesi* (2.34.67–68).

40. 7.635–36.
41. 3.1.3–4.
42. On the meaning of *puro fonte* see Wimmel, 229–30, and Kambylis, 158–59, as well as 110–21 on Callimachus' use of water symbolism in general.
43. 3.1.19–20. For a comparison of *mollia serta* with *molli umbra* and *mollia prata* (Prop. 3.3.1, 18), see Kambylis, 148, n. 80.
44. 7.504, 524.
45. 3.3.41–42.
46. The violence implicit in the taming of the stag is also discussed in an important article by Vance, who sees the taming as a perversion by the civilized Latins of the stag's true nature.
47. 7.485; 11.571–72, 568.
48. 11.581–82.
49. 62.42.
50. This detail is absent from the Homeric original (*Il.* 1.234–39).
51. 7.392. It may be more than a curiosity that Iulus' dogs are female (*rabidae*, 7.493). Virgil, when he chooses, can also have a male hunting dog (e.g., *Aen.* 12.751). For a penetrating discussion of the episode in book 5, see Nugent.
52. 12.946–47.
53. 1.29.

Chapter 5. The Shield of Aeneas

1. From the enormous bibliography of writing on the shield of Aeneas, I have found the following most useful, listed in chronological order: Lessing, ch. 18, 91–97; W. W. Fowler, 103–104; Drew, 26–31; Otis, 341–42; C. Becker, 111–27; Eichholz, 45–49; Griffith, 54–65; McKay, 145; Binder, 150–282; Eden (1973), 78–83; Eden (1975), on *Aen.* 8.608–731; West, 1–6; Gransden, on *Aen.* 8.608–731; Williams (1981), 8–11; Dubois, 41–51; Romeuf, 143–65; Hardie (1986), 336–76; Clausen, 80–81; Lyne (1987), 207–209; Ravenna (1988), 739–42; Cairns, 97–102; Quint (1989), 1–32; J. Thomas, 303–308; Heffernan (1993), 30–35; Quint (1993), 19–31; Gurval, 209–47.

The search for a design in Virgil's placement of its discrete episodes has been one of the major foci in scholarly discussions of the shield. I have found no presentation that is wholly successful, and have therefore limited my discussion of any potential patterning to the signposts that the poet himself offers.

Nor am I in more than partial accord with the general interpretative bias of this century's criticism that sees the shield as largely an emblem of Roman martial accomplishment and, in particular, of the civilizing mission of Augustus. For Fowler (103–104), e.g., the scenes on the shield are evidence for a series of Roman escapes from peril, with Actium being the most impressive of all. Drew's allegorical interpretation finds the shield exemplifying the four virtues (*clementia, iustitia, pietas*, and *virtus*) on the *clupeus aureus* offered by senate and people to Augustus in 27 B.C.E. (*RG* 34.2).

His reading is varied by Otis (341–42), who sees the episodes as displaying the triumph of *virtus, consilium,* and *pietas* over violence in Roman history. Hardie (336–76), especially, interprets the shield as imaging the victory of Augustan rationality over the chaos of non-Roman barbarism. His views are essentially followed by Cairns, Clausen, and Quint, though the latter, in both his treatments, is fully aware of equivocal aspects of the ekphrasis. My own critique is most in sympathy with that of Gurval to which I am indebted both in general and in detail.

2. For a full discussion of the symbol of the wolf see Dulière. The Lupercal is the subject of a detailed study by Lavagne.

3. For the location of the Lupercal see Richardson, s.v.; for the Augustan restoration, *RG* 19.

4. Virgil displays a fondness for such doubling throughout the poem. We range, for instance, from the twin snakes or twin sons of Atreus in book 2 to the "twin blights with the name Dread Ones" (*geminae pestes cognomine Dirae*) who are at Jupiter's service as the epic comes to an end (12.845).

5. 8.680.
6. 8.697.
7. 8.678–81.
8. 8.682–84.

9. Part of the intent of these lines therefore parallels a major motif of Jupiter's prophecy at 1.257–96, especially lines 292–93 which assure us that in the new Augustan dispensation Remus will give laws with his brother, Romulus.

10. To add this further idea of enclosure may be one reason why Virgil transfers the occurrence of the rape of the Sabine women from the Consualia (Livy 1.9; Servius on *Aen.* 8.636) to the Ludi Circenses. It should be noted, however, that the Altar of Consus was located at the Circus (see Richardson, s.v. *Consus*).

11. On this point see Gurval, 219.
12. Livy 1.23.1.
13. Livy 1.28.11.
14. *Geo.* 3.267–68.
15. Livy 1.28.11.
16. On the problematics of the Gallic capture of the Capitolium see Skutsch, on Enn. *Ann.* 227–28; Horsfall (1981), 94–95.
17. Livy 1.11.6; *Aen.* 2.250–55.
18. Cf., e.g., *Aen.* 5.558–59.
19. Cf. *geo.* 4.98–99 of bees: *elucent aliae et fulgore coruscant/ardentes auro.*
20. 10.137–38. *Subnectens* is the reading of *P.* and *R. M.* reads *subnectit.* For the phrasing see also *Aen.* 5.558–59, a passage which suggests that *circulus* at 10.138 surrounds neck, not hair.
21. On the placement and purpose of these lines see especially Gurval, 228.
22. In fact, the majority of the pre-Actian vignettes consist of two scenes linked together.

23. If only for reasons of chronological order, Cato the Younger and not his great-grandfather the censor must be the subject of Virgil's lines.

24. *Il.* 18.483, 606–607.

25. 5.588–91, 594–95. The *lusus Troiae* has therefore two links with ekphrasis, through its comparison to the Labyrinth with the ekphrasis of Daedalus that opens book 6, and through its equation to the disciplined play of dolphins with the shield of Aeneas and its centerpiece.

26. The vocabulary shared between lines 671–75 and the opening verses of Catullus 64 (cf. 64.7 alone—*caerula verrentes abiegnis aequora palmis*) suggests deliberate allusion on Virgil's part. The beginning of Catullus' great poem is echoed in Virgil's impressive new start, and his depiction of the grand, ambiguous enterprise of the *Argo*, with its consequent meditation on humanity's moral decline and on the equivocal figure of Achilles, remains appropriately in the intellectual background as Virgil commences his longest portrayal of the initiation of Augustan Rome, in the waters off western Greece.

27. 1.142.

28. 8.40, 86.

29. Compare here the apparent horror of Anchises (and his narrator) at the action of the original Brutus, who had his sons put to death "for beautiful liberty's sake" (*pulchra pro libertate* [*Aen.* 6.821]).

30. We think, for instance, of the flame on Lavinia's head (*Aen.* 7.71–80) and its anticipation of the marriage of Latium and Troy.

31. 6.779.

32. 3.11–12. Cf. Enn. *Ann.* 190 Skutsch.

33. N.B. the triple repetition of *Italia* at 3.523–24. On landing, Anchises sees four white horses which he considers an omen of war. There will be peace, he announces, if they learn to withstand the reins of concord (*frena concordia*). The implication is that the war Aeneas will become involved with centers on *discordia*, i.e., that it smacks of civil strife. Virgil's mention of the Itali on the shield (as well as of *Discordia* at 702) may be meant to recall this earlier moment of discord in relation to the present battling.

34. 10.272–75. The simile varies one at *Iliad* 22.26–31 and furthers the link between Aeneas and Achilles that Virgil fosters from the beginning of the epic. We should also note, in relation to the depiction of Augustus on the shield, that the lines immediately preceding the simile depict flames pouring forth from the helmet of Aeneas.

35. The phrase is echoed from Ennius *Andromacha* 89 Jocelyn.

36. Unless, of course, we are meant to think of Delos before the stabilizing birth of Apollo.

37. *Caede nova* and perhaps *Neptunia* (cf. Hor. *Epode* 7.3 and, more obliquely, 9.7) may refer to the battle of Naulochus. The language of the whole is reminiscent of Vir. *geo.* 1.489–92, where civil war is also the subject.

38. *Aen.* 7.25 and 3.521; *geo.* 2.34.
39. This and one at Prop. 3.11.43, where the context has much in common with the present passage, are the first appearances of the word in Latin.
40. Cf. the use of *ferrum* shortly before at 694. Lines 701–702, which come at the center of the Actium episode, parallel each other and are noteworthy for their slowness.
41. 12.853, but the whole context, from 845 to 855, has bearing on the present moment on the shield.
42. The other noteworthy absence from the Roman divinities is Juno. Only Minerva represents the Capitoline triad. Are we to think that even now Juno harbors negative thoughts against the (Trojan) Romans?
43. 6.570. *Sanguineo* (703) keeps the color red from *rubescunt* still before our eyes.
44. Cf. the parallel usages at 6.602 and 12.754.
45. *C.* 1.37.
46. 4.644.
47. 8.64.
48. 3.64 (on which see the comments of Williams [1970]), 6.410.
49. For a detailed examination of the ambiguities of the phrase see Dyson.
50. Pliny *H.N.* 7.47. For further references see Maltby, s.v.
51. And once again we ponder the conundrum Virgil regularly poses for his reader when dealing with violence with its positive as well as negative potential. For the former I think especially of the revivifying efforts of Aristaeus at the end of the fourth georgic with his parallels to Octavian campaigning in the east who, in the final lines, "gives laws to willing peoples" (*geo.* 4.561–62).
52. 8.628, 710; 724.
53. For uses of the title before Virgil see *OLD* s.v. On the etymologies see Maltby, s.v.
54. 8.726.
55. 8.633–34.
56. *Ante aram* (640); *ante aras* (719).
57. *Vestis* (659, 720).
58. *Templo* (653), *templis* (718) (cf. also the allusion to the temple of Apollo); *matres* (666), *matrum* (718).
59. 8.653, 680.
60. 8.645.
61. 8.690–91.
62. *Vellere* (650); *ruebant* (648), *ruere* (689); *innaret* (651), *innare* (691).
63. 8.719.
64. *OLD* s.v. 4b. Cf. also 3 (to lay paving stones) and 7 (to overthrow one's enemies).
65. 3.23.
66. 2.537.

67. 12.922 (thunderbolt), 923 (whirlwind) with which cf. 12.855 and Putnam (1995), 205–206.

68. 2.461. Virgil would have originally seen the phrase *postis superbos* at *De Rerum Natura* 4.1178, where it is applied to the doorposts of a mistress who scorns the *exclusus amator*.

69. 8.196.

70. 2.503–505.

71. Conington, on *Aen.* 2.504, can even speak of Aeneas as "forgetting himself" (*The Works of Virgil*, ed. J. Conington and H. Nettleship, London, 1884).

72. 8.620.

73. 8.198–99, 259.

74. 8.265, 618.

75. On this point see Putnam (1995), 30–33.

76. *Vita Donati* 22 (ed. Hardie).

77. *N.A.* 17.10.2–3 (trans. Rolfe).

78. 1.52, 51.

79. 1.150–51.

80. 1.153.

81. 12.951–52.

82. 8.649.

83. 1.55.

84. In this discussion I am, of course, privileging two caves, out of several in the *Aeneid*, and two moments of indignation, of which the shield itself offers yet another instance. (And the material in-between, detailing the hero's story, in one case, the saga of Rome, in the other, cannot lay claim to surface parallels.) But Virgil, as this chapter illustrates elsewhere, is fond of such an emphasis on beginnings and endings, and there is no need to undervalue their significance here.

85. *Il.* 19.19.

86. Virgil may wish us to speculate, however, on whether or not Aeneas sensed any parallelism between Dido and Cleopatra and, if he did, what he would have made of the connection.

87. Unlike Homer's Achilles, who responds only after the shield has arrived (and the ekphrasis concluded), Aeneas is allowed to react to his armor before as well as after the ekphrasis. It is doubly through his eyes that we do our reading.

88. Not that Homer's shield lacks its own distancing from its context. It describes a world which, on the face of it, is unknown to Achilles, short-lived warrior who will not be allowed to know the rhythms and revolving continuities of life.

89. Macr. *Sat.* 1.24.6–7. Cf. Servius' repunctuation of *Aen.* 8.383 to connect the phrase *genetrix nato* with Thetis (and Achilles), not Venus and Aeneas.

90. 8.373, on which see the comments of Gransden.

91. The reader was made aware already in book 1 of insincerity in Venus' rhetoric, especially from her addresses there to Jupiter and Juno.

92. *DRN* 1.34; *Aen.* 8.394.
93. The tale is first told by Homer as the subject of Demodocus' second song in *Odyssey* 8.
94. *Aen.* 8.403–404.
95. There is irony, too, in Virgil's playing with the conventions (and vocabulary) of Catullus and the elegists at one of the major moments in his epic where he is directly rivaling Homer.
96. 8.408–14.
97. *Il.* 12.433–35.
98. *Arg.* 3.291–98, 4.1062–67.
99. Such a strong reversal of gender in an erotic context is a further reminder of Catullus' poetry and of the frequency with which his masculine first-person speakers adopt feminine roles.
100. 8.611.
101. 2.589–90.
102. 3.66 (*sese offert ultro*).
103. 8.615, 405.
104. 4.133.
105. 6.211.
106. 6.142, 629, 637.
107. 8.612–13.
108. 6.816, 817–19, 833.
109. 8.393.
110. 8.609, 617.
111. 8.729.
112. 1.647–55.
113. 1.673.
114. 1.679.
115. 1.709.
116. 1.714.
117. 1.718.
118. 4.508, 8.627.
119. 2.31, 34.
120. 2.43–44.
121. 2.49.
122. 2.189, 252, 264.
123. 2.62, 196.
124. 2.57–61.
125. 2.242–43.
126. 2.244.
127. 12.946–47, 8.394 (*devinctus amore*—Virgil's only use of the verb *devincio*).
128. 2.15; 8.377, 401, 442, 612.

129. 2.237–38.
130. 65 Skutsch (68 Vahlen 3).
131. 8.633; *DRN* 1.35–36.
132. *DRN* 1.37.
133. 1.75–76.
134. 1.70–71.
135. 12.569.
136. 12.583.
137. 1.82–83.
138. 1.71.

139. The echo in this phrase of the Labyrinth's *inextricabilis error* (*Aen.* 6.27) is one of several ways in which Virgil links the ekphrasis of Daedalus' temple doors with that of the shield.

Chapter 6. The Baldric of Pallas

1. I have learned much from the sensitive treatment of Virgil's Danaids by Spence. Other valuable commentary on the ekphrasis and the tangential problems it raises can be found in Conte (1970, trans. 1986), who sees the sons of Aegyptus as primarily emblematic of youths who die unmarried. (He is followed in essence by Lyne [1989], 158.) See also Barchiesi (1984), 33–34 and especially 71–72 on the iconographic content of the *balteus*. Hardie (1993, 33) sees in the belt "the symbolism of the ephebe cut down on his wedding night" which Turnus transfers to himself. The following essays also have much of value for a student of the Danaid ekphrasis: Breen, D. Fowler (1987), and R. N. Mitchell.

2. Both Conte (1986, 187) and Fowler (192) give special emphasis to Virgil's use of *foede* here. Conte quotes Servius *ad Aen.* 2.55 where he equates *turpe* with *crudele*. Livy has a pertinent instance (6.22.4) where *turpe* comes close to being an antonym to *civiliter* (*foede . . . in captis exercere victoriam*). Here, too, in victory no leniency is offered the defeated.

The connection with the Iphigeneia passage in Lucr. *D.R.N.* 1.85 (and cf. 1.62) is clear. Cf. Hardie (1984), 406–12.

3. The language describing the *balteus* and Turnus' assumption of it is close to the words Virgil uses to describe sinners in the Underworld (*Aen.* 6.624): *ausi omnes immane nefas ausoque potiti* (All dared an enormous crime and claimed what they dared).

4. 5.794.

5. Iulus describes the action in terms of *furor* at 5.670.

6. The verb *foedo*, as used by Virgil, means to make black and blue from scratches or blows (*Aen.* 4.673 repeated at 12.871, 11.86) or to blacken or deface, literally, with blood from wounds or filth or dust (2.286, 502; 3.227; 7.575; cf. 2.55 on the "wounding" of the wooden horse). It also means metaphorically to darken with the sight of

death (2.539). In many of these instances a sense of moral repugnance hangs over the context. The same holds true for Virgil's use of the adjective *foedus*. It twice characterizes the filth of the Harpies (3.216, 244), and Turnus applies it in the superlative to his antagonist Drances, in allusion more to the underhanded craft of his rhetoric than to any disfigurement of body. *Fama* in book 4, one of the *Aeneid*'s less attractive beings, is styled *dea foeda* (4.195). She is an evil (*mala*) who pursues her dismal work at night, engendered out of anger and sharing traits with Homer's personified strife (4.174, 178 and 176–77, with which cf. *Il.* 4.442–43).

7. 7.619.

8. One of the ancient etymologies of the noun *foedus* ("treaty") connected it with *foede*. See, e.g., Festus 84: *foedus appellatum ab eo, quod in paciscendo foede hostia necaretur*. (For other examples see Maltby s.v. *foedus*.) If Virgil means any resonance here it is possibly to suggest the difference between the divisive horror of human murder and victimization and the demand of animal sacrifice as accompaniment to the forging of a treaty which would bring enmity to an end (in the *Aeneid* cf. 8.641, 12.170–71 and 213–15 where the violence is graphically described).

9. It requires no great leap of the imagination to connect the Gates of Sleep, whose description concludes book 6, with the Gates of War, one of the most prominent symbols of the subsequent book, or to link Aeneas' escape out of the Underworld (and into the text of the last second half of the epic) through the gate of false dreams with the advent of civil war which Juno's opening of the *Belli portae* betokens.

10. 12.31, and cf. 6.612–13 of those tortured in the Underworld who *arma secuti/impia* as well as *geo.* 1.511 (*Mars impius*).

11. It is well to remember the many occasions in the poem when night abets scenes of cruelty and violence. Among them we could count the Rhesus episode in the Dido murals (1.469–73; N.B. the phrase *multa . . . caede cruentus* at 471), the descent of night over doomed Troy (2.250), Palinurus and the lethal combination of *Nox* and *Somnus* at his death, night and Helen's treachery to Deiphobus (6.513), and the murderous nocturnal adventure of Nisus and Euryalus in book 9. When Aeneas arrives on the scene in book 10, the gleaming of his shield is compared to the sinister red glow of "bloody comets" (*cometae sanguinei*, 272–73).

12. *Il.* 16.459–60; *Aen.* 10.469–71.

13. With 10.495 cf. *Il.* 16.863.

14. *Il.* 17.205.

15. We learn from 11.91–92 that Turnus has in his possession all the armor of Pallas except spear and helmet. He seems actually to use, that is to wear, only the sword-belt.

16. Virgil leaves unexplained the patronymic Eurytides. Two candidates for the Eurytus or Eurytion in question seem feasible. First is Eurytus, king of Oechalia and father of Iole, beloved of Hercules. The second, which I consider more apt because of the theme of violence on a wedding night common to his tale and to that of the Danaids, is Eurytion (or Eurytus in Ovid's *Metamorphoses*), the centaur who, accord-

ing to Homer (*Od.* 21.285), gets drunk at the wedding feast of Hippodameia and Pirithous. For references to him in Latin literature see Prop. 2.33.31 (and cf. 2.2.9–10), Ovid. *A.A.* 1.593 and *M.* 12.220–28, where the centaur seizes the bride herself and is slain by Pirithous. For variations on the occasion of Eurytion's (Eurytus') behavior and his fate, see Dio. Sic. 4.70, Hyg. *Fab.* 33, Apollodorus *Bib.* 2.5.6.

17. The evidence is set forth with sobriety by Garvie, 163–233. See also the more concise summary by Winnington-Ingram, 284–86. For the speech of Aphrodite see Aes. fr. 44 in *Tragicorum Graecorum Fragmenta*, ed. Radt (Göttingen, 1985). It comes from Athenaeus (13.600a–b), who tells us that the speaker is Aphrodite.

Aeschylus' treatment of the myth is the subject of two essays by Zeitlin (1990, see especially 105–106 and 113, n. 8, for further bibliography, and 1992).

18. The connection of Turnus with Io and hence with her descendants, the Danaids, deserves separate treatment. See also Breen (63–71), Kellum (174), Ross (160–63), and O'Hara (78–81).

19. The sparing act of Hypermestra and the ancestry of Hercules form the climax of the Danaid myth as described by Prometheus in Aes. *P.V.* 846–73. Pausanias (2.20.7) informs us that Hypermestra was brought to judgment by Danaus and (2.21.1) that she won the trial. We are also told by Pausanias (2.19.3–7) that, to celebrate her victory, Hypermestra dedicated a statue of Aphrodite in the sanctuary of Apollo Lycius and (2.16.1) that Lynceus succeeded to the throne of Argos on the death of Danaus.

20. The main reference by Plato is at *Gorg.* 493a (cf. also *Rep.* 363d). The first surviving mention of Danaus in Latin is apparently in fr. 1 (Morel 93) of Varro Atacinus' translation of the *Argonautica* of Apollonius Rhodius (cf. 1.133), followed by Cic. *Par. St.* 44, where Danaus is mentioned with his daughters. Lucretius (*D.R.N.* 3.935–37, 1008–11), who leaves them unnamed, finds in them an analogy to those who for whatever reason have not allowed themselves to enjoy their earthly existence to the full and who therefore suffer in life what superstition claims that the Danaids endure in death. The sisters figure in standard lists which Horace (*c.* 2.14.18–19, 3.11.21–29), Tibullus (1.3.80–81), and Propertius (2.1.67, 4.11.27–28) offer of those who pay for sublunar crimes with perpetual punishment in the afterlife. (At 4.7.63–68 Propertius places Hypermestra in the Elysian Fields.) Once in the *Ibis* (177–78) and twice in the *Metamorphoses* (4.364–65, 10.43–44) Ovid mentions them, on the second occasion momentarily relieved of their suffering by the song of Orpheus just as they are in Horace *c.* 3.11 by the sounds of Mercury's lyre. Cf. also ps.-Ver. *Culex* 245–47 and, in Neronian literature, Seneca *Med.* 748–49 and *H.F.* 498–500 and 757 (with the comments of Finch on 750–59).

21. *C.* 3.11.46.

22. On eccentricities in Virgil's treatment of the damned, see Putnam (1990).

23. 11.178–79.

24. The references to the portico in prose are Aug. *RG* 19; Vell. Pat. 2.81; Suet. *Aug.* 29.3; Cass. Dio 53.1.3.

25. Prop. 2.31.3–4.
26. *Am.* 2.2.4.
27. *A.A.* 1.73–74.
28. *Tr.* 3.1.61–62.
29. For the Danaids in art see the detailed article by Keuls (1986). Her survey offers only one sure example of the Danaids portrayed as murderers before the Palatine statuary, namely, on an Apulian bell crater of the fourth century B.C.E. (p. 338). It is important also to note that in late Republican wall painting and on stone reliefs the Danaids are uniformly shown as water-carriers. See also Keuls (1974), 117–58.

A late scholium to Persius (on 2.56) mentions that there were equestrian statues of the sons of Aegyptus opposite those of the Danaids, but the logic of such a portrayal, given the circumstances of the myth, the exigencies of space, and the silence of the literary sources, tell against such a possibility.

30. His views are set forth in greatest detail in P. Zanker (1983). They are summarized in (1987), 91, trans. (1988), 85–86 ("guilt and expiation"). His interpretation develops from that of Carcopino, especially 280–85 and Gagé, 529, on the Danaids as noninitiates.

31. Two exponents of this view are Lefèvre, 12–16, and Simon, 21–24.

32. Quint (1993), ch. 2, "Repetition and Ideology in the *Aeneid*," 50–96. On p. 78 he distinguishes between revenge that posits further vengeance and revenge that brings vendetta to a stop. Perhaps Augustus meant to create the image of revenge mastered by monumentalizing it, but the cyclicity of the *Aeneid* tells another tale.

33. Kellum, 169–76, and in particular 173–76.

34. Cf. Virgil's use of *impius* and *barbarus* to describe a Roman soldier at *ecl.* 1.70–71.

35. *C.* 2.14. 18–19; 3.11.25, 30–31. Horace's judgment is an important aid to interpreting the morality of Aeneas' action at the poem's end. The *pietas* of vendetta (i.e., that which Aeneas may be construed to owe Evander) must not be allowed to take ethical precedence over the *pietas* of *clementia* (i.e., what Aeneas experienced in the words of his father). The point deserves further development in relation to the end of the *Aeneid*. Because the *pietas* (if such it be) of vengeance rules the poem's conclusion, no reconciliations are possible nor any type of higher "marriage."

36. *RG* 3.1–2, for the boast; 34.2, for the shield.

37. 4.495–97 (on which see Spence, 18).

38. 7.574–75, 535–36. We note the connection of *foedo* with incipient civil war.

39. 2.499–503.

40. Virgil uses *ara* or *altaria* five further times after 501 as the passage unfolds (513, 514, 515, 523, 550). The first human victim is Laocoön, who dies in the stead of the false sacrifice, Sinon.

41. 2.539.

42. In one particularity here Virgil may also be following Homer. We are twice

reminded during Achilles' killing of Hector that the latter is wearing Patroclus' armor, once by the narrator (*Il.* 22.323) and once by Achilles (331).

43. 2.541–42.
44. 12.930.
45. 12.949.
46. 10.541.
47. 10.537.
48. 6.35.
49. 10.523–25.
50. 6.91.
51. 6.115–17.
52. 12.946–47.
53. 7.392.
54. 4.376.
55. 1.25–29. Cf. also *saeva* and *ira* (4) and *dolens* (9).
56. 4.469–73.
57. Virgil could have chosen a figure representing female fury, Agave, for instance, to serve as analogy for Dido, but he did not. Dido, even in her wildness, is deliberately compared to a male figure, as if the masculine emblematization of political order, which Virgil regularly adopts, were still hers, but now hopelessly transformed by emotion.
58. It is possible that Virgil was also thinking of the ugly criminality of the figure of Orestes as conceived by Euripides, but the presence of the Furies makes Aeschylus the paramount model for Virgil.
59. Another possible allusion to tragedy may lie in the figure of Io, suffering metamorphosis into a cow, as emblem on the shield of Turnus (7.789–92). We know that Accius wrote a tragedy devoted to her (*Scaenicorum Romanorum Fragmenta*, ed. Klotz [Oldenbourg, 1953], I, pp. 252–53). It is a reasonable assumption that the metamorphosis came early in the dramatization, before any acts of forgiveness, return to human shape, or apotheosis took place.
60. The speech that Aeschylus gives to Aphrodite has something in common with many of the utterances of Athena at the end of *Eumenides* (cf., e.g., 903–908), proclaiming the bounteousness of nature. We may likewise be meant to think of the alteration of Furies into Eumenides when we contemplate Juno's apparent renunciation of anger in her speech to Jupiter at 12.808–28. But it is *furiae*, not Eumenides, who hold Aeneas in their grip at the poem's end.

Conclusion

1. Pöschl (1962), 53.
2. Otis, 391.
3. Hardie (1986). See also Cairns, 102.

Bibliography

For references to periodicals, the bibliography follows the abbreviations adopted in *L'Année Philologique* (Paris, 1924–).

Alpers, S. "*Ekphrasis* and Aesthetic Attitudes in Vasari's *Lives.*" *JWI* 23 (1960): 190–215.
Anderson, W. S. "Vergil's Second *Iliad.*" *TAPA* 88 (1957): 17–30.
Arkins, B. "New Approaches to Virgil." *Latomus* 45 (1986): 33–42.
Austin, R. G., ed. *P. Vergili Maronis: Aeneidos: Liber Primus.* Oxford, 1971.
———. *P. Vergili Maronis: Aeneidos: Liber Sextus.* Oxford, 1977.
Barchiesi, A. *La Traccia del Modello.* Pisa, 1984.
———. "Rappresentazioni del dolore e interpretazione nell'Eneide." *A&A* 40 (1994): 109–24.
Barkan, L. *Transuming Passion: Ganymede and the Erotics of Humanism.* Stanford, 1991.
———. "The Beholder's Tale: Ancient Sculpture, Renaissance Narratives." *Representations* 44 (1993): 133–66.
Bartsch, S. *Decoding the Ancient Novel.* Princeton, 1989.
Baxandall, M. *Patterns of Intention.* New Haven, 1985.
Becker, A. S. "The Shield of Achilles and the Poetics of Homeric Description." *AJP* 111 (1990): 139–53.
———. "Reading Poetry through a Distant Lens." *AJP* 113 (1992): 5–24.
———. "Sculpture and Language in Early Greek Ekphrasis." *Arethusa* 26 (1993): 18–30.
———. *The Shield of Achilles and the Poetics of Ekphrasis.* Lanham, Md., 1995.
Becker, C. "Der Schild des Aeneas." *WS* 77 (1964): 111–27.
Binder, G. *Aeneas und Augustus.* Meisenheim, 1971.
Boswell, J. *Christianity, Social Tolerance and Homosexuality.* Chicago, 1980.
Boyd, B. W. "*Non Enarrabile Textum:* Ecphrastic Trespass and Narrative Ambiguity in the *Aeneid.*" *Vergilius* 41 (1995): 71–90.
Boyle, A. J. "The Canonic Text: Vergil's *Aeneid.*" In *Roman Epic,* ed. A. J. Boyle. London, 1993, 79–107.

Breen, C. C. "The Shield of Turnus, the Swordbelt of Pallas and the Wolf." *Vergilius* 32 (1986): 63–71.
Brown, R. D. "The Structural Function of the Song of Iopas." *HSCP* 93 (1990): 315–23.
Cage, C., and L. B. Rosenfeld. "Ekphrastic Poetry in Performance." *Text and Performance Quarterly* 9 (1989): 199–205.
Cairns, F. *Virgil's Augustan Epic.* Cambridge, 1989.
Carcopino, J. *La Basilique pythagoricienne de la Porte Majeure.* Paris, 1943.
Clarke, J. R. "The Decor of the House of Jupiter and Ganymede at Ostia." In *Roman Art in the Private Sphere,* ed. E. K. Gazda. Ann Arbor, 1991, 89–104.
Clausen, W. *Virgil's Aeneid and the Tradition of Hellenistic Poetry.* Berkeley, 1987.
Clay, D. *Lucretius and Epicurus.* Ithaca, 1983.
———. "The Archeology of the Temple to Juno in Carthage." *CP* 83 (1988): 195–205.
Conte, G. B. "Il balteo di Pallante." *RFIC* 98 (1970): 292–300, repr. in *Il genere e i suoi confini.* Torino, 1980, 96–108. Trans. in *The Rhetoric of Imitation.* Ithaca, 1986, 185–95.
Drew, D. L. *The Allegory of the Aeneid.* Oxford, 1927.
Drexler, W. "Ganymedes." In *Ausfürliches Lexicon der griechischen und römischen Mythologie,* ed. W. H. Roscher, 1.2 (1886–90): 1595–1603.
Dubois, P. *History, Rhetorical Description and the Epic.* Cambridge, 1982.
Duckworth, G. "The *Aeneid* as a Trilogy." *TAPA* 88.9 (1957): 1–10.
———. *Structural Patterns and Proportions in Vergil's Aeneid.* Ann Arbor, 1962.
Dulière, C. *Lupa Romana.* Institut Historique Belge de Rome, 1979.
Dyson, J. T. "*Caesi iuvenci* and *Pietas Impia* in Virgil." *CJ* 91 (1996): 277–86.
Eden, P. T. "The Salii on the Shield of Aeneas: *Aeneid* 8, 663–66." *RhM* 16 (1973): 78–83.
Eden, P. T., ed. *A Commentary on Virgil: Aeneid VIII. Mnemosyne Supp.* 35: Leiden, 1975.
Edgecombe, R. S. "A Typology of Ecphrases." *CML* 13 (1993): 103–16.
Eichholz, D. E. "The Shield of Aeneas: Some Elementary Notions." *PVS* 6 (1966–67): 45–49.
Elsner, J., ed. *Art and Text in Roman Culture.* Cambridge, 1996.
Enk, P. J. "De Labyrinthi Imagine in Foribus Templi Cumani Inscripta." *Mnemosyne* 4.11 (1958): 322–30.
Feeney, D. C. *The Gods in Epic.* Oxford, 1991.
Fitzgerald, W. "Aeneas, Daedalus and the Labyrinth." *Arethusa* 17 (1984): 51–65.
Fowler, D. "Vergil on Killing Virgins." In *Homo Viator: Classical Essays for John Bramble,* ed. Michael Whitby, P. Hardie, and Mary Whitby. Bristol, 1987, 185–98.

———. "Narrate and Describe: The Problem of Ekphrasis." *JRS* 81 (1991): 25–35.
Fowler, W. W. *Aeneas at the Site of Rome.* Oxford, 1918.
Friedländer, P. "Ganymedes." *RE* 7.1 (1910): 737–49.
———. *Johannes von Gaza und Paulus Silentiarius.* Leipzig, 1912.
Frontisi-Ducroux, F. *Dédale: Mythologie de l'artisan en grèce ancienne.* Paris, 1975.
Gagé, J. *Apollon Romain.* Paris, 1955.
Garvie, A. F. *Aeschylus' Supplices: Play and Trilogy.* Cambridge, 1969.
Gazda, E. K. "A Marble Group of Ganymede and the Eagle from the Age of Augustine." In *Excavations at Carthage: 1977,* ed. J. H. Humphrey. Ann Arbor, 1981, 125–78.
Genette, G. "Boundaries of Narrative." *NLH* 8 (1976): 1–13.
———. "Frontiers of Narrative." Trans. A. Sheridan, in *Figures of Literary Discourse.* Oxford, 1982, 127–46.
Gransden, K. W., ed. *Virgil, Aeneid Book VIII.* Cambridge, 1976.
Griffin, J. *Latin Poets and Roman Life.* Chapel Hill, 1986.
Griffith, J. G. "Again the Shield of Aeneas *(Aeneid* VIII. 625–731)." *PVS* 7 (1967–68): 54–65.
Gurval, R. A. *Actium and Augustus.* Ann Arbor, 1995.
Hagstrum, J. *The Sister Arts: The Tradition of Literary Pictorialism and English Poetry from Dryden to Gray.* Chicago, 1958.
Hardie, P. "The Sacrifice of Iphigeneia." *CQ* 34 (1984): 406–12.
———. "Imago Mundi: Cosmological and Ideological Aspects of the Shield of Achilles." *JHS* 105 (1985): 11–31.
———. *Virgil's Aeneid: Cosmos and Imperium.* Oxford, 1986.
———. *The Epic Successors of Virgil.* Cambridge, 1993.
Heffernan, J. A. W. "Ekphrasis and Representation." *NLH* 22 (1991): 297–316.
———. *Museum of Words.* Chicago, 1993.
Hollander, J. "The Poetics of Ekphrasis." *Word and Image* 4 (1988): 209–19.
———. *The Gazer's Spirit.* Chicago, 1995.
Horsfall, N. "From History to Legend: M. Manlius and the Geese." *CJ* 76 (1981): 298–311.
———. "Dido in the Light of History." *PVS* 13 [1973–74]: 1–13, repr. in *Oxford Readings in Vergil's Aeneid,* ed. S. J. Harrison. Oxford, 1990, 127–40.
———. *Virgilio: L'epopea in alambicco.* Naples, 1993.
Hubbard, T. K. "Nature and Art in the Shield of Achilles." *Arion* 2 (1992): 16–41.
Jocelyn, H. D., ed. *The Tragedies of Ennius.* Cambridge, 1967.
Johnson, W. R. *Darkness Visible.* Berkeley, 1976.
Kambylis, S. *Die Dichterweihe und ihre Symbolik.* Heidelberg, 1965.
Kellum, B. "The Temple of Apollo on the Palatine." In *The Age of Augustus,* ed.

R. Winkes (*Archaeologia Transatlantica* 5 [Louvain and Providence, 1985]), 169–76.
Keuls, E. *The Water Carriers in Hades: A Study of Catharsis through Toil in Antiquity*. Amsterdam, 1974.
———. "Danaides." *LIMC* 3.1 (1986): 337–43.
King, K. C. "Foil and Fusion: Homer's Achilles in Vergil's *Aeneid*." *MD* 9 (1982): 31–57.
Knauer, G. N. *Die Aeneas und Homer* (*Hypomnemata* 7: Göttingen, 1964).
Koerner, J. J. *Die Such nach dem Labyrinth*. Frankfurt, 1983.
Krieger, M. *Ekphrasis: The Illusion of the Natural Sign*. Baltimore, 1992.
Kris, E., and O. Kurz. *Legend, Myth and Magic in the Image of the Artist*. New Haven, 1979.
Kurman, G. "Ecphrasis in Epic Poetry." *CLS* 26 (1974): 1–13.
Laird, A. "Sounding out Ekphrasis." *JRS* 83 (1993): 18–30.
———. "*Ut figura poesis:* Writing Art and the Art of Writing." In *Art and Text in Roman Culture*, ed. J. Elsner. Cambridge, 1996, 75–102.
Landels, J. G. "A Hellish Note." *CQ* 8 (1956): 219–20.
Lausberg, H. *Handbuch der literarischen Rhetoric*. Munich, 1960.
Lavagne, H. "L'antre du Lupercal et les Lupercalia." In *Operosa Antra*. Ecole Française de Rome, 1988, 203–25.
Leach, E. W. "Ekphrasis and the Theme of Artistic Failure in Ovid's *Metamorphoses*." *Ramus* 3 (1974): 102–42.
———. *The Rhetoric of Space*. Princeton, 1988.
Lefèvre, E. *Das Bild-Programm des Apollo-Tempels auf dem Palatin* (*Xenia* 14: Konstanz, 1989).
Lessing, G. E. *Laocoön*. Trans. E. A. McCormick. Baltimore, 1984.
Lonsdale, S. H. "Simile and Ecphrasis in Homer and Virgil." *Vergilius* 36 (1990): 7–30.
Lowenstam, S. "The Pictures on Juno's Temple in the *Aeneid*." *CJ* 87 (1993): 37–49.
Lyne, R. O. A. M. *Further Voices in Vergil's Aeneid*. Oxford, 1987.
———. *Words and the Poet*. Oxford, 1989.
Maltby, R. *A Lexicon of Ancient Latin Etymologies*. Arca Monographs 25. Leeds, 1991.
McKay, A. G. *Vergil's Italy*. Greenwich, 1970.
Meltzer, F. *Salome and the Dance of Writing*. Chicago, 1987.
Mitchell, R. N. "The Violence of Virginity in the *Aeneid*." *Arethusa* 24 (1991): 219–37.
Mitchell, W. T. J. "Spatial Form in Literature: Toward a General Theory." In *The Language of Images*, ed. W. T. J. Mitchell. Chicago, 1980, 271–99.
———. *Iconology: Image, Text, Ideology*. Chicago, 1986.

Moorton, R. F. "The Innocence of Italy in Virgil's *Aeneid.*" *AJP* 110 (1989): 105–30.
Moulton, C. "The End of the *Odyssey.*" *GRBS* 15 (1974): 153–69.
Nagy, G. *The Best of the Achaeans.* Baltimore, 1979.
Nänny, M. "Chiasmus in Literature: Ornament or Function?" *Word and Image* 4 (1988): 51–59.
Nisbet, R., and M. Hubbard, eds. *A Commentary on Horace: Odes II.* Oxford, 1978.
Norden, E., ed. *P. Vergilius Maro: Aeneid Buch VI.* Stuttgart, 1957.
Nugent, S. G. "Virgil's 'Voice of the Women' in *Aeneid* V." *Arethusa* 25 (1992): 255–92.
O'Hara, J. J. *Death and the Optimistic Prophecy in Vergil's Aeneid.* Princeton, 1990.
Onians, J. "Abstraction and Imagination in Late Antiquity." *Art History* 3 (1980): 1–23.
Otis, B. *Virgil: A Study in Civilized Poetry.* Oxford, 1963.
Patterson, L. "Rapt with Pleasaunce: Vision and Narration in the Epic." *ELH* 48 (1981): 455–75.
Perkell, C. *The Poet's Truth.* Berkeley, 1989.
Pichon, R. *Index Verborum Amatorium.* Paris, 1902.
Pöschl, V. *Die Dichtkunst Virgils.* Innsbruck, 1950. Trans. G. Seligson, as *The Art of Vergil.* Ann Arbor, 1962.
———. "Die Tempeltüren des Dädalus in der Aeneid." *WJA* 1 (1975): 119–33.
Pucci, P. *The Violence of Pity.* Ithaca, 1980.
———. *Odysseus Polutropos.* Ithaca, 1987.
Putnam, M. C. J. *The Poetry of the Aeneid.* Cambridge, Mass., 1965. Repr. Ithaca, 1988.
———. "Aeneid 7 and the Aeneid." *AJP* 91 (1970), 408–30. Repr. in *Essays on Latin Lyric, Elegy, and Epic.* Princeton, 1982, 288–310.
———. "Virgil's Lapiths." *CQ* 40 (1990): 562–66.
———. *Virgil's Aeneid: Interpretation and Influence.* Chapel Hill, 1995.
Quinn, K. *Virgil's Aeneid: A Critical Description.* London, 1968.
Quint, D. "Epic and Empire." *CLS* 41 (1989): 1–32.
———. *Epic and Empire.* Princeton, 1993.
Ravenna, G. "L'*Ekphrasis* poetica di opere d'arte in Latino." *Quad. Ist. Fil. Lat. Pad.* 3 (1974): 1–52.
———. "Ekphrasis." in *Enciclopedia Virgiliana.* Rome, 1988, 2:183–85.
———. "Scudo di Aenea." in *Enciclopedia Virgiliana.* Rome, 1988, 4:739–42.
Richlin, A. *The Gardens of Priapus.* Oxford, 1992.
Romeuf, J. "Les Peintures du Temple de Carthage." *Ann. Lat. Mon. Arv.* 2. (1975): 15–27.

———. "Le Bouclier d'Enée." *REL* 62 (1984): 143–65.
Rosand, D. "Ekphrasis and the Generation of Images." *Arion* 1 (1990): 61–105.
Ross, D. O. *Virgil's Elements.* Princeton, 1987.
Rowland, R. J. "Foreshadowing in Vergil, Aeneid, VIII, 714–28." *Latomus* 27 (1968): 832–42.
Rutledge, H. "Vergil's Daedalus." *CJ* 62 (1967): 309–11.
Saslow, J. M. *Ganymede in the Renaissance.* New Haven, 1986.
Segal, C. P. "*Aeternum per saecula nomen,* the Golden Bough and the Tragedy of History: Part I." *Arion* 4 (1965): 617–57.
———. "*Aeternum per saecula nomen,* the Golden Bough and the Tragedy of History: Part II." *Arion* 5 (1966): 34–72.
———. "The Song of Iopas in the Aeneid." *Hermes* 99 (1971): 336–49.
———. "Dido's Hesitation in *Aeneid* 4." *CW* 84 (1990): 1–12.
———. *Singers, Heroes, and Gods in the Odyssey.* Ithaca, 1994.
Selden, D. "Ceveat Lector." In *Innovations of Antiquity,* ed. R. Hexter and D. Selden. New York, 1992, 461–512.
Shapiro, H. A. "Jason's Cloak." *TAPA* 110 (1980): 263–86.
Shapiro, M. "Ecphrasis in Virgil and Dante." *CLS* 42 (1990): 97–115.
Sichtermann, H. *Ganymed.* Berlin, 1953.
Simon, E. *Augustus: Kunst und Leben in Rom am die Zeitenwende.* Munich, 1986.
Skutsch, O., ed. *The Annals of Quintus Ennius.* Oxford, 1985.
Spence, S. "Cinching the Text: The Danaids and the End of the *Aeneid.*" *Vergilius* 37 (1991): 11–19.
Stanley, K. "Irony and Foreshadowing in Aeneid I." *AJP* 86 (1965): 173–98.
Szantyr, A. "Bemerkungen zum Aufbau der vergilischen Ekphrasis." *MH* 24 (1970): 28–40.
Thomas, J. "Le Sens Symbolique de la Bataille d'Actium." *Euphrosyne* 19 (1991): 303–308.
Thomas, R. "Virgil's Ecphrastic Centerpieces." *HSCP* 87 (1983): 175–84.
Vance, E. "Silvia's Pet Stag: Wildness and Domesticity in Vergil's Aeneid." *Arethusa* 14 (1981): 127–38.
Vasaly, A. *Representations: Images of the World in Ciceronian Oratory.* Berkeley, 1993.
Walker, A. D. "Enargeia and the Spectator in Greek Historiography." *TAPA* 123 (1993): 353–77.
Weber, C. "Gallus' Grynium and Virgil's Cumae." *ARCM* 1 (1978): 45–76.
West, D. A. "Cernere erat: The Shield of Aeneas." *PVS* 15 (1975–76): 1–6. Repr. in *Oxford Readings in Vergil's Aeneid,* ed. S. J. Harrison. Oxford, 1990, 295–304.
Williams, R. D. "The Pictures on Dido's Temple." *CQ* 10 (1960): 145–51.
———. "The Shield of Aeneas." *Vergilius* 27 (1981): 8–11.

Williams, R. D., ed. *P. Vergili Maronis: Aeneidos: Liber Tertius.* Oxford, 1962.
———. *The Aeneid of Virgil: Books 7–12.* London, 1973.
Wimmel, W. *Kallimachos in Rom. Hermes Einzelschriften* 16: Wiesbaden, 1960.
Winnington-Ingram, R. P. "Aeschylus." In *The Cambridge History of Classical Literature: Greek.* Cambridge, 1985, 284–86.
Zanker, G. "Enargeia in the Ancient Criticism of Poetry." *RhM* 124 (1981): 297–311.
———. *Realism in Alexandrian Poetry.* London, 1987.
Zanker, P. "Der Apollontempel auf dem Palatin: Ausstattung und politische Sinnbezüge nach der Schlacht von Actium." *An. Rom. Inst. Dan.*, supp. 10 (1983): 21–40.
———. *Augustus und die Macht der Bilder.* Munich, 1987. Trans. A. Shapiro as *The Power of Images in the Age of Augustus.* Ann Arbor, 1988.
Zeitlin, F. "Patterns of Gender in Aeschylean Drama: *Seven Against Thebes* and the Danaid Trilogy." In *Cabinet of the Muses: Essays in Honor of T. Rosenmeyer,* ed. M. Griffith and D. Mastronarde. Atlanta, 1990, 103–15.
———. "The Politics of Eros in the Danaid Trilogy of Aeschylus." In *Innovations of Antiquity,* ed. R. Hexter and D. Selden. New York, 1992, 203–52.

Index

Achates, 5, 27, 77, 85
Achilles, 4, 11–12, 14, 26–29, 33–47 passim, 63–64, 68, 91, 94, 136, 167–69, 180, 193, 202–03, 218–19, 231, 236, 238, 244
Actium, 16–17, 121–22, 136–37, 139, 145, 147–48, 150–52, 154, 157, 183, 199, 209, 214, 234
Aeolus, 68, 138, 163–65, 179, 187
Aeschylus, 9, 15, 195–96, 207, 242, 244
Agamemnon, 47, 207
Agrippa, 122, 139–40, 142, 160
Alcinous, 49, 53
Allecto, 20, 102–03, 105–07, 111, 118, 205, 233
Alliteration, 28–29, 57, 61, 104, 121, 130, 170, 177
Amata, 19–20, 45, 47, 105, 118, 205
Amor. *See* Cupid
Anchises, 5, 16, 75, 89, 91, 95, 137, 141, 167, 173–75, 197, 204, 227, 230–31, 236
Ancus Marcius, 174
Andromache, 63, 222
Antony (Marcus Antonius), 16, 142, 159, 161, 199–200
Aphrodite. *See* Venus
Apollo, 1, 17–18, 44, 64, 75, 78, 81, 114, 117, 146, 151, 154, 160, 187, 200, 203, 219, 222, 224–25, 230, 236
Apollo Palatinus, temple of, 15, 17, 51, 121, 198–99, 211, 216
Apollonius Rhodius, 13–14, 59–64, 91, 93–94, 171–72, 180, 200, 221, 242

Araxes, 151–52, 157–58, 165–66, 187, 210
Ares. *See* Mars
Arethusa, 106–07
Argus, 21–22
Ariadne, 5, 13–14, 77, 80–83, 86, 206, 223, 226, 229
Artemis. *See* Diana
Ascanius, 6, 66, 85, 97, 99, 103–05, 111, 116, 120, 137, 176–77, 222, 233
Assonance, 28, 61, 104, 121, 130, 170, 177
Attis, 65–66, 222
Augustus, ix, 6, 11, 15–18, 51, 83, 95, 121–22, 130, 133, 138–42, 148–51, 154–62, 174, 177, 179, 187, 191, 197–218 passim, 234, 236–37
Aventine, 125

Brutus, 174, 236

Cacus, 160–62
Caesar, Julius, 135, 150, 158, 174
Callimachus, 113–14, 234
Calypso, 1
Camilla, 1, 19, 46, 89, 102, 106, 116–17, 218, 222
Capitolium, 128–30, 134, 142, 148, 157
Carthage, 4, 23–24, 26, 42–43, 52–53, 84, 86, 176, 217
Catiline, 134–35, 137, 140
Cato, 17, 134–35, 137, 140, 158, 236
Catullus, 13–15, 60, 65, 117, 206, 226, 236, 239
Chiasmus, 28, 31–32, 58, 84, 102, 129–30, 221

Circe, 1, 19, 102, 225–26
Circus Maximus, 123
Clementia, 10, 16, 47, 69, 73, 82, 90–91, 118, 166, 196, 200–02, 204–07, 213, 227, 230, 234, 243
Cleopatra, 16, 122, 142, 145, 147–51, 158–59, 174, 199, 238
Cloanthus, 2, 5, 11, 55, 65
Cloelia, 17, 127–28, 135, 140, 157–58
Clonus, 8, 190, 194–95
Clupeus aureus, 16, 201, 211, 216, 234
Cocles, 17, 127–28, 135, 140, 157–58
Creon, 93–94
Crete, 77, 137
Creusa, 68, 95, 227
Cumae, 75, 84
Cupid, 14, 51, 85–86, 176–77, 218, 233
Curia Julia, 16, 216
Cybele, 60, 65
Cyclopes, 63

Daedalus, 1, 5–7, 10, 13–15, 17, 23, 51, 74–75, 77–88, 90–91, 95–96, 211, 216, 223–31, 236, 240
Danaid Porticus, 15, 17, 198, 200, 242–43
Danaids, 8–11, 15–16, 20–21, 190–201, 203, 205, 211, 221, 240–43
Daphnis, 108–09
Deiphobe. *See* Sibyl
Deiphobus, 241
Demodocus, 25, 47–49, 51–54, 219–20, 239
Descriptio, 1, 98, 104, 116, 215, 231
Diana, 11, 17, 36–37, 44, 53, 85, 116, 203–04, 219, 225
Dido ix, 1–5, 7, 9–11, 17, 20, 23–26, 36–39, 41–54, 69, 85–88, 95, 97, 101, 117, 148, 173, 175–77, 180, 201–02, 204–07, 216–20, 222–23, 228–30, 233, 238, 241, 244
Diomedes, 28–29, 35, 37, 39–41, 45, 47, 217, 219

Dirae. *See* Furies
Discordia, 105–07, 145–46, 184–86, 236
Dolor, 5, 14, 20, 71–73, 82–83, 90–91, 94–95, 205, 217, 229–31, 244
Donatus, 162

Eclogues, 7, 83, 98, 107–10, 183–87, 233
Egypt, 142, 149
Ekphrasis: and allusion, 12, 60, 98, 106, 113, 119, 159; and atemporality, 2, 32, 36, 38, 50, 55, 58, 154, 201, 217; and centrality, 28–29, 31, 154; and circularity, 7, 12, 29, 31, 33, 58–59, 65, 69, 73, 79, 122, 154, 156, 160, 166, 205, 210–11, 221; and focalization, 3, 24, 212, 217, 228; and gender, 3, 19, 42, 44, 54, 216, 219; and genre, ix, 3, 6, 11, 15, 22, 98, 106–07, 109–10, 112–16, 118, 181, 206; and memory, 4, 10, 72–73; and narrativity, ix, 3, 10, 14, 21, 25, 30–32, 36, 53–54, 102–03, 110, 166–67, 190, 208, 212; notional, 1–2, 18, 30, 50, 97, 131, 189, 208; and repetition, 7, 21, 31, 39, 58, 70, 155–56, 160, 201, 205–06; and simile, 11, 19, 37, 209; and synecdoche, ix, 3, 7, 10, 26, 46, 61, 74, 97, 166, 188, 205, 209, 214
Enargeia, 58, 215
Ennius, 141, 180–81, 225, 236
Epicurus, 182
Erato, 223
Euphrates, 156
Europa, 22
Euryalus, 45, 66, 89, 206, 241
Eurydice, 67, 229
Evander, 89, 161, 189, 197, 204, 222, 232

Furies (Fury), 9, 15, 47, 90, 118, 146, 160, 205–07, 229–30, 235, 244

Galaesus, 111–12, 201, 233
Gallus, 106–09

INDEX

Ganymede, 4, 11, 13, 20–21, 55–60, 64–74, 102, 210, 221–22
Gauls, 128–35, 142, 152, 156
Gellius, Aulus, 162, 225
Georgics, 67, 83, 98, 107–10, 183–87, 233

Hardie, Philip, 214
Harpies, 84, 241
Hector, 12, 32–33, 35, 37–41, 46, 63, 68, 71, 85, 91–92, 94, 192–93, 203, 219, 244
Heffernan, James, 3
Heinze, Richard, 212
Helen, 24, 62–64, 85, 90, 172–73, 175, 220, 231, 241
Hephaistos. *See* Vulcan
Herbert, George, 191
Hercules, 17, 62, 161–62, 193–96, 241–42
Hermes. *See* Mercury
Hollander, John, 1
Homer, ix, 1, 13, 40, 48, 50, 53–54, 59–60, 63, 71–72, 90, 97, 136–37, 168–69, 180, 193, 195, 217, 221, 238, 241–43. See also *Iliad; Odyssey*
Homeric Hymn to Aphrodite, 59
Horace, 16, 111–13, 148–50, 196–97, 199, 201, 229, 242–43
Hypermestra, 9–10, 16, 195–97, 199–200, 207, 210, 242

Icarus, 5, 77–79, 81, 95, 223–27, 230
Iliad, 12, 14, 24, 27, 33, 37–38, 43, 46, 59, 61–62, 64, 68, 70, 85, 91, 94, 119, 167, 171, 192, 194, 231, 236
Ilione, 85, 176
Ilioneus, 106
Inachus, 18–19, 22
Io, 18–22, 102, 210, 226, 242, 244
Iopas, 25, 48, 51–53, 220
Ira, 71–72, 96, 118, 191, 205, 228, 230–31, 244

Iris, 87
Isis, 145
Ithaca, 1
Iulus. *See* Ascanius

Jason, 62–64
Johnson, W. R., 213
Juno, 1, 8, 17, 20–23, 43, 47, 59, 70–73, 82, 85, 87, 102, 105–07, 117–18, 138, 163, 166, 173, 191, 204–06, 210, 217, 228, 230, 237–38, 241, 244
Jupiter, 17, 20–22, 56–57, 59–60, 63, 65–67, 69–71, 73, 89–90, 92, 123–24, 129–30, 132, 145, 159–60, 165, 170, 192–93, 221, 230, 238, 244
Juturna, 145, 185, 230

Kellum, Barbara, 199
Krieger, Murray, 2, 205

Labor, 26–27
Labyrinth, 5, 14, 80, 137, 225–26, 228–29, 236, 240
Laocosn, 177, 243
Latins, 9
Latinus, 7, 19, 43, 47, 100, 102, 106, 117, 185, 191–92, 204, 225, 232
Latium, 1, 15, 20, 84, 89, 99, 102, 104, 107, 166, 185
Latona (Leto), 17, 36
Lausus, 45, 66, 89
Lavinia, 89–90, 205, 207
Lessing, G. E., 168
Libertas, 135, 139, 157
Livy, 124–26, 130
Lucretius, 170, 181–83, 218, 231, 242
Lupercal, 121–22, 154, 180–81, 235
Luperci, 132
Lynceus, 16, 195–97

Macrobius, 51, 70–71, 169, 232–33
Maecenas, 83

Manlius Torquatus, 17, 128–29, 134–35, 156
Marcellus, 31, 95, 174
Mars, 48, 52, 64, 119–20, 124, 139, 145, 152–53, 155, 170, 179, 181–83, 187, 218, 241
Medea, 172
Memnon, 34, 37–39, 41, 85
Mercury, 21, 224, 242
Metamorphosis, 99–100, 102, 110, 112
Metonymy, 103–04, 106, 139, 142–43
Mettus Fufetius, 124–26, 130, 134–35, 152, 157
Minerva, 8, 13, 31–32, 35, 39–40, 44–45, 47, 64, 72, 82, 92, 95, 145, 171, 177–79, 217–18, 228, 237, 244
Minotaur, 77–78, 80, 86, 88, 226
Moschus, 21–22
Mulciber. *See* Vulcan

Nausicaa, 53
Neoptolemus. *See* Pyrrhus
Neptune, 65, 138, 145, 157, 164, 191, 224, 228
Nile, 147–49, 151
Niobe, 17
Nisus, 45, 89, 241
Numa, 133, 152

Octavian. *See* Augustus
Odysseus, 39–40, 48–50, 53, 67, 92, 194, 219, 224, 227
Odyssey, 23, 25, 47, 49, 52–53, 61–62, 70, 91, 93–94, 192–94, 220, 224, 230, 239
Orestes, 9, 11, 20, 207, 244
Orpheus, 59, 67, 207, 220, 229, 242
Otis, Brooks, 212
Ovid, 59, 160, 192–200, 241–42

Palatine, 121, 151–52, 154, 156
Palinurus, 95, 241

Palladium, 39–40, 218
Pallas, 2, 5, 8–11, 15, 20, 45, 66, 68, 89–90, 173, 189, 192–93, 195, 197–98, 203–04, 206, 211, 221–23, 228–29, 231, 241
Pallas Athena. *See* Minerva
Paris, 47, 70–71, 219
Pasiphaë, 5, 77–78, 80, 84, 86–87, 228–29
Patroclus, 40, 71, 192–93, 244
Peleus, 13–14
Penelope, 92, 219
Penthesilea, 4, 11, 34–39, 41, 46, 85, 116, 218
Pentheus, 11, 20, 207
Phaeacia, 1, 47
Phaeacians, 48, 51, 53
Philetas, 113
Pietas, 16–17, 47, 82, 159, 164, 197, 201, 223, 227, 234–35, 243
Plautus, 39
Pliny the Elder, 150, 221
Pompey, 174
Porsenna, 102, 127–28, 135, 139, 157, 165, 226
Pöschl, Viktor, 212
Priam, 26–27, 32, 35, 39–41, 43, 46, 91–92, 161, 176, 202–03, 231
Propertius, 15, 51, 98, 113–15, 198, 200, 233, 242
Pyrrhus, 43, 202–03, 231

Quint, David, 199

Remulus Numanus, 66, 222
Remus, 135, 154, 159–60, 235
Rhesus, 28, 39–40, 43, 217–18
Romulus, 121, 123–24, 128–29, 135, 140, 150, 154, 160, 187, 235

Sabines, 150
Saevitia, 26, 28, 37

INDEX

Salii, 132
Sappho, 206
Saturn, 159–60, 232
Scylla, 85
Servius, 51, 130, 180, 224, 238
Sextus Pompeius, 15
Sibyl, 75–76, 78, 88–89, 117, 173–74, 196, 203–04, 227
Silvia, 1, 15, 21, 97–99, 101–03, 105–06, 108–10, 112, 114, 118
Sinon, 40, 86, 178, 220, 232, 243
Statius, 91, 93–94, 231
Superbia, 223
Sychaeus, 44, 87

Tarentum, 111–12
Tarquinius Superbus, 127, 135, 174
Tatius, 123–24, 129, 135
Theseus, 13, 93, 226
Thetis, 13–14, 169
Tiber, 84, 89, 112, 138, 148
Tibullus, 51, 242
Tragedy, 8–9, 15, 25, 60, 97, 193, 195, 205, 244
Troilus, 29–30, 35, 37, 39–40, 43, 45, 85, 218

Troy, ix, 2, 11, 27, 33, 42, 45, 47–48, 84, 97, 161, 175–77, 179, 202
Tullus Hostilius, 125–27
Turnus, ix, 2, 9–12, 18–22, 31, 38, 45–46, 66–72 passim, 82, 89–91, 95, 97, 102, 105, 118, 141, 162, 165–66, 173, 178, 187, 189–93, 195–97, 203, 207, 210, 218, 221, 223, 226, 230, 240, 244
Tyre, 42
Tyrrhus, 99, 111

Ulysses. *See* Odysseus

Venus, 7, 9, 19, 48, 52, 63, 68, 72, 85–86, 117, 126, 145, 169–79, 182–83, 191, 195, 207, 218, 233, 238, 242, 244
Violentia, 89
Virgil. See *Eclogues; Georgics*
Vulcan, 2, 3, 6–7, 10, 12–13, 17, 21, 23, 48, 52, 84, 120–39 passim, 142–45, 147–48, 151–53, 155–56, 160–64, 167–76, 178–79, 181–82, 186, 188, 204, 214, 216, 228

Zanker, Paul, 199
Zeus. *See* Jupiter